£22.05N+

THE RHETORIC
OF THE
REFORMATION

THE RHETORIC
OF THE
REFORMATION

PETER MATHESON

T&T CLARK
EDINBURGH

T&T CLARK LTD
59 GEORGE STREET
EDINBURGH EH2 2LQ
SCOTLAND

First published 1998

ISBN 0 567 08593 7

British Library Cataloguing-in-Publication Data
A catalogue record for this book is available from the British Library

Typeset by Waverley Typesetters, Galashiels
Printed and bound in Great Britain by MPG Books, Bodmin

For Anna

CONTENTS

ABBREVIATIONS

AvG   Peter Matheson, tr. and ed., *Argula von Grumbach: A Woman's Voice in the Reformation*. T. & T. Clark: Edinburgh, 1995.

CR   C. G. Bretschneider, ed., *Corpus Reformatorum. Melanchthons Opera*. Halle, 1834ff.

CW   Peter Matheson, tr. and ed., *The Collected Works of Thomas Müntzer*. T. & T. Clark: Edinburgh, 1988.

LW   *Luther's Works* (the 'American Luther'), eds. J. Pelikan and W. Lehman. 55 Vols. Concordia: Philadelphia & St Louis, 1955ff.

MSB   *Thomas Müntzer: Schriften und Briefe*. In collaboration with Paul Kirn edited by Gunther Franz (Quellen und Forschungen zur Reformationsgeschichte, Vol. XXXIII) Gerd Mohn: Gutersloh, 1968.

W   *D. Martin Luther's Works*. Kritische Gesamtausgabe. Weimar, 1883ff.

WBr   *Briefe*.

WTr.   *Tischreden*.

CHAPTER 3

B   *Von beiden gestaldten der heyligen Messze*. Wittenberg, 1521.

D   *Dialogus oder ein gesprech buchlin. Von dem grewlichen und abgottischen missbrauch/ des hochwirdigsten Sacraments Jesu Christi*. n.p., 1525.

E   *Erklerung des x. Capitels Cor. I Das Brot das wir brechen: ist es nitt ein gemeinschaft des leybs Christi . . .* Augsburg, 1525.

CHAPTER ONE

INTRODUCTION

They have no place for the fine graces
of poetry. The great forgiving spirit of the word,
fanning its rainbow wing, like a short bird
falls from the windy sky. The sea heaves
in visionless anger over the cramped graves
and the early daffodil, purer than a soul,
is gathered into the terrible mouth of the gale.

Ian Crichton Smith, from *The Long River*, 1955.

As a movement to renew and reform the Church the various Reformations of the sixteenth century – Humanist, Catholic, Protestant, Radical – were committed to the struggle against moral and educational abuses, to taking the lid off ancient wrongs, to toppling the tyrant and the sycophant. By necessity such actions involved polemic.

Words were minted, therefore, to sharpen issues, alert minds, awaken emotions, and to motivate the hesitant to action. But such polemic was more than a means to bring about certain changes in Church and society. It had a heuristic function as well as an instrumental one. Its aim was to let truth emerge from the clash of competing views. In the scholastic 'game' of the medieval university the disputation had set up thesis against counter-thesis, person against person. This whole exercise had something of the flavour of a tournament. The conventions permitted and even fostered extremism, confrontation and aggression in the interests of the ultimate resolution of apparently contradictory views.

1

As the Reformation began to take root the disputation left the cloistered realm of the university for the Rathaus, or Town Hall, the inn and the home, and – through the new medium of the printing press – went on to address the wider forum of public opinion. In school, monastery and sodality, in rural congregation and regal court, traditional practices and authoritative norms were interrogated by the criteria of Scripture, reason and conscience. Or such was the theory. It was a popular as well as an academic assumption that, through this process, the truth would out. Pamphlet after pamphlet records the insistence that both sides be heard. As reformer and conserver clashed, the body public would act as jury, and come to an informed and just verdict. Under the proper conditions polemic would elicit the truth, or at least that which best served the common weal.

And indeed it is a fact that it was only as the guardians of the old verities responded to the initial provocations of the Reformers with a counter-polemic, which kindly pointed out their heretical and schismatic implications, that they realised the full extent and intent of their innovations. In 1520 Luther warmly thanked Alfeld, for example, at the beginning of the *Babylonian Captivity* for driving him on to think through his position much more radically. The blunt cudgel swung by reaction, quite as much as the adulation of excited followers, confirmed, strengthened and deepened the Reformers' tentative ideas. The fresh wounds of polemic, the rapid transitions from words to threats to persecution, sharpened the mind as no university debate had ever done. It drove Reformers from desk, lectern and pulpit to the calm or angry analysis of authority and power-structures.

The various Reformations – Catholic and Protestant – constituted, then, a fascinating battle for the mind and heart of those who were hurting and those who were thinking – often one and the same thing – of monks and nuns and secular clergy, but also of the laity – teachers, counsellors, artisans and aristocrats, women and men, merchants and literati, students and peasants and miners. As editions of the pagan and Christian classics poured out for the more sophisticated, vernacular Scriptures spoke to those hungry for clear answers, and preachers and pamphlets offered their services in interpreting them.

Polemic, however, to be successful, had to be directed not only at corrupt institutions and threadbare belief systems but at those who personified them, or even profited from them. Polemic soon became personal; groups and individuals were held up to ridicule and abuse. In turn, of course, those who were attacked – the hierarchy, monks, friars, scholastic theologians – retorted with counter-abuse, both sides often moving swiftly from vindication to vindictiveness. A growing number of disputes within the Reforming camp soon developed as well.

In a Church afflicted by a crisis of authority, in a society and culture swirling with a heady mix of anger and anticipation, how was theology best 'done', how was an authentic piety to be nurtured, how the true face of the Church to be discerned: through polemic or by dialogue? If there was something far wrong, as Erasmus argued, about sermons breathing out fire and fury, was there not, on the other hand, much to be said for the view that the peace of the Church was frequently hard to distinguish from its sleep?

We should be clear from the outset, however, that it is far from the case that dialogue was the irenic alternative of the humanist to the polemic of the theologian. The picture is infinitely more complicated. In the 1520s, at least, Luther was much more aware than militant humanists such as von Hutten of the need to bear with the weak and carry the case by the better argument. If, however, in Luther's formulation, the true preaching of the Word of God always causes 'uproar' (*uffrur*), how is the ensuing conflict to be managed? What forms of theological disputation and dialogue are socially acceptable? To what extent do apparently religious conflicts reflect social and political tensions?

The sixteenth century offers a perhaps unparalleled array of answers to such questions. The various alternatives displayed not only different theologies and pieties, but different patterns of communication. All the major players, from Erasmus to Luther to Loyola, and many of the minor ones proved extraordinarily inventive in producing new styles of addressing people, new 'languages'. The traditional theological tome almost disappeared as Biblical commentaries poured out, as hymns, catechisms, sermons, dramas, pamphlets in every shape and form rode pick-a-back on the now fashionable quest for a literate Gospel. People's mental furniture and the gestures of love we call liturgy, their inner and cultic worlds, were transformed by the vernacular Bible, song-book, catechism. Mysticism became popular and even populist, lay preachers fleshed out apocalyptic images, women wondered about emulating the initiatives of Deborah, Judith, and Esther, and even the peasant became *witzig*, 'up with the play'. Civic disputations brought theology into the public arena. Local sodalities or 'prophecies' catered for the learned, while more modest groups gathered in an 'upper room' or an inn; zealous new converts slung a plethora of new bridges between academia and church praxis. Domestic and intimate forms such as letter and poem became public knowledge through print. Prophecy and profit were married by the enterprising printing-house. Colloquies and councils, Imperial Diets and princely courts saw scholars and power-brokers rubbing shoulders in the heady glare of public expectation.

The militant language of the Reformation is certainly unmistakeable. In his 1520 best-seller, the *Appeal to the German Nobility*, Luther leads an assault troop against the besieged city of clerical privilege, sounding the trumpet against triple walls defending Jericho, or is it Babylon or Rome? The wood-cut adorning one pamphlet depicts the word of God as a cannon. No small part of the entertainment value of Reformation literature was its war-game character: ritual challenges, calls to battle, epic stories of heroism abounded! Luther himself was often portrayed as the German Hercules.

In today's very diverse interpretations of the Reformation, whether the apocalyptic one of Oberman, or the anti-clerical one of Goertz,[1] the clash of ferocious antagonisms between the Old Church and the Reformers is one of the few fixed points. In Lindberg's terms, old symbols of security tottered.[2]

'The Devil never sleeps, and we, too, must wake up', is the burden of countless Reformation preachers and pamphleteers. An precedented struggle was breaking out. Martin Luther, Argula von Grumbach, the woman reformer from Bavaria, and the radical liturgist and peasant leader, Thomas Müntzer, all believed that the Reformation was provoking the devil to un-heard-of ingenuity.

The Reformation, then, stirred up much emotion, as well as spreading light. It was a struggle for power as much as for truth. The crisis in belief paralleled, to some extent reflected, to some extent precipitated, a shift in power-relationships. It reflected, as much as it generated itself, frustrations, hopes and dreams stoked up over the years. A long tradition of humanist, anti-clerical and national polemic was fanned into flame. Better lay education made a gradual shift of power from clergy to laity inevitable; a struggle for control over social welfare, education and health sharpened in imperial cities, princely territory and the new nation state.

The Reformation pamphlet, on which this book will focus, is not literature in the normal sense of the word. It is too agitatorial

---

[1]   Heiko A. Oberman, *Luther – Man between God and the Devil.* Tr. Eileen Walliser-Schwarzbart (Image Books: New York, 1992); Hans-Jürgen Goertz, *Pfaffenhass und gross Geschrei; die reformatorischen Bewegungen in Deutschland 1517–1529* (Beck: Munich, 1987); Peter A. Dykema and Heiko A. Oberman (eds.), *Anticlericalism in Late Medieval and Early Modern Europe,* Studies in Medieval and Reformation Thought, vol. 51 (Brill: Leiden, 1993).

[2]   Carter Lindberg, *The European Reformations* (Blackwell: Oxford and Cambridge, Mass., 1996), p. 41.

for that. Wherever it has flourished, in sixteenth-century Germany, seventeenth-century England, or nineteenth-century Scotland, pamphlet literature has always indicated a struggle for the mind. It is thought tailored to action. It may educate and divert; but its primary concern is to challenge its readers' assumptions, to inculcate specific attitudes and to encourage particular commitments or actions. The reader becomes the juror in a trial in which the whole of society is in the dock, and where religious and cultural identity is at stake.[3] Yet the Reformation pamphlet's zeal to spread its ideas cannot be simplistically equated with propaganda, certainly not as the twentieth century has come to know it.[4]

If, then, a struggle for power accompanied the intellectual and spiritual quest of the Reformation, a struggle between clergy and laity, patricians and guilds, prince and nobility, between the social élite and the common people, as well as between rival groups of theologians and clerics and laity, how does this tussle for power relate to the struggle for truth? Did the polemic of the pamphlets, with its verbalised aggression, sharpen perceptions, and marshal arguments and attitudes hitherto restricted to particular regions and groupings for a wider audience, or did it simply line up largely conscript forces into an unedifying trench warfare which soon ground to a halt? How did the confessional stance of writers more at home in the pulpit enhance or inhibit the quality of the arguments? What was the influence of the raw prophetic and polemical traditions within Scripture itself? Was polemic at its best when it was

[3]   Among Reformation historians Ozment presents the most up-beat portrayal of a 'Revolution of the Pamphleteers', which he sees as based on the plumb-line of Scripture and the spiritual equality of laity; he agrees, however, that the vision they outlined in the pamphlets always represented a blueprint, not a reality. Steven Ozment, *Protestants: The Birth of a Revolution* (Doubleday: New York, 1992), pp. 45–66.

[4]   Cf. Harald Lasswell, Daniel Lerner and Hans Speier (eds.), *Propaganda and Communication in World History*. 3 Vols (University Press of Hawaii: Honolulu, 1980).

playful and controlled? How did it relate to the educational outreach of humanist and reformer, to the works of devotion which had dominated the early years of printing? What attempts were made to mediate between the various parties which emerged? And why did such irenic attempts falter so quickly when they were launched?

The word 'polemic' comes from the Greek, *polemos*, battle, fight, or war, and is akin to the Latin *pello, bellum. Logomachia*, warring about words, is mentioned negatively in the New Testament.[5] In the Reformation period humanist reformers such as Bucer and Melanchthon were critical of wars of words, distinguishing between real conflicts and verbal ones. Today, too, the term 'polemics' tends to carry negative associations, evoking the bigoted clash of religious and political ideologies, the slanging matches of party hacks in parliament, or the tedious predictability of aggressive personal rivalries. It is often seen as counter-productive, forcing the opponent into a corner, and limiting the proponent to a pre-programmed, inflexible stance.

Yet the underdog has always resorted to polemic. In the mean streets of every large city graffiti say the unsayable, articulate the pain and anger of the marginalised in memorable over-simplifications. The cartoon is the most obvious example of the revenge which the powerless exact on society's makers and shakers. In the totalitarian régimes of the twentieth century black humour has at least enabled the voiceless to remain sane, to maintain their aesthetic and moral and intellectual distance, to pillory a humourless régime. In the oppressive atmosphere of the West German post-war 'Wirtschaftswunder' of the 1950s and 1960s, political cabaret did much to clear the turgid air with its verbal acrobatics and brilliant songs, while across the Berlin Wall Wolf Biermann's passionate lyrics and memorable melodies rocked the pretences of the Democratic Socialist Republic. Dennis Potter's pungent television dramas punctured

5   James 4:2.

the complacencies of a Thatcherite Britain. The long tradition of American and British investigative journalism is a form of socially redemptive polemic.

Polemic, then, is both necessary and useful. It enables us to see things as they are. Its caricatures are nearer to the truth than the smooth rhetoric and facile images beloved of politician, businessman and media mogul. It encourages us to laugh at those whom we would otherwise tend to fear. It has an apotropaic function.[6] We have, says Paul Speratus, himself fresh from imprisonment, to face our opponents courageously and defiantly (*trutzlich und tröstlich*). His anger at the tyranny of the clergy stems ultimately from love, and is accompanied by a readiness to bear the cross.[7] His polemic is directed against any fearful acceptance of the prohibitions on preaching and publishing. Marc Lienhard makes the point that fear of the clergy, awe and respect for the theological and social authorities which had hitherto determined what acceptable discourse was, always had to be overcome before any new ideas could begin to be entertained.[8]

The positive features of polemic are evident. By laying bare the 'realities', however unpalatable, of a situation, it provides

[6]   One of the many intriguing points made by my colleague in the University of Otago, Dr John K. Hale, in 'Milton and the Rationale of Insulting', a paper given to the conference on 'Freedom and Modernity? Early Modern Studies in the Pacific', Wellington, 4–7 August 1994; he characterises insulting as 'a deeply humanist exploit', tracing its Classical roots in Aristotle, and notes both its playful or ludic role, in lightening a heavy discourse with a 'licensed release of aggression', and its seriousness as a counterpart to praise, ensuring the disparagement and ridicule of those who deserve it; Milton's 'abusive charisma', for example, derives from Quintilian's *inventio*, it is the fruit not only of a quick intellect but of *urbanitas*; it pleases and teaches and is not to be confused with angry, emotion-laden outbursts.

[7]   *Aus lieb zurne ich also . . . ; Wie man trotzen soll aus Kreuz wider alle welt* (H.-J. Köhler et al. (eds.), *Flugschriften des frühen 16. Jahrhunderts* (Microfiche-Serie, Zug, 1977ff.):168/456 – Wittenberg, 1524), Fiiiʳ.

[8]   Marc Lienhard, 'Mentalité populaire . . . a Strasbourg en 1522–1523', in M. Kroon and M. Lienhard (eds.), *Horizons Européens de la Réforme en Alsace* (Librairie Istra: Strasbourg, 1980), p. 39.

diagnostic tools by which problems can be honestly faced and remedies attempted. By asking the right questions, and asking them in a way which cannot be swept aside, the first steps have been taken to undermining false certainties and clearing the way for alternative solutions. It has been argued that the Reformation's advocates went beyond the personal attacks of the humanists, adapting satire to mobilise public opinion for a positive, creative programme.[9] It is no accident that the phrase 'to take the lid off' occurs so often in the writings of Thomas Müntzer and other sixteenth-century pamphleteers. In Augean stables muck-raking can be regarded as an honourable profession. As Josef Schmidt has pointed out, the demasking character of satire, measuring perceived deficiency against agreed moral norms, cohered well with Luther's 'central aim, to reform or recreate evangelical Christianity'. The satirical code excites ridicule, but its primary aim is to disclose and highlight the incongruities in a situation.[10]

Thus polemic also has a heuristic function. Its undoubted aggressive components can shock its targets into revising their perceptions. Where the polemical 'game' is properly played the participants can ascertain the lacunae in their knowledge, the weak points in their arguments, the limitations in their 'blik', or world-view, as they allow themselves to be challenged and stretched by the polemic of an opponent. Jewish culture, of course, has always relished the cut and thrust of such debate.

The clash of view and counter-view also empowers onlookers by offering them a range of options. Polemic of this kind, for all its divisive features, presupposes an ultimate community of

[9]   Cf. Barbara Könneker, 'Vom "Poeta Laureatus" zum Propagandisten: Die Entwicklung Huttens als Schriftsteller in seinen Dialogen von 1528 bis 1521', in *Colloque international d'études humanistes: L' humanisme allemand 1440–1540*: XVIIIe colloque international de Tours (Fink: Munich, 1979), pp. 303–19.

[10]   Gerhard Dünnhaupt, 'Luther the Satirist: Strategies and Function of his Satire' in idem (ed.), *The Martin Luther Quinquennial* (Wayne State University Press: Detroit, 1985), pp. 32–43, esp. p. 34.

minds and values. Rules and boundaries and referees are recognised. While argument proceeds, on lines that are neither compelling nor arbitrary, there is an alternative to repressive tolerance or coercion or violence. Individual freedom and community concerns can be married.[11] When, on the other hand, debate is suppressed and challenge interpreted as personal insult, one suspects a provincial society and a petty mind. Polemic may be as essential for healthy thought as conflict to an effective democracy.

Finally, polemic has a liberating role. It is illuminating to note who dislikes polemic, for it empowers those who have nothing to pit against oppression but their minds and their mouths.[12] It is the extreme, all-or-nothing language of the dreamer.[13] It articulates their frustration and distress and sets it within a larger context. It provides information and analytical tools for those whose influence and status in society have lagged behind their social and cultural importance. The 'structural analysis' of liberation theology is a good contemporary example. Inhibiting barriers based on traditional roles and loyalties, and sentimental myths and

[11]   Chaim Perelman and Lucy Olbrechts-Tyteca, *The New Rhetoric: a Treatise on Argumentation*, tr. John Wilkinson and Purcell Weaver (University of Notre Dame Press: Notre Dame, Ind., 1969), p. 514.

[12]   Fierce social, professional and hierarchical opposition to lay literacy in Church and state triggered constant and determined efforts to limit its spread; cf. Klaus Schreiner, 'Grenzen literarischer Kommunikation. Bemerkungen zur religiösen und sozialen Dialektik der Laienbildung im Spätmittelalter und in der Reformation', in Ludger Grenzmann and Karl Stackmann (eds.), *Literatur und Laienbildung im Spätmittelalter und in der Reformationszeit*, Germanistische Symposien, V (Metzler: Stuttgart, 1984), pp. 1–23.

[13]   Hans-Jürgen Goertz is one of the few to look at dreams in the Reformation period: 'Träume, Offenbarungen und Visionen in der Reformation', in Rainer Postel and Franklin Kopitzsch (eds.), *Reformation und Revolution. Beiträge zum politischen Wandel unter den sozialen Kräften am Beginn der Neuzeit*, Festschrift für Rainer Wohlfeil zum 60. Geburtstag (Stuttgart, 1989), pp. 171–91.

individualistic pieties can be seen for what they are. Polemic, then, is indispensable if the disenfranchised are to have a good conscience about creating and deploying networks of resistance. It may be not only superficial but oppressive to contrast it with a 'constructive approach', or to characterise it as 'a stereotyped aggressive stance'.[14]

It was no mean task to challenge the power of century-long ideas and values, and those who throw themselves into commitments are frequently ready to climb over corpses to attain their ends. Mosellanus' comment after the Leipzig debate between Luther and Eck that the former had come over as full of life and fun, but that everyone wished he was less fierce and biting in his criticisms reminds us that such emotional engagement frequently swings from one extreme to the other. One only has to think of Sir Thomas More![15]

Polemics should not, then, be confused with coarseness of expression or personal abuse, with what the Germans call 'Grobianismus'. Undoubtedly resoluteness does often degenerate into rudeness, and one can see why. Haug Marschalck, for example, listing Biblical precedents for drastic vocabulary, argued, as Luther so often did, that the monstrous evil of the Reformation's opponents could not be defeated 'with a gentle voice, and a discreetly opened mouth'; ordinary people would not be reached without forthrightness. Luther's natural inclination was to be mild, good, gentle, pure and merciful, but the abuses in the Church and the exploitation of the laity

---

[14] Hans-Christoph Rublack, 'Anticlericalism in German Reformation Pamphlets', in Dykema and Oberman (eds.), *Anticlericalism*, pp. 461–90, esp. pp. 481f.

[15] *In Gesellschaft ist er lustig, scherzhaft, lebhaft und immer freudig . . . Nur den einen Fehler tadeln all an ihm, daß er im Schelten etwas zu heftig und beißend sei*; Martin Hurlimann (ed.), *Martin Luther. Dargestellt von seinen Freunden und Zeitgenossen Johannes Mathesius, Philipp Melanchthon, Lucas Cranach u.a.* (Berlin, 1933), p. 81; cf. Alistair Fox, *Thomas More: History and Providence* (Basil Blackwell: Oxford, 1982).

forced him to be outspoken and aggressive.[16] Only drastic language, Luther himself argued, could reveal the fantasies of his opponents for what they were. One has to snarl like a dog to be heard. (The word he uses is *mordacitas*.) Posterity will understand this. After all, the prophets and Paul spoke equally trenchantly; it is also because we have become so habituated to their words that we no longer sense this. To speak moderately is to ensure that one is ignored. Even in the womb of Rebecca, Jacob and Esau had to fight for the upper hand.[17]

Language, then, reflects our anthropology. For Luther life is a struggle, in reality as well as theology, and the dauntless courage and unshakeable faith on which contemporaries so often commented was certainly reflected in his drastic language.[18] It has to be remembered that the threat of coercion and violence, the resort to feudal levy or mercenary troops, to prison and torture and stake was never far away. Christian princes and their theological advisers had long known that the mailed fist was the best way to deal with schismatics and heretics, and the latter, too, had learned from the Hussites to be proactive. In principle, at least, Luther eschewed physical violence, though his close alliance with the Saxon court qualifies this. It is ironic, indeed, that it is precisely his outrage at what he sees as the physical violence of Müntzer and the Papacy, for

[16]   . . . *jr boßhait mit menschen leer in die götlych warhayt zu vermischen, mocht nit leiden mit sanffier stymm vnd mytt halbem mund wyder fochten werden*; Haug Marschalck, *Ein Spiegel der Blinden*, A 3 b 27ff., quoted in Gottfried Blochwitz, 'Die antirömischen deutschen Flugschriften der frühen Reformationszeit (bis 1522) in ihrer religiös-sittlichen Eigenart', ARG 27 (1931), p. 183 n. 5; a study of how the Reformers themselves justified their use of polemical language would be rewarding.

[17]   *Video enim ea, quae nostro saeculo quiete tractantur, mox cadere in oblivionem, nemine ea curante*; W Br. 2, 168/3–11.

[18]   Andrea Körsgen-Wiedeburg offers good examples of this: 'Das Bild Martin Luthers in den Flugschriften der frühen Reformationszeit', in Horst Rabe et al. (eds.), *Festgabe für Ernst Zeeden* (Aschendorff: Münster, 1976), pp. 154–6.

example, which provokes his most outrageous verbal violence. This was preferable to physical coercion, though of course it could also trigger the latter.

Our language reflects also our concept of God. Argula von Grumbach, for example, like so many of the Reformers, read Scripture as witnessing to a tempestuous, caring but also chastising God, a God of conflict and not of harmony. Luther declared that the Gospel, truly preached, always creates *uffrur*, turns things upside down. Wherever Christ is born, Herod appears, warned Thomas Müntzer, meaning that justice and truth always attract their polar opposites.[19] Argula von Grumbach's favourite Scriptural quotations tell of human traditions and wisdom being swept aside (Matthew 15:8; 1 Corinthians 3:19), of princes and potentates being overturned, of the poor and voiceless finding advocates, of children and women ruling (Isaiah 3; Psalm 146:3; Hosea 8:4). For God brings not peace but the sword, sets family against family, parents against children (Matthew 10:35), and uproots everything false (Matthew 15:13). Confrontation and radical change are inevitable. And it is the yeast of the word, mixed, as the parable has it, by a woman, which will effect this (Matthew 13:33, 10:42). God will strike the earth with the rod of his mouth, slaying the wicked with the breath of his lips (Isaiah 11:4). Hidden scandals will be revealed, mendacity banished (Matthew 10:26; Hosea 4:1).[20]

The Christian God is a polemical God, but effects transformation without physical violence. 'The word of God must be our weapon. We must not hit out with weapons, but love our neighbour, and keep peace with one another, as the Lord says in John 13, "That is how you will be recognised as my disciples." In Isaiah 33 the Lord says that the word, which

---

[19] Peter Matheson (ed. and tr.), *The Collected Works of Thomas Müntzer* (T. & T. Clark: Edinburgh, 1988; henceforth CW), p. 282.
[20] Peter Matheson (ed. and tr.), *Argula von Grumbach: A Woman's Voice in the Reformation* (T. & T. Clark: Edinburgh, 1995; henceforth AvG), pp. 79, 84, 90, 122, 133, 142, 148, 158, 180, 188.

proceeds from his mouth, will never be without fruit.'[21] One notes the limitless faith in such redemptive words. One precious fruit of such words is that they 'open fists'. God works through the seed of the word to effect change non-violently.[22] In her long poem, refuting the outrageous claim that her womanly 'garrulity' stemmed from licentiousness, she turns the other cheek, linguistically, and declines to descend to the level of her opponent, 'Johann of Landshut'. Yet she does not cede an inch on the substance of the accusations against her, and her own polemical response, delving deep into Scripture to illustrate women's true role under God, has genuine heuristic value. No one reading it empathetically could see women or Scripture in the same way again. Polemics, then, has its value.

Yet the century of polemic and confessionalism was also a utopian one which yearned for order, harmony, justice and peace. It saw the emergence of some of the most moving literature ever penned against the folly of war, and determined efforts to launch a diplomatic network, which would obviate the necessity for immediate resort to hostilities. It also witnessed attempt after attempt to resolve conflict by peaceful colloquy. Polemics may be out of favour in contemporary Western society, but curiously there is equally little disposition to pay serious attention to mediation. Institutions such as the Ecumenical Movement or the United Nations are hardly in fashion. Hence we may have to guard against a certain predisposition to be dismissive of the irenic initiatives of the sixteenth century.

By irenics is meant a determined attempt to listen carefully, to tune one's ears to the alien language and expectations of the

---

[21] AvG, 133.

[22] 'Words Open Fists' is the title, based on Quintilian's distinction between the closed fist of dialectic and the open hand of dialogue, of Horst Schorlemmer's remarkable account of the peaceful transformation of the former East Germany in 1989 into a democratic state; *Worte öffnen Fäuste: Die Rückkehr in ein schwieriges Vaterland* (Kindler: Munich, 1992).

other. This requires patience and preparation, time and trust. While polemic uses the swift cut and thrust of debate, dialogue is built on imaginative empathy, on creating a safe environment in which vulnerability becomes possible.[23]

Secondly, it involves a willingness to rephrase one's own concepts and concerns to make them accessible to the other. This requires an awareness of the varieties of discourse, or language games, and an ability to commute between one and the other, instead of discussants talking by one another, because they are so busy refuting arguments or presenting alternative accounts of past or present conflicts. In genuine dialogue one crosses imaginatively to the territory of the partner and seeks to uncover the communality of perceptions and interests. Guido Calogero has described this commitment to dialogue as the absolute basis for a liberal ethic, a 'freedom to express our belief and to try and convert others to it, with the obligation to let others do the same with us, and to listen to them with the same willingness to understand their truths and make them ours that we demand of them for our own'.[24] Facilitators can enable conflicting parties, by the use of role-play and other boundary-crossing devices, to explore the world through the eyes of the other. Insights can be preceived as complementary rather than

---

[23] Some modern business and communication handbooks appear to instrumentalise dialogical, or listening skills simply as techniques to win others over: cf. Albert Thiele, *Die Kunst zu überzeugen. Faire und unfaire Dialektik* (VDI Verlag: Düsseldorf, 1990); Schorlemmer, on the other hand, emphasises that true dialogue always names the uncongenial, and therefore can only be practised where there is freedom from fear, violence and domination, from the tyranny of 'correct' vocabulary (*Worte öffnen Fäuste*, p. 252); the Second Vatican Council offered a helpful definition of dialogue: see Austin Flannery (ed.), *Vatican Council II. The Conciliar and Post Conciliar Documents* (Talbot Press: Dublin, 1975), pp. 1005–14.

[24] Guido Calogero, 'Why Do We Ask Why? Some Observations on the Ethics of Dialogue: The Will to Understand as the Absolute Foundation of Liberalism and Morals', *Actes des XIe Congrès International de Philosophie*, vol. XIV (North Holland Pub. Co.: Amsterdam), pp. 260–5; quoted in Perelman and Olbrechts-Tyteca, *The New Rhetoric*, p. 56.

exclusive. Participants can escape from their own provincial 'dialects' and move towards being understood by an in principle 'universal audience'.[25] Irenics, like polemic, has a heuristic function.

The issue of power must also be squarely faced in mediation. Mediation works only where both sides come to recognise clearly where their interests conflict, and where they coincide, and where there is a readiness to hammer out a creative com-promise which respects the essential interests of both parties. An irenical solution liberates both sides from the waste of energy and time, and from a confrontation which may well develop into angry, wasteful, and even bloody conflict.

The Reformation, of course, saw determined attempts at colloquy, between Old Church and New, between Lutherans and Zwinglians, between Reformed and Anabaptists, as well as polemic. All language, in Erasmus' view, was mediatorial, mirroring the ultimate harmony of the cosmos.[26] A successful act of communication created a bridge between people. Holy Scripture itself was the supreme example, the bridge from God to humanity. Here was the basis, together with the recovered knowledge of the Early Church, for agreement on doctrine, morality, Church and social structures. God's language would reconcile all mere human differences.

It is at times of stress and challenge that new language is always minted. Luther himself has been been unforgettably

---

[25] Perelman and Olbrechts-Tyteca argue that the highest point of unanimity is reached when there is agreement on the 'universal audience', but point out that the latter is a construct of each individual; *The New Rhetoric*, pp. 31–5.

[26] Cf. the unpublished article by Manfred Hoffmann, 'Language and Reconciliation: Erasmus' Ecumenical Attitude'; and ibid., *Rhetoric and Theology: the Hermeneutic of Erasmus* (University of Toronto Press: Toronto, 1994), pp. 211–27; Marjorie O'Rourke Boyle, *Erasmus on Language and Method in Theology* (University of Toronto Press: Toronto, Buffalo, 1977).

described as a 'language event', a *Sprachereignis*.[27] On the most
obvious level both Renaissance and Reformation saw an
extraordinary burgeoning of languages. The renewing of ancient
tongues, such as Latin, Greek and even Hebrew, was accompanied, as is so often the case, by an energising and coming of
age of vernacular ones. Language-smiths of outstanding
creativity flourished, from Erasmus to Luther, Cranmer to
Rabelais. With the advent of the printed book and tract,
language hurdled the old barriers of estate and caste and nation,
and to some extent new ideas became accessible to women,
and to the common folk.[28] The recovery of learning was made
permanent, knowledge advanced simultaneously in widely
separated regions, lay people gained immediate access to
enhanced resources.[29] The potential for informing people and
engaging their participation was unprecedented. As Roger
Chartier has said so well, images and texts were now given a
more substantial presence and a more familiar reality.[30] These

[27]   Gerhard Ebeling, *Luther: an Introduction to His Thought* (Fortress:
Philadelphia, 1970); the bland English translation, 'Luther's linguistic
innovation', fails to catch the dramatic, explosive character of his discourse,
of language which was itself event.

[28]   Cf. Peter Matheson, 'Breaking the Silence: Women, Censorship and
the Reformation', *Sixteenth Century Journal* XXVII/I (1996), pp. 97–109.

[29]   William Bouwsma, 'The Renaissance and the Broadening of
Communication', in Lasswell et al. (eds.), *Propaganda and Communications*
Vol. 2, *The Emergence of Public Opinion in the West*, pp. 3–40.

[30]   There is a very extensive literature on the printing press; cf. Elizabeth
Eisenstein, *The Printing Press as an Agent of Change: Communications and
Cultural Transformations in Early Modern Europe* (Cambridge University
Press: Cambridge, 1979); very suggestive is Roger Chartier (ed.), *The Culture
of Print: Power and the Uses of Print in Early Modern Europe*; tr. Lydia G.
Cochrane (Polity Press in association with Basil Blackwell: Cambridge/
Oxford, 1989), esp. pp. 1–10; Mark U. Edwards, *Printing, Propaganda and
Martin Luther* (University of California Press: Berkeley/London, 1994)
warns, esp. pp. 37–40, of the danger of underestimating the 'multiplier effect'
of the printed book and its role in reaching a mass audience between 1518
and 1546 there may well have been some six million books or pamphlets,
excluding Bible translations, in circulation.

are not just connections which later historians have made. In 1521 Eberlin von Günzburg spoke of a new stirring in the German nation, a revival which he attributed to God: 'profound insight, keen and sensible initiatives, superb work in all the crafts, discovery of all sorts of literature and of all the useful languages, the new and useful skill of printing, a desire for evangelical teaching, a delight in all that is true and honest'.[31]

To cap it all, in the wake of the educational and linguistic surge and the technical revolution of printing came the enthusiasm for Scripture. Erasmus' call for a philosophy of Christ, which yoked philosophy firmly to daily life, on the one hand, and to Scripture on the other, was the culmination of a long humanist drive to ally philosophy with rhetoric.[32] Scripture emerged as the Word above all words, relativising the professional codes of canon-lawyers and clerics and scholastics. In vernacular, printed form it was accessible as never before. It has been suggested that by mid-century about a million copies of the German Bible existed. Even though only a minority of laity had direct access to Scripture, and a quite tiny minority to the written exegesis of it, its mana, or prestige, could not be questioned. Argula von Grumbach's contemptuous dismissal of canon law and philosophical speculation and her call for total dependence on the divine light of Scripture is typical: 'Philosophy can avail nothing. . . . Jurisprudence cannot harm me. What I have written to you is no woman's chit-chat, but the word of God. . . .'[33]

---

[31] *Subtile sinn/ scharpffe vernünfftige anschleg/ maisterliche arbeit in allen handtwercken/ erkantnüß aller geschrifften vnd aller fürderlichen sprachen ein new nützlich kunst der buchtruckery/ begird ewangelischer lere/ ain gefallen ab aller warheit vnd eberkeit* [sic]. *Ein klägliche klag an den christlichen römischen kayser Carolum. . . . Der erst bundts gnoß* (Fiche 1584–5/4092), Aii[v]; he was not uncritical at times, however, of the mercenary motives of the printers: *Mich Wundert, daß kein Geld im Land ist* (Fiche 142/388), Biiii[v].

[32] Cf. Jerrold E. Seigel, *Rhetoric and Philosophy in Renaissance Humanism* (Princeton University Press: Princeton, 1968).

[33] AvG, 89f.

The élan of the Reformation period is mirrored in a plethora of ways: in its songs, its music, its wood-cuts, its art, its sermons. This book will concentrate on the pamphlets of the early 1520s. It will be less concerned with their doctrinal or ethical content than with their discourse, their genres, their communicative tools, their style.[34]

The style of the Reformation pamphlets mirrors the uproar in countless individual minds and hearts, reflects a society in perplexed and joyous upheaval. We are the way we interact. We write the way we are.[35] Style is far more than the aesthetic garment in which substance is clothed, concepts and ideas are 'presented'. As Hans Speier has said, where language is used not merely informatively, but playfully, aesthetically, and metaphorically, it enables one to live with the 'dreadfully incomprehensible' by inventing verisimilitudes to the comprehensible.[36]

This, surely, is as true of Luther, say, as of Shakespeare. In his analysis of Luther's vernacular sermons, Leroux draws on the work of Kenneth Burke, Chaim Perelman and Lucy Olbrechts-Tyteca, and argues convincingly that 'figurative language may be as rhetorically important to argument as it has been assumed to be aesthetically in literature'. Figures are not just decorative, they bring about a change in perspective. 'Critical sensitivity to style contributes to understanding how a discourse functions.' By tracing not only how Luther focuses his writing, but also gives it 'presence', wardrobing his ideas in

---

[34]   Much of the older literature and not a little of the newer is concerned with determining how 'Lutheran' writings are, how central the formal and material principles of the Reformation; the pioneering article by Gottfried Blochwitz mentioned in n. 16 above is vitiated by this obsession.

[35]   A vivid analysis of the interactive nature of writing and reading is given by Deborah Brandt, *Literacy as Involvement: The Acts of Writers Readers and Texts* (Southern Illinois University Press: Carbondale and Edwardsville, 1990).

[36]   Hans Speier, 'The Communication of Hidden Meaning', in Lasswell et al. (eds.), *Propaganda and Communication*, Vol. 2, p. 262.

attractive form, and finally establishing 'communion' with the
audience, we come to understand his writings as a form of
stylised speech, address, outreach. Printed sermons are, of
course, a particularly useful example of literature on the edge
of a predominantly oral, popular culture. Leroux's image of
Luther as a choreographer of thought is a striking and helpful
one.[37]

Writers such as Brandt and Leroux and Ivan Illich remind us
that 'lay literacy' is far more than a technical accomplishment
in reading and writing, made possible by new technologies or
communicative techniques, it implies 'a new type of space in
which social reality is reconstructed', it has implications for
memory and conscience. The book becomes the decisive
metaphor through which the self is conceived.[38] Through what
is often termed 'passive literacy' even those not able to write or
even read themselves came to recognise the authority of the
printed word.

The Reformation pamphlet facilitated the dance of ideas on
a remarkably accessible stage. In today's Pacific Island cultures
dramas are interrupted by the audience. They are expected to
be interactive. Similarly the sixteenth-century pamphlet was
written for an interactive situation. It is impossible to read them
without being aware of the rhythms, repetitions, alliteration,

[37]   Neil Richard Leroux, 'Style in Rhetorical Criticism: the Case of
Martin Luther's Vernacular Sermons' (PhD, University of Illinois, 1990),
esp. pp. 7, 289. I am indebted to Leroux for the formulation that Luther
approaches texts as a choreographer, p. 267; John W. O'Malley has pointed
out that for all Luther's allegiance to the text of Scripture in his sermons,
following the homiletic, patristic, and 'grammatical' tradition, he also uses
elements of the classical *contio*, the *genus deliberativum*, calling for decision
and action; together with the doctrinal content, there is a polemical
demarcation from opponents, and a 'practical agenda that required decision'.
'Luther the Preacher', in Dünnhaupt, *The Martin Luther Quinquennial*, pp.
3–16, esp. p. 13.
[38]   Ivan Illich, 'A Plea for Research on Lay Literacy', in David Olson
and Nancy Torrance (eds.), *Literacy and Orality* (Cambridge University Press:
Cambridge, 1991), pp. 28, 40.

antitheses, and parallels of oral culture. It may be helpful to conceive of them as a carnival procession of pertinent and impertinent images, of maskings and unmaskings, of knotty questions and triumphantly simple answers. Long before the novel such writings enabled alternative worlds to be presented. A good example is Eberlin von Günzburg's 'Wolfaria', a utopian vision of the German nation, renewed morally, educationally, socially, and spiritually, and resting on the communal ethos of a peasant republic.[39]

Dreams of truth, justice, freedom could be launched on a flood of cheap paper and smudgy print. In their immediacy, evocativeness, concreteness, and stridency these pamphlets caught the contemporary imagination. Verbal images of Jerusalem and Babylon, Christ and Antichrist, jostled alongside simple, rough-hewn wood-cuts, in which peasants and women routed clerical pretensions and challenged university experts. In their interactive dialogue, creative irreverence, shafts of wit, and 'principled audacity'[40] these often anonymous pamphlets seemed indeed to represent the *vox populi*, to conjure up that anonymous and elusive animal, public opinion.

In their pages theology and piety became, for a while, *kurzweilig*, entertaining. And yet, at the same time, it had never been more serious. For really good play, as every teacher knows, is the most intense, concentrated work. One of the achievements of the pamphlet may have been to recover the playfulness of religious discourse. Its closeness to the dance, song, poetry, and ritual of oral culture enabled it to touch people in new depth.[41]

[39] Gottfried Geiger, 'Die reformatorischen Initia Johann Eberlins von Günzburg nach seinen Flugschriften', in Rabe et al. (eds.), *Festgabe für Zeeden*, pp. 178–201.
[40] A memorable phrase used by the journalist John Pilger to describe New Zealand's defiance of the nuclear weapon powers.
[41] Cf. Eric Havelock, 'The Oral-Literate Equation', in Olson and Torrance, *Literacy and Orality*, pp. 1–27.

'Manners makyth the man.' The manner in which the pamphlet was conceived, written and structured, presupposed an eager, reading public, an emergent public opinion, the convergence of interests of reforming clerics and impatient laity. Yet, as Hans Speier has said, 'the audience seeks the meaning that it needs'. Mark Edwards has now documented this, drawing our attention forcefully to the way in which the printed book packaged ideas. There can be a chasm between the intentions of the writer, the presentation of the printer, and the reception by the reader.[42] The medium may not be the message, but it certainly conditions it. The traditional stepping-stones in the progress of the Reformation are radically shifted if we look, as Edwards has suggested, less at the gradually shifting doctrinal perceptions of an academic, Latinate minority, and more at the warm reception given by a much broader spectrum of the population to Luther's devotional and vocational emphases, to his championing of Scripture, and to the personality of the reformer; '. . . the story takes a different form if you structure it around communication and ask what those with an engaged interest would know about Luther and when they would know it'.[43]

The very term 'Laie', 'lay person', while deriving from the Greek *laos*, people, was understood in the medieval period not only to identify non-clerics, but to denominate the 'illiterate', those without Latinity. By the sixteenth century, with the spread of humanism in lay circles one distinguished between the intelligent, *kluge*, laity who had Latin and the 'simple', *einfeltige*, laity, who at best could read German. In turning to the German language, reformers such as Luther, von Hutten, Eberlin von

[42]   Speier, 'The Communication of Hidden Meaning', p. 281; Mark Edwards, *Printing, Propaganda and Martin Luther*, draws our attention forcefully to the importance of the packaging of ideas by the printed book and argues convincingly for more attention to be given to the reception of the Reformers' messages by the public.

[43]   Edwards, *Printing, Propaganda and Martin Luther*, p. 171.

Günzburg had to emphasise that they were not 'ashamed' to do this.[44]

The recourse to the vulgar language, the *lingua franca*, meant a break with an élitist view of education and religion and Church; there were no longer to be 'two kinds of Christians', 'spiritual' and 'worldly', using two different languages. The translation of the best learning into common coin provided the previously untooled with the leverage, information and authority to change society as well as to inform their own minds.[45] If previously the concept of literacy had been 'the great instrument of the power and influence of the *clerici*'[46] and only small 'textual communities' such as those of the Waldensians or Hussites had been able to challenge this, the combination of the vernacular with printing changed all that. It is no surprise to find countless pamphlets insisting on the right of lay people to have access to 'German books'.[47]

It is true that the Reformers did not talk of universal human rights to be informed, or to contribute to the new emergent Church and society. Their discourse is, rather, of a freedom based on baptism, an obligation based on election. But their heady mix of polemic and irenics assumed, often explicitly, a

[44]   *Ich will . . . mich gar nichts schemenn, deutsch den ungeleretenn layen zupredigen und schreiben*; W 6, 203.

[45]   Cf. Georg Steer, 'Zum Begriff "Laie" in deutscher Dichtung und Prosa des Mittelalters', in Grenzmann and Stackmann, *Literatur und Laienbildung*, pp. 764–8.

[46]   R. I. Moore, 'Literacy and the Making of Heresy, c. 1000–1150', in Peter Biller and Anne Hudson (eds.), *Heresy and Literacy 1000–1530*, Cambridge Studies in Medieval Literature, 23 (Cambridge University Press: Cambridge, 1994), p. 24.

[47]   There is a lively debate among medievalists and Reformation historians about the relationship between literacy and the spreading of heretical or unorthodox views; cf. Bob Scribner, 'Heterodoxy, Literacy and Print in the Early German Reformation'; Peter Biller, 'Heresy and Literacy: Earlier History of the Theme'; and R. N. Swanson, 'Literacy, Heresy, History and Orthodoxy; Perspectives and Permutations for the Later Middle Ages', in Biller and Hudson, *Heresy and Literacy 1000–1530*, pp. 255–78; 1–18; 279–93.

critical readership, which would toss provocations around and find them either winning or wanting. To its Catholic opponents such as Murner or Hauer it appeared not only to erode professionalism but to stoke the fires of anarchy, 'We have all become priests these days, whether we're men or women.'[48] There was significant conservative opposition to printing, and recent scholarship has emphasised the difficulties faced by Catholic writers in overcoming the theoretical as well as practical difficulties which popular access to printed books began to pose.[49]

If reformist theology followed humanism in regarding godly learning and living as inseparable, but went further by removing the sacred distance between priest and people, the pamphlet is the literary expression of this new self-understanding. In its form, language, and accessibility it threw open the doors of Scripture, theological reflection, moral decisions, and Church reform to those who could not read Latin, who had neither time nor energy for reading great tomes, but who wished to become subjects of their own destiny, temporal and eternal, and who wished to make connections between themselves and the people of God in all times and all places. The pamphlet's pages offered hospitality to those who had previously been regarded as part-time, or second-class Christians, just as the introduction of vernacular worship gave practical form to the principle of the priesthood of all believers. The importance of the pamphlets as texts is that they flesh out a dawning awareness of Church and society as inclusive, as places where everyone had a say, even the old mother of Ulm, even the peasant. Such communal literature expressed the conviction that books, especially the Book of books, were too important to be left to the bookish.

[48]   M. H. Guchmann, *Die Sprache der deutschen politischen Literatur in der Zeit der Reformation und des Bauernkrieges* (Akademischer Verlag: Berlin, 1974), p. 38.
[49]   David V. N. Bagchi, *Luther's Earliest Opponents: Catholic Controversialists, 1518–1525* (Fortress Press: Minneapolis, 1991).

It is understandable, therefore, that the Reformation pamphlet could only be a temporary phenomenon. Every society seeks to foster social harmony and a degree of unanimity about values, and exercises sanctions to enforce its conception of unquestionable truths. The media have to reflect its reading of the world, to transmit the social inheritance to the next generation, and to link together society's constituent parts.[50] The crisis, or rather the redistribution of authority which the pamphlets mirrored and encouraged could not be expected to last, and the censorship of prince, magistrate, theologian and inquisitor soon reined in its creativity. Access to information was access to power. One person's liberation meant another's displacement. The verbal uproar of polemic could quickly lead to social chaos. It had an incendiary dimension, and there is a sense in which the Peasants' War was to be its step-child, although the radicals would rightly deny, as Müntzer and Hergot did, that *von buchern oder von schreyben auffrur kommen, es kumpt alles aus gottes macht.* The insurrection was God's doing, not that of books.[51] Secular and religious authorities, however, had a common interest in defining and refining the zones of demarcation, and were quick to reimpose them.

Even without such social control, moreover, as Chrisman has pointed out, there were considerable limits to the effectiveness of printed communications. Few ideas found general acceptance throughout the whole of society. Educational standards and social loyalties varied too much: 'diffusion took place among specific groups; different forms of knowledge

---

[50] Perelman and Olbrechts-Tyteca, *The New Rhetoric*, p. 571; W. Phillips Davison, 'The Media Kaleidoscope: General Trends in the Channels', in Lasswell et al. (eds.), *Propaganda and Communication,* Vol. 3, pp. 191–248, esp. p. 196.

[51] Hans Hergot, *Von der newen Wanderung eynes Christlichen lebens,* quoted in Carlos Gilly, 'Das Sprichwort "Die Gelehrten die Verkehrten", oder der Verrat der Intellektuellen im Zeitalter der Glaubensspaltung', in *Forme e destinazione del messaggio religioso. Aspetti della propaganda religiosa nel cinquecento* (Olschki: Florence, 1991), p. 277.

appealed to different interests'.[52] Lay culture and clerical culture tended to go their own ways, even in Protestantism. The Latinate culture of humanism, well endowed financially and institutionally anchored, continued to dominate the form of cultural and political life of post-Reformation Europe, while a resurgent scholasticism, Protestant as well as Catholic, was to determine its values.

Yet the genie was out of the bottle, and nothing was ever to be quite the same again. Polemic may have begun to harden into propaganda by mid-century, and mediatorial dreams into rather stylised colloquies, but the playfulness of the pamphlet, with its wood-cut, its earthy style, and its wild, utopian optimism had become part of the lasting European heritage. The dance of ideas it initiated may have heralded the Peasants' War, but it also offered an alternative to coercive and violent solutions which continues to allure us.

[52]   Miriam Chrisman, *Lay Culture, Learned Culture, Books and Social Change in Strasbourg, 1480–1599* (Yale University Press: New Haven, 1982), pp. 281, 284.

CHAPTER TWO

THE EMERGENCE OF A PUBLIC OPINION

When Songs Become Water
. . . the newsprint of mutiny
is as medicine
on the fingertips,
and the beat of the press printing mutiny
is like the pounding of tortillas in the hands.

Martin Espada, *City of Coughing and Dead Radiators.*[1]

'Words are thrall but thocht is free.' This piece of folk wisdom can still be seen chiselled in stone above seventeenth-century doorways in Scotland. Certainly no one who has had to survive times of censorship and repression can doubt the explosive power of the word when it breaks out of that thralldom. Frequently it begins with brief scrawled slogans or snatches of doggerel or song, with caricature and flysheet or graffiti on a wall. Perhaps the pamphlet, however, is the most reliable evidence, like a periscope sticking out of the ocean, of that vast, submarine force of discussion and dissent, which we call public opinion.

Literary activity such as the Reformation pamphlets are evidence, then, of a dissonance between the values embraced by the power-brokers in society and an articulate and crusading minority, which may or may not be speaking for a wider

---

[1]   Martin Espada, *City of Coughing and Dead Radiators* (W. W. Norton: New York, 1993), p. 80.

constituency. It frequently claims to be the voice of 'the people'. It certainly provides otherwise inaccessible information; allows the social control of views to be circumvented; forges an underground network of communication, and helps to form an alternative consensus. Such a process enables participation in social and political decision-making by those previously excluded. It empowers marginalised groups such as 'lay', or non-expert people, women, the young and impatient, ethnic or cultural minorities. Such explosions of pamphlet literature both reflect and themselves encourage a wide variety of other mini-forms of communication: group gatherings, meetings, protests, petitions, webs of correspondence. An independent force gradually emerges to confront the received wisdom and challenge the controlled flow of information from the authorities, a 'fourth estate', a body of opinion which state and society have to take into account, if only by attempting to refute or domesticate or repress it. It develops its own maxims and criteria. Instead of the traditional door keepers, charismatic leaders emerge who incarnate and model and propagate the new attitudes. Long before the development of opinion polls attempted to measure it, and politicians pretended to ignore it, public opinion exercised its own field of power and magnetism; and political and ecclesiastical trimmers of every kind set their course by it.

But was there a public opinion as early as the sixteenth century? Jürgen Habermas has argued that public opinion is a bourgeois creation which did not emerge until the nineteenth century, based on the newspapers, periodicals, books, but also on the clubs and salons of that century. Its presuppositions are the 'private space' of people, who allow themselves the right to think their own thoughts; the availability of safe areas, little laboratories of new ideas, where heterodox concepts can be teased out; universal access to public media which can carry the bacilli though the body politic; a rational principle or norm; and finally a central forum such as a parliament, to focus the emergent views. One can see the arguments for Habermas' position: the robust self-confidence of the middle class, their organisational skills, their literacy, their pragmatic drive to relate thought to experience and to critique experience by further thought.[2] Balzer, however, was one of the first to contend that all the criteria named by Habermas are already satisfied in the Reformation period.[3] And many others would today argue a similar case. Most of the conditions set by Habermas had been satisfied. The humanists, after all, had already underlined the rights and duties of individual judgement, while Luther and his followers emphasised the priesthood of all believers, based on baptism. 'Inner space' had, in any case, always been a mark of the mystical and spiritualist tradition. Sodalities and less formal groups in or around monasteries and colleges and the cities flourished for the exchange of ideas, while popular preachers and the printing press spread ideas so fast that stunned onlookers thought there must be angels at work;[4] civic

---

[2]   Jürgen Habermas, *Strukturwandel der Öffentlichkeit. Untersuchungen zu einer Kategorie der bürgerlichen Gesellschaft* (Luchterhand: Darmstadt-Neuwied, 1962); a pioneer in outlining some of the cultural and political preconditions for the development of a public opinion was Louise W. Holborn, 'Printing and the Growth of a Protestant Movement in Germany from 1517–1524', *Church History* 11 (1942), pp. 123–37; still valuable is A. G. Dickens, *Luther and the German Nation* (Edward Arnold: London, 1974), pp. 102–34; cf. E. C. Erik Midelfort, 'Toward a Social History of Ideas in the German Reformation', in Kyle C. Sessions and Phillip N. Bebb (eds.), *Pietas et Societas. New Trends in Reformation Social History (Essays in Memory of Harold J. Grimm)* (Sixteenth Century Journal Publishers: Kirksville, Miss., 1985), pp. 11–22; probably the single most influential book in this area is Bob Scribner, *For the Sake of Simple Folk: Popular Propaganda for the German Reformation*, Cambridge Studies in Oral and Literary Culture, 2 (Cambridge University Press: Cambridge/London, 1981).

[3]   Bernd Balzer, *Bürgerliche Reformationspropaganda. Die Flugschriften des Hans Sachs in den Jahren 1523–1525* (Germanistische Abhandlungen, 42: Stuttgart, 1973), pp. 11–13.

[4]   Myconius: 'as if the angels themselves were the *Botenläufer*'; quoted by Werner Lenk, 'Martin Luthers Kampf um die Öffentlichkeit', in Gunter Vogler (ed.) with S. Hoyer and A. Laube, *Martin Luther. Leben − Werk Wirkung* (Akademie Verlag: Berlin, 1986), p. 59.

colloquies and Imperial Diets acted as sounding-boards for ideas; Scripture functioned as a plumb-line or norm.

The debate about the genesis of public opinion, moreover, can no longer be contained within the categories set by Habermas. The definition of what constitutes the 'public', is, after all, a rather subjective enterprise. Tribal society is eminently public in nature, and indeed totalitarian propaganda aims to reduce public opinion to a tribal consensus again. Most historians would accept today that a public opinion emerged in the Reformation period. Wohlfeil speaks of a forum for reform ideas, a *reformatorische Öffentlichkeit*. The German term has the connotation of openness, transparency, rather similar to what is meant today by the 'public square'.[5] J.-F. Gilmont has called for a more quantitative and systematic approach to the study of the Reformation pamphlet to document this, a concern now being met by studies such as those of Mark Edwards.[6]

What appears to be happening is that in the Reformation period, as the traditional guardians of cultural and religious values were challenged, a plurality of new voices emerged. Often these clustered around a charismatic individual, with whom

[5]   Rainer Wohlfeil, 'Reformatorische Öffentlichkeit', *Einführung in die Geschichte der deutschen Reformation* (Beck: Munich, 1982), pp. 123–33; Hans-Joachim Köhler, 'Erste Schritte zu einem Meinungsprofil der frühen Reformationszeit', in Volker Press und Dieter Stievermann (eds.), *Martin Luther: Probleme seiner Zeit* (Stuttgart, 1986, pp. 244–65); H.-J. Köhler (ed.), *Flugschriften als Massenmedium der Reformationszeit*, Klett-Cotta: Stuttgart, 1981; cf. the older, but still valuable article by Helga Trompert, which traces the emergence of a less confessional, functional approach, and warns against the uncritical use of modern categories of market research and mass communications: 'Die Flugschriften als Medium religiöser Publizistik: Aspekte der gegenwärtigen Froschung', in *Kontinuität und Umbruch: Theologie und Frömmigkeit in Flugschriften und Kleinliteratur an der Wende vom 15. zum 16. Jahrhundert* (Klett-Cotta: Stuttgart, 1978), pp. 211–21.

[6]   J.-F. Gilmont, 'Pour une typologie du "Flugschrift" des débuts de la Réforme. A propos d'une recherche entreprise à Tübingen', *Revue d'Histoire Ecclésiastique* 78.2 (1983), pp. 788–809; Mark Edwards, *Printing, Propaganda and Martin Luther*, passim.

people could identify. Pamphlets, one is inclined to argue, are built around personalities, around heroes and anti-heroes rather than abstract issues. It is in such personalities that the issues are crystallised: Reuchlin and the Dominicans, Luther and the Pope, Zell and Murner, Argula von Grumbach and Hauer. Luther himself, of course, became the most famous person in the whole of Germany. It has been computed that more than three million copies of his different writings circulated, that one-fifth of the entire pamphlet literature of the first three decades of the century flowed from his pen. The very ferocity of the attacks on him worked in his favour. The papal nuncio, Aleander, catches well the star status of Luther as he enters Worms. People rush forward to touch him, as if he were a holy relic. 'I suspect he will soon be said to be working miracles.'[7] He is emphatically larger than life. Public opinion focused on such 'public people', people's people.

It would be a mistake, however, to see public opinion as a 'trickle-down' phenomenon dependent on Luther, Karlstadt and other writers. Sometimes the boot was on the other foot, and the 'opinion-makers' themselves came under pressure. Luther himself, for example, was quite conservative in liturgical matters, but was eventually persuaded to produce a German vernacular Mass, by the accumulated pressure of letters and requests from all sides, including the secular authorities. Public opinion had become for him a sign that this was the will of God.[8] Moreover, public opinion was highly selective, and was fed by countless sources. It identified only with those aspects of Luther's teachings, such as his positive Scriptural piety in the early days, which suited its own predilections. It had little grasp of the niceties of theological issues. It gained profile as an alternative opinion, at first reflecting, but then transcending regional and sectional

---

[7] Quoted from Hurlimann, pp. 81f.

[8] *Nu aber so mich so viel bitten aus allen landen mit geschrifft und brieffen, und mich der weltlich gewalt darzu dringet, kunden wyr uns nicht wol entschuldigen und ausreden, sonder mussen darfur achten und halten, es sey der will Gottis*; W 17.1, 459/25–27.

concerns. Virtually every account of the spread of the Reformation in the towns, for example, notes the alliance between a popular preacher and what Lienhard calls 'les pulsations d'une opinion publique', a 'popular mentality', which begins in the heated disputations of inns such as the *herberg zur äxst* in Strasbourg, and eventually forces the hand of the Council.[9] There is an ongoing dialectical relationship between grass-roots tensions and the articulation of discontent by leaders such as Luther.

Pamphlets, then, are a literature of crisis, cultural, political, social and religious. Behind every pamphlet lies the collapse of a previous consensus, while it itself frequently proffers a way out, if not the way out.[10] But it is also a literature of exploration, excitement, even exhilaration. Successful pamphlets are those which reflect and at the same time spread and modify the 'pulsations' of oral discourse. It is not just that words are no longer held 'in thrall'. The unthinkable is being paraded in public; moreover it is driving for support, seeking to convict, determined to universalise itself. As Chrisman has pointed out, 'The early years of the Reform were marked by a pamphlet war, not a battle of books.'[11]

This, then, is not literature for its own sake, scholarship for its own sake. It is confessional, activist, cause-related, in

[9]   Marc Lienhard, 'Mentalité populaire', p. 38.

[10]   Berndt Hamm has pointed to the phenomenon of 'compression', *Verdichtung,* in the early modern period, a concern by theologians to reduce, order, simplify reality in the face of its growing complexity: 'Das Gewicht von Religion, Glaube, Frömmigkeit und Theologie innerhalb der Verdichtungsvorgänge des ausgehenden Mittelalters und der frühen Neuzeit', in Monika Hagenmaier and Sabine Holtz (eds.), *Krisenbewusstsein und Krisenbewältigung in der frühen Neuzeit . . .* (Peter Lang: Frankfurt, 1992), pp. 163–96; this is an interesting alternative to the more fashionable view of religion as a form of social control; as a concept however, it appears too all-encompassing and ill-defined to offer much analytical purchase on reality.

[11]   Miriam Chrisman, *Lay Culture, Learned Culture, Books and Social Change in Strasbourg, 1480–1599* (Yale University Press: New Haven, 1982), p. 12.

Foucault's terms, conflictual discourse. The struggle for truth is also a struggle for power. In Richard Cole's striking phrase 'words in print became virtual missiles'; almost by their nature pamphlets were bound to be polemical; he points out that the printer himself was often a preacher or priest.[12] Bernd Moeller underlines the civic provenance of the pamphlet and sees conversion of the reader as its primary aim.[13] Were the pamphlets, then, proto-catechisms for a new utopia, anticipating the *Systembruch*, the turn-around, the break with the whole previous system? Were they charters of human rights, rather similar to the manifestos of the Peasants' War? Were they, as they are often dubbed, pieces of propaganda?

Certainly pamphlets were weapons to thump opponents, as well as means to mobilise supporters. They were portrayed on wood-cuts as arrows, cannons, or clubs, and one obvious outcome of the verbal violence of the pamphlet was iconoclasm, the smashing of non-verbal images. There are also connections to be explored with the Peasants' War, with the structural, repressive violence which followed it, and indeed with the long dreary succession of religious wars for a century to come. But pamphlets were much more than pieces of polemic. They were information packs. With their armoury of arguments, precedents, information, they equipped supporters to pursue effective campaigns, and of course lent them moral support. Wohlfeil sees this as going well beyond the previous sectoral communication processes of the authorities or of humanism.[14]

[12]   Richard G. Cole, 'Reformation Printers: Unsung Heroes', *Sixteenth Century Journal* 15.3 (1984), pp. 327–39.

[13]   Bernd Moeller, 'Stadt und Buch: Bemerkungen zur Struktur der reformatorischen Bewegung in Deutschland', in W. J. Mommsen (ed.), *Stadtbürgertum und Adel in der Reformation: Studien zur Sozialgeschichte der Reformation in England und Deutschland* (Stuttgart, 1979), pp. 25–39.

[14]   Wohlfeil, *Einführung*, pp. 123–33.

This new public opinion, however, did not emerge overnight. The Wycliffite and Hussite movements were forerunners.
The humanist reform – a republic of letters from Hungary in
the East to England and Spain in the West, from the Baltic
in the North to Florence or Rome or Naples in the South,
produced new libraries, dictionaries, styles of letter-writing
and humour, which certainly transcended national boundaries
and later confessional allegiances. It also produced a new
breed of opinion-makers, lawyers, diplomats, teachers,
academics, and clergy, too. It was strongly lay and civic in
ethos. Although generally Latin-speaking, it nevertheless
challenged the old élites and could be accompanied by a
relish for the vernacular. As Lenk has said, it forced the
defenders of the Old Church to move from pronouncement
to disputation.[15] The ferocity of much humanist polemic
against the Papacy has tended to be underestimated. The
Roman pasquils, for example, and the German nationalist
attacks on Curial decadence helped, as Stadtwald has shown,
to create the Rome which 'Luther loved to hate'.[16] And as Martz
has said, 'We should not think of the Renaissance humanist
as a peaceful person, he is an expert in language, not in self-
control.'[17]

This humanist *via rhetorica* certainly offered an alternative
opinion, literate, articulate and determinedly reformist, but
was its social base broad enough to constitute a public opinion?
Certainly its alliance with the printing-press, its network of
sodalities, its trans-regional outreach, its challenge to Church
and university conventions, and its transmission through key

[15]   Lenk, 'Martin Luthers Kampf', p. 55; the most recent treatment in
Erika Rummel, *The Humanist-Scholastic Debate in the Renaissance and
Reformation* (Harvard University Press: Cambridge, Mass./London, 1995).
[16]   Kurt Werner Stadtwald, 'When O Rome Will You Cease to Hiss?
The Image of the Pope in the Politics of German Humanism' (PhD,
University of Minnesota, 1991), pp. 250, 246.
[17]   Louis L. Martz, 'Thomas More: The Search for the Inner Man',
Moreana 26 (1989), p. 409.

opinion-makers such as patrons, teachers, preachers, poets and counsellors, made it a community of discourse well on the way to becoming an independent force to be reckoned with. It saw itself as addressing the 'judgement of the whole world', *totius orbis iudicium,* as Mosellanus once put it, but of course by that the world of the intellectuals was meant. Its social range was limited.

At first inextricably tied up with the humanist one, the reform and reformation movement, including its Lutheran forms, reached still wider circles through its vernacular rhythms, rhymes, proverbs, liturgies, broadsheets, by its directness and coarseness, through its immediacy and its apocalyptic content, through a more populist style, a dashing use of wood-cuts, above all, though, through a rediscovered Bible.[18] In Eberlin von Günzburg's ringing phrase, *Der Pawr wirt witzig,* 'the peasant wised up, got the picture'.[19] The Bible gave the ordinary person access to a norm by which he could form his own opinions.[20]

Sermons, too, reminded the humble laity that though they had to work day and night, and knew no Latin, that put them side by side with 'Jesus our saviour [who] was a lay person, too, a carpenter, unlearned in the eyes of those whom the world

[18]   An undoubtedly humanist production, such as T. W. Best (ed.), *Eccius Dedolatus: A Reformation Satire* (Kentucky University Press: Lexington, 1971), pp. 63f., emphasised the unlearned nature of the first disciples and warned the scholastic theologians that the laity were now opening their eyes to the abuses around them.

[19]   Ludwig Enders (ed.), *Johann Eberlin von Günzburg. Sämtliche Schriften,* Vol. 1 (Neudrucke deutscher Literaturwerke . . . Halle, 1896), p. 65.

[20]   A monk in Upper Alsace was reported to have complained that uneducated laity, peasants and even gossiping women had 'gobbled up heavenly wisdom'; quoted by Franziska Conrad, *Reformation in der bäuerlichen Gesellschaft: zur Rezeption reformatorischer Theologie im Elsass* (Veröffentlichungen des Instituts für europäische Geschichte Mainz. Vol. 116; Steiner: Stuttgart, 1984), p. 2.

respected and saw as spiritual'.[21] We need to see the hunger for sermons, a vernacular liturgy, the thirst for German pamphlets, the endless debates and discussions, the insistence on Divine Law, Scripture, as part of a dawning hope in a new active literacy, a dignity for ordinary folk, a literate, lay discipleship or priesthood. All these 'mini-media' are related. Against all the odds, they enabled Biblical images, models, and teachings to resurface in vivid contemporary form. Who could ever have believed this possible unless it had happened? We wonder much too little at the 'Scripture-riddenness' of the sixteenth century. Patriarchs, prophets and apostles wandered through sixteenth-century books and minds. Reformers identified themselves or were identified with prophets and apostles. The Bible formed public opinion; while at the same time public opinion reshaped the Bible. To a significant extent a people's Bible emerged to replace a clericalised Bible.

With an estimated 5 per cent literacy in Germany at the time such changes in mental furniture, not to mention social change, could not of course have been achieved by books and pamphlets alone. It has been calculated that in the thirty years following 1518 at least six million vernacular treatises about the Reformation appeared, at least one for every two people, and one has to remember the multiplier effect of the semi-public reading of pamphlets, so the 5 per cent literacy figure may be a rather conservative one. In the towns it stretched to above 30 per cent. Nevertheless it appears that it was the intimate connection with the other mini-media which enabled a critical mass to be achieved, so that traditional authorities and taboos could be toppled.

It was the face-to-face encounters which really shifted hearts and minds, the civic talk-ins, endless discussions in inns and mills, monasteries and student lodgings, non-verbal events such

---

[21]   *Ob ir schon nit pfaffen oder münch seyt, kein latin künnen, tag und nacht mußt arbeiten . . . Jhesus unser heyland was auch ein ley, vor den würdigen und geistlichen der welt ungelert und ein zymmerman*; Martin Bucer, *Deutsche Schriften* 1, 85/16–19.

as processions, demonstrations and other acts of symbolic aggression; above all the electric excitement of innovative preaching. Slogans chanted in the streets one day would garnish the front page of a pamphlet the next. The visual images projected by broadsheets, wood-cuts, portraits, medallions were certainly also of incalculable importance.[22] It was a time when the boundaries between the oral and the written word, the literary and the visual, the Latinate and the vernacular, the literate and the semi-literate were extraordinarily fluid. Writer and artist worked together, author and printer, cleric and layman; printing popularised and laicised art, scholarship, literature. The current consensus of opinion may be best expressed in Robert Scribner's image of pamphlets as one 'voice' in the Reformation's musical score.[23]

There is certainly a complex dialectic between event and image and word. Lee Palmer Wandel has reminded us that acts are more vulnerable than texts.[24] The latter tend to survive; the former are caught for posterity only in textual form, or in the precarious web of popular memory. The pamphlet was one part of a communications process, of a new stirring of consciousness, a psycho-drama of staggering proportions in which old traumas were exorcised and new personas tried out. Many of the concepts contained in the pamphlets would have been received at second or third hand, either through listening to them being read out, or by reference to them in conversations, sermons, informal meetings. Social, cultic, pedagogic occasions would all have deployed pamphlets, but filtered them to meet their own specific needs.

[22]   One particularly attractive edition of these visual images is: Hermann Meuche (ed.), *Flugblätter der Reformation und des Bauernkrieges: 50 Blätter aus der Sammlung des Schloßmuseums Gotha,* catalogue by Ingeburg Neumeister (Insel: Leipzig, 1975).

[23]   Robert Scribner, 'Flugblatt und Analphabetentum. Wie kam der gemeine Mann zu reformatorischen Ideen?', in Köhler, *Flugschriften als Massenmedium,* p. 75.

[24]   In her fascinating reflection on 'Strubelhans and the Singing Monks', in Hagenmeier and Holtz, *Krisenbewusstsein . . . ,* pp. 307–15.

38

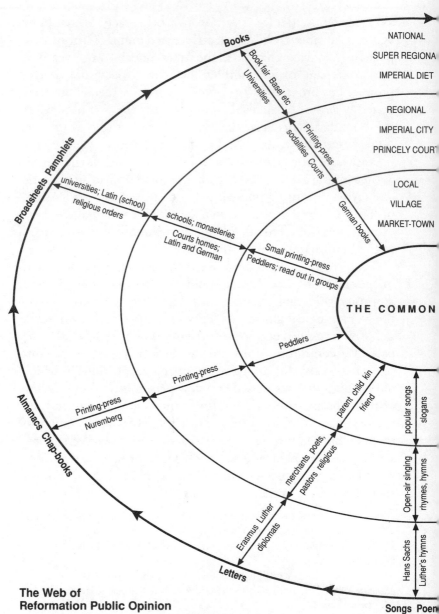

The Web of
Reformation Public Opinion

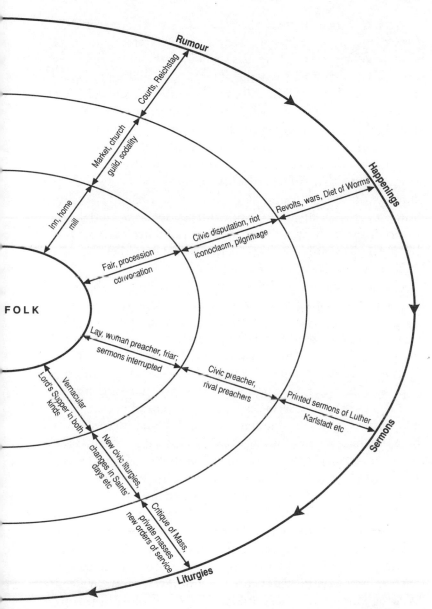

We have, then, to read these pamphlets in terms of their genesis and their reception. Strong-text characterisations of literacy, so beloved of academics, may miss the point noted by those who work today on the interface of oral and literate cultures that literacy is involvement, is in intimate dialogue with conversation, story-telling, song and dance. 'Instead of viewing the oral as antagonistic to the literate it is necessary to understand better how the oral sustains the literate.' Literacy is not an 'abstract, text-engined technology' but 'instead appears as something that flourishes only in local forms, as part of "how we do things around here". It is by nature and necessity pluralistic and in flux.' Text and context, semantic and social relationships are inseparable. 'Writing pulls into sharp focus the means by which we make the world together.' It is a 'thickening history of the "we"'.[25]

The Reformation pamphlet can be seen best, perhaps, as part of a popular movement to 'make the world together', rather than as a propaganda movement co-ordinated by a few gifted intellectuals. We would be talking about a plethora of 'mini-media', rather than about mass-media. Thomas Müntzer, for example, frequently refers to his work as 'speaking, printing, singing'. In other words he saw his printed writings as complemented by his sermons, and by the radical new liturgies in German, which aimed to train the whole congregation. Then there was his patient pastoral work, his special instructions to the advanced few in the 'upper room', and of course his letters. We have to be cautious that we do not overestimate the role of the printed word on its own in changing opinions.

These judgements may be particularly apposite to a form of literature so close to oral culture in its language, immediacy and ephemeral nature as the pamphlet, the *Flugschrift,* or 'fleeting writing'! Personal experience may support the insight that today's modern equivalents to pamphlets – films, videos, TV programmes, the most brilliant pieces of journalism – are

[25]   Deborah Brandt, *Literacy as Involvement,* pp. 7, 30f.

in themselves seldom sufficient to shift attitudes unless reinforced by the intimate face-to-face encounter, sharing the stress and excitement of an experience and then reflecting on it, working closely with a group over a sustained period of time. A good example in the New Zealand context is the *hui* in which the sharing of ideas is complemented by that of food, music, ritual, a common roof.

Attempting to construct a diagram which will portray the way in which Reformation attitudes and ideas spread is a salutary exercise, because no visual depiction can do justice to the complexity and speed of the process. Yet since the degree of consensus established is dependent on the 'universality' of the communication network and the nexus between new concepts and new technology it is important to make the attempt.

The web-form which has been chosen sets Herr und Frau Omnes, 'The common folk', at the centre. In one sense, of course, that is a fiction. The 'ordinary, average person' has never existed, and never will; he and she is a construct of our élitist or populist imaginings. Yet we children of the new communication age may well tend to underestimate the creativity and receptivity of peasant and artisan communities, especially if we think in anachronistically individualist terms. It was through the events of communal life, the seasonal markets, the patterns of the liturgical year, the round of feasts and festivals, so vividly portrayed in Richard Wunderli's *Peasant Fires*,[26] that news and views will often have trickled down, and reactions to them been articulated.

Around the outer rim of the web are noted the various 'media' which carried such news and views. The power of rumour can hardly be overstated in this era, especially when the drum of public anger and expectation was stretched as taut as it was in the early 1520s. Extraordinary events on the national or regional stage such as the Indulgence Controversy or the Diet of Worms

---

[26]   Richard Wunderli, *Peasant Fires: The Drummer of Niklashausen* (Indiana University Press: Bloomington and Indianapolis, 1992).

triggered off rumours, which were ornamented with sensationalist and miraculous elaborations as they spread. The same is true of more localised events, Lenten disturbances, the marriage of prominent clergy, iconoclastic outbursts. Sermons by parish priests or itinerant preachers responded to these events and were catalysts of others. Songs and rhymes imprinted controversies and personalities on the popular consciousness. Letters from children at distant schools and towns, or from kinsfolk and friends, put a familial face on social and ecclesiastical upheaval. Almanacs, broadsheets and pamphlets encapsulated in symbolic and verbal form hitherto unasked questions, and outlined programmes of action for those who could read, or be read to, or could at least compare the familiar iconography of saints and martyrs with the new role models and satirical caricatures. Books, of course, in German and Latin, flooded the homes of the literate and semi-literate as never before. And all these media interacted synergistically with one another in the secular and sacramental life of each village and town.

One has to recognise that even small settlements such as Lenting, not far from Ingolstadt, in which Argula von Grumbach spent much of her life, or Thomas Müntzer's Allstedt in Electoral Saxony, would be hosts to this wide range of media. That fact that Allstedt had its own printing press for a while reminds us that the traffic of ideas flowed in two directions, from the local scene, which was, after all, the dominant one for the overwhelming mass of the population, to the 'periphery' of the great towns and courts, as well as vice-versa. In larger cities such as Nuremberg or Strassburg such media would be dramatically augmented by grand cycles of sermons, by theatrically staged civic disputations, such a feature of the Reformation in the cities, and by spontaneous convocations in times of crisis in front of the town hall. New ideas, of course, have always spread along the trade routes, and trading centres such as Strassburg or Nuremberg put a premium on accurate information. The infant art of diplomacy, closely linked to business and trading interests as well as to politics, was also reliant on a steady, accurate stream of instructions and reports. Thus although the sixteenth century had almost nothing corresponding to today's mass-media, it did boast an intricate, complementary, and remarkably effective variety of what we might call 'mini-media'.

The spokes of the wheel, or radiating arms of the web, illustrate another key feature of the evolution of public opinion: the plethora of different loci in which news and ideas were received, exchanged, processed and 'broadcast': the local inns, mills, bath-houses, markets; peripatatetic messengers, hawkers and colporteurs of all kinds; pulpits and the temporary stage of wandering players; great houses, and more modest homes, maintaining contacts with family, friends, with patrons and clients; networks of trade and business. At a more sophisticated level there were the administrative, legal and diplomatic links between court and country, town hall and village, bishop's residence and clergy, provincials of orders and religious houses. Schools, academics and universities, the traditional transmitters of knowledge, were now comple-mented by the informal 'republic of letters' of the humanists, the printing-houses and their distributive networks, the great sounding-boards of provincial and national Diets. Town clerks such as Lazarus Spengler of Nuremberg, and the legal counsellors of magistrates and princes, played a key role in transmitting information. Nor should one underestimate the importance of the chancelleries of little courts such as that of Albrecht of Mansfeld, which sent Luther information and warned him, for example, of the danger awaiting him at Augsburg in 1518.[27] Not infrequently for individuals or groups these networks overlap to a bewildering degree. Argula

[27] W 15, 244, quoted in Siegfried Bräuer, 'Die Reformation in Grafschaft Mansfeld', *Protokoll Band zum Kolloquium anlässlich der ersten urkundlichen Erwähnung Eislebens am 23 November 1994* (Vol. 1, Veröffentlichungen der Lutherstätten Eisleben, Stekovics: Halle, 1995), p. 40.

von Grumbach, for example, who systematically ordered pamphlets from Spalatin in Wittenberg, also wrote widely, had children studying in distant Reformation centres, exploited her kinship contacts, and travelled herself!

Finally, one has to remember that local, regional, and trans-regional areas are all in two-way contact with one another. Information and ideas spread upward to opinion-makers such as Bucer or Luther from local and regional centres, as well as downward from them to the remote areas. All the major Reformers groaned at the size of their correspondence, and their rooms were littered with papers full of questions, requests, complaints, information. The 'reception' of ideas flowed both ways! A great army of intermediaries, such as preachers and printers and teachers, all added their own imprint to this two-way traffic.

Perhaps enough has been said to demonstrate that sixteenth-century processes and networks of communication are markedly different from those of our day, and that we have to be circumspect about describing sixteenth-century communication in modern categories of mass persuasion. Ozment, for example, describes the Reformation as a revolution, and speaks of the 'revolution of the pamphleteers'. Nor does he hesitate to use the term 'propaganda', though not in a pejorative way, to describe its literature, as do a host of other writers, including Cole, Edwards, Lienhard and Scribner.[28] Others speak of the Reformers launching 'literary offensives'.[29] Lenk describes Luther as a deliberate propagandist, *ein Stratege der Öffentlichkeitsarbeit,* who used his sermons as a laboratory for his writings, a *Prüffeld seiner Publizistik.* For all the value of Lenk's insights in many other respects, this may be to confuse our perceptions with Luther's intentions.[30] One

[28]   Steven Ozment, *Protestants: The Birth of a Revolution.*
[29]   Halbach, pp. 185–94.
[30]   I have pointed elsewhere to the problem of seeing Argula von Grumbach's work in these modernising terms; cf. Matheson, 'Breaking the Silence', p. 107.

fears that such large language sets off quite incorrect chains of assumptions.[31]

There are strong arguments for avoiding the term 'propaganda' altogether in relation to the pamphlet, in view of its modern associations with massive media penetration and a manipulative ethos. Propaganda involves the systematic and often cynical propagation by an interested party of tendentiously presented views. The aim is simply to influence public opinion, to 'sell' ideas. The function of the recipient is a purely passive one. Even the polemical pamphlet, on the other hand, is interested in argument, and takes the partner in argument seriously, even if only as opponent.

In his moving speech in 1982 accepting the award of the Hans and Sophie Scholl Award, Franz Fühmann explicitly contrasts the extraordinarily brave leaflets of the Scholls and their group, who called for resistance to Hitler, with the bland, pervasive propaganda of the Third Reich. The former are read in secrecy and excite the alarmed recognition of shame and complicity; they have a strange 'inescapable' quality and end with words which could be appended to most Reformation pamphlets: 'We are not silent; we are your bad conscience. . .'. The latter poured predictably out of every newspaper and radio.[32]

It may be salutary to note the comment of one of the best experts in the field, Hans-Joachim Köhler, who suggests that the agitatorial and polemical content of the pamphlets may

---

[31] One unfortunate by-product is rather curious modifications of the term 'revolution'; Heinz Scheible, in an article which seeks to put a theological grid on the pamphlets, refers to the Reformation as a 'conservative revolution'. 'Reform, Reformation, Revolution. Grundsätze zur Beurteilung der Flugschriften', *Archiv für Reformationsgeschichte* 65 (1974), pp. 108–34, esp. p. 133.

[32] Franz Fühmann, 'Wahrheit und Würde, Scham und Schuld. Rede bei der Entgegennahme des Geschwister-Scholl-Preises', in *Den Katzenartigen wollten wir verbrennen. Ein Lesebuch* (Deutscher Taschenbuch Verlag: Munich, 1988), pp. 261–72.

have been overestimated while the breadth of the themes they tackled, their reliance on discursive argument, and their importance as sources of information have been underrated.[33]

It is all too easy to read back the manipulative intentions of modern propaganda and advertising into sixteenth-century pamphlets. Analyses such as those of Balzer suggest that instead of categorising pamphlets in ideological terms, such as Catholic or Protestant, or in terms of literary genre, such as satires, dialogues, or epistles, we use a functionalist description: either they conduct personal polemic or they are programmatic or propagandistic.[34] The problem is that the Reformers appear as slightly disguised marketing executives, conducting amateurish market-research, and using verbal and visual material to mould people's behaviour. At the very least, more differentiation is required. Far from seeing the Ninety-Five Theses as programmatic, Luther regarded them as opening up a necessary debate.

There can be no objection to functionalist categories if they in fact represent what was actually happening. The term 'propagandist' may have some justification, for example, in relation to the nationalist and humanist pamphlets of an Ulrich von Hutten, or to the confessional literature of the second half of the century.[35] But it is quite another matter when applied to authors in the 1520s whose primary motivation was pastoral or theological. The widespread currency of the term 'propaganda' in the secondary literature is no argument for its continuance. Quite the contrary. If it is as misleading as has been suggested above it should be abandoned.

[33]   Köhler, 'Meinungsprofil', pp. 261f.

[34]   Cf. the critique by Ninna Jørgensen, *Bauer, Narr und Pfaffe: Prototypische Figuren und Ihre Funktion in der Reformationsliteratur* (Acta Theologica Danica, vol. XXIII; Brill: Leiden, 1988), esp. p. 12.

[35]   Cf. for example, von Hutten's *Die Anschauenden*, with its contrasts of the moral Germans and the 'womanly' Italians, its crude anti-clericalism and anti-papalism, the threat of a conspiracy of the sheep against their bloodthirsty shepherd; Lenk, 'Martin Luthers Kampf', esp. pp. 51, 60, 66; Stadtwald, 'When O Rome . . .' offers countless examples of such humanist polemic.

The Reformation pamphlet was generally, after all, a secondary product: it began as a sermon, or a meditation, or a private letter, or a contribution to a debate. Its arguments often went from mouth to mouth, or hand to hand as a manuscript, before it reached print. We need to ask in a much more specific way why and in what particular circumstances a Karlstadt or an Argula von Grumbach decided to entrust a passionately felt and intimately communicated personal concern to wider scrutiny through print, in principle addressing a universal public. The answer may lie in their understanding of evangelisation and liberation and in their personal distress and sense of vocation rather than in a concern for the techniques or social strategies of propaganda.

In other words, the original homiletical, pastoral, liturgical, confessional aims linger on in the new pamphlet form. To understand the impact of the Reformation pamphlet we must first reflect on the excitement with which sermons were listened to, the vernacular Scriptures read, the new pastoral advice given in the confessional received. When Luther began to move around 1518 to writing in German as well as in Latin it is Luther the pastor, the spiritual advisor, the ethicist, whose voice is heard in these pamphlets, not the academic controversialist, and certainly not the propagandist for a programme of structural reform. It is, above all, the preacher of a new Gospel of grace, not Indulgence. The sermons of Luther, or Müntzer, or Bucer, for example, are themselves immensely complex, and evidence a whole spectrum of intentions, including pedagogical and pastoral ones as well as proclamatory or exhortatory ones. Preacher and people alike were conceived as being *coram Deo*, in the presence of God, as the art of the period makes abundantly clear. Printing, too, was conceived as a God-given art, to enable people to learn Scripture and recognise the Romanists for what they were. It may be necessary to repeat these commonplaces to remind ourselves that the audience was an end not a means, a congregation rather than a political rally. Hence any simplistic reduction of the pamphlet to the agitatorial concerns of a Goebbels or for that matter a modern public relations executive does not begin to do justice to their complex genesis, nor does it explain why they touched people at so many levels.

The authors experienced a compulsion to preach and write. Their writings are littered with prayers, blessings, curses, lyrical exclamations, groans of despair. They have a doxological quality. Similarly, if we turn to their reception the pamphlets would not have been read as a contemporary newspaper or periodical is read, but much more like almanacs, or devotional guides, or reflections to guide one's daily life. The author often addressed the reader intimately as if she or he were the latter's spiritual adviser, confessor, priest, teacher, moral mentor. Room needs to be found in our interpretation of them for this dialogical nature of the pamphlet, its ' I–Thou' nature, its position on the rim between oral and literary culture, so that the religious intentions and expectations of its writers and readers are taken seriously, and the excitement with which the first pamphlets were read can be recreated. If one were to look for one area in which books and pamphlets most obviously moulded opinion and created social change the curiously neglected answer would have to be in worship, both private and public. The Church service was the most pervasive social gathering of sixteenth-century Europe. Vernacular collections of liturgies and hymns, prayers and sacramental practices transformed it, as well as devotional life in the family. Preachers sometimes found their laity were ahead of them in access to new books by Luther and others and had to amend their reading and practices accordingly.[36]

To make another obvious point: the teaching of the priesthood of all believers was not only part of the content of

---

[36]   One is reminded that this was the area where Vatican 2 created most change in our own time; Matthew Zell claimed his 'flock's' reading of Luther had proved the catalyst for him, his 'shepherd' role as preacher necessitating his reading of the Lutheran books his parishioners had long been devouring, whatever the law might say. *Christeliche Verantwortung*, ciij[r].

many of the pamphlets. It informed their whole ethos. It was assumed that the conscience of the reader was to be activated, empowered to tussle with the issues treated, and to do so on the basis of Scripture, as well as common sense and experience. This is at some considerable distance from the mere instrumentalisation of opinion. It is worth remembering, too, that the sixteenth-century reader or listener was not immunised to the impact of ideas and symbols in the way we are today. There was nothing comparable to the saturation of the intellectual market with which we have to contend. In many cases people will also have operated with a naive container view of truth, and assumed that whatever was in print was gospel truth. The apparent consensus of a galaxy of pamphleteers who all seemed to want reform and offer a new and simpler way to salvation will have swept many off their feet.

None of this is to argue, however, a return to an idealised view of the impact of the religious pamphlet. Thanks to the careful statistical and analytical work of Köhler and Chrisman, Zorzin and Edwards on the distribution and numbers of editions we can assess it much more accurately. The content analysis of Moeller and others is also crucial. Writers such as Mark Edwards have reminded us that the actual form of the publication, as determined by the printer's skills, and commercial interests, significantly modified the message of the author. The bluff simplicity of the pamphlet form, its cheap paper, rough print, accessibility and relative cheapness, the blatant directness of title page and wood-cuts, itself constituted a message. The perceived character of the author, whether accurate or not, greatly influenced the chances for the acceptance of the message. Long ago, moreover, Balzer was pointing out that the message of the pamphlet 'only has a chance when its contents coincide with the cognitive structure of the group it is addressing'.[37] Köhler, too, has underlined the active,

[37]   Balzer, p. 26.

not passive role of the reader.[38] Oberman talks of the 'fermentation phase in which audiences became active participants'.[39] The filters applied by the readers in their reception of the material meant that women read it differently from men, lay from clergy, town-dwellers from those in the country or at court. This would often have meant that the reader never got beyond the first page, either because of boredom or fury! Public opinion, then, was certainly formed by the pamphlets, but public attitudes also determined which and what part of the pamphlets would hit home. The relationship is a subtle one.

When we move on to radical writers, such as Müntzer, the language of the pamphlets becomes rougher, more dialect-limited, and the appeal becomes markedly less cosmopolitan. There is often little trace of the linguistic genius of an Erasmus or a Luther. One is poignantly reminded of the scrubby leaflets of the IRA and UDA in Belfast in the 1970s and 1980s, of an under-class seeking its voice. It is not always clear whether a wider public is being addressed, or a narrower group of the elect. Great caution is in place, however, about regarding all radicals as separatists, targeting what we would call today a sectarian, or sectional audience, uninterested in a wider public opinion. Karlstadt, after all, was to emerge as the greatest spokesperson for the laity in the Reformation. What the semi-literate correspondents of Thomas Müntzer remind us of, moreover, as does the literature of the Peasants' War, is that there was often an intentional outreach among the radicals to the semi-literate, to a wider public opinion. Only unheard-of over-simplification, Müntzer argued, could get through to the wooden, thick, foolish people, *grob, tolpelisch und knuttelisch volk*, who were yet, somehow, to be God's chosen instruments. Too much sophistication and literacy can block the road to

[38]   Köhler, 'Meinungsprofil', p. 246.
[39]   Heiko O. Oberman, *The Impact of the Reformation* (T. & T. Clark: Edinburgh, 1994), p. ix.

Christian truth![40] Müntzer saw printing as having an eschatological function, as being an almost miraculous weapon to gather the elect, who were the unlearned, the raw outcasts of society. He saw his own imminent trial in universal terms. 'So if I am to be brought to trial before the Christian people then an invitation, announcement and communication must be sent to every nation. . . .'[41] It would placard the wickedness of the authorities 'for the whole world to see, then you can count on the understanding of all Christian people. . . . Thus by putting it into print . . . you will be able to argue your case before other governments. . . . For the common man (God be praised) is acknowledging the truth almost everywhere.'[42]

It was the radicals, too, such as Müntzer who extended the potential audience of their message beyond Christendom. 'To be honest, my most beloved brothers, I cannot hide my preference for giving the most elementary instruction to heathens, Turks and Jews about God. . . .'[43] Although therefore there is an undeniable tendency of the radicals at times to see themselves in counter cultural terms as the remnant, the little band of the righteous, there are also universalist tendencies in their thinking which greatly expand the horizons of public opinion.

Why did the excitement of pamphlets and sermon-tasting vanish so quickly? Peter Blickle has developed the thesis of an incipient communal reformation, whose promising beginnings in the early 1520s were then crushed by the later magisterial

---

[40]   CW, 234; 'for where cleverness abounds, deviousness abounds too'. CW, 121; Paul Speratus uses almost identical language about the need for simple, crude language to get through to ordinary folk, and free them from their deference to the traditional authorities: *mus ich mit den groben/ knorrigen/ storrigen/steltzer kopffen eyn grobe disputatzn und frag halten*; *Wie man trotzen soll aufs Kreuz*, Fiche 168/456 (Wittenberg, 1524), Eiii.

[41]   CW, 111.

[42]   CW, 133f.

[43]   CW, 316; cf. *Ein brüderliche warnung*, 42, where the 'Father' prays: *lassz herr alle menschen nit verderben, es seyen Juden, Türcken oder Heyden.*

reformation.[44] The very energy with which this interpretation is refuted in some quarters is itself illuminating. Hans-Joachim Köhler, who is not unsympathetic to the concept of the communal reformation, does point out that at the very most only some 10 per cent of the pamphlets made any reference to specifically peasant concerns, although those which do so derive from the regions and the period which the Blickle school sees as the high-point of the 'peasant reformation'. Köhler suggests that the interest of common folk in whatever effected their salvation should not be underestimated, and that a pastoral awareness of this may well be reflected in the reformers' use of the image of the 'pious peasant' in the pamphlets.[45] One remembers that the figure of Karsthans himself appears to be based on an actual historical person who visited Strasbourg, and with whom the Reformer Matthew Zell had to deny having extensive contacts.[46] Nor can the prominence of the poor and the humble in the prophetic and apostolic books of Scripture be forgotten! It does appear to be the case that many of the Radical Reformers read Scripture in the light of the common folk they saw around them, and in turn saw the latter through the lens of Scriptural promises and expectations. Again, the relationship is not a simple one.

It would seem, on the face of it, not improbable that the demise of the communal reformation and the rapid decline in

[44]   The most recent summary by Peter Blickle, 'The Popular Reformation', in Thomas A. Brady, Heiko O. Oberman and James D. Tracy (eds.), *Handbook of European History 1400–1600. Late Middle Ages, Renaissance and Reformation*, 2 Vols. (Brill: Leiden, 1994–95), Vol. 2, pp. 161–92.

[45]   '"Der Bauer wird witzig". Der Bauer in den Flugschriften der Reformationszeit', in *Zugänge zur bäuerlichen Reformation. Bauer und Reformation* Vol 1. (Chronos: Zürich, 1987), pp. 187–218; Jørgensen, on the other hand, sees the figure of the peasant as a purely literary construct: *Bauer, Narr und Pfaffe*, passim.

[46]   Lienhard, 60, n. 61; *Christeliche Verantwortung über Artikel, ihm vom bischöflichen Fiskel entgegengesetzt*. Wolfgang Köpfel: Strassburg, 1523 (Fiche 1570/4074), K iiii.

pamphlet literature may be linked, and that there are connections here also with the closing of the brief window of opportunity which had opened up to women readers, writers and preachers. The role of peasants and women was often linked. An indignant monk in Upper Alsace noted in 1522 that illiterate laity, peasants and even gossiping women felt they had gobbled up the whole of heavenly wisdom.[47]

How did women contribute to the development of a public opinion? We know that inns and mills acted as places for male bonding, but it was harder for women outside a convent to gather together to talk, though men appear to have been anxious about their conversations over spinning and weaving in the *Gunkelstube*.[48] Argula von Grumbach argued that public opinion had already made the obscurantism of the Ingolstadt theologians 'notorious throughout the entire world'[49] and sketched the outlines of a network of women's opposition. If she were martyred 'a hundred women would emerge to write against them'.[50] Johann Eberlin von Günzburg emphasised the new role of women as well as other lay people, not only in Germany but throughout Europe.[51] This whole question of the role of women is only beginning to be aired, and much more research requires to be done, but the opportunities opened up to women by printing and by humanist and reformist ideas soon disappeared. Censorship moved in swiftly to shut down

[47]   J. Westenhoeffer (ed.), *Die Reformationsgeschichte von einem Barfüsser-Mönch* (Leipzig, 1882), p. 10, quoted in Franziska Conrad, *Reformation in der bäuerlichen Gesellschaft. Zur Rezeption reformatorischer Theologie im Elsass* (Franz Steiner: Stuttgart, 1984), p. 2.

[48]   Cf. Lyndal Roper, *The Holy Household. Women and Morals in Reformation Augsburg* (Clarendon Press: Oxford, 1989); Peter Matheson, 'A Reformation for Women', *Scottish Journal of Theology* 49.1 (1996), pp. 39–56.

[49]   AvG, 82.

[50]   AvG, 120.

[51]   *Der erst bundtsgnoss*, Aii^v; cf. Gottfried Geiger, 'Die reformatorischen Initia Johann Eberlins von Günzburg nach seinen Flugschriften', *Festgabe für Zeeden*, pp. 178–201.

the initiatives of Catholic women authors such as Constance Pirckheimer, or Protestants such as Katharina Zell, or later on Marie de Dentière. Nor is the case much different in the radical camp. Although women figured prominently among Müntzer's followers, they were regarded in a patriarchal light in most radical groups. The 'prophetess', Ursula Jost, a follower of Melchior Hoffman, appears to be the only radical woman to have written a book.[52]

In a handwritten comment on Argula von Grumbach's pamphlet to Duke Wilhelm, a furious reader has scrawled: 'née von Stauff; née the hellish brothel of Luther'. This is a timely reminder that pamphlets written by women were often read in a maelstrom of emotions, of almost incoherent rage.[53] The few, scattered instances of Protestant women writers such as Katherine Schütz, or Zell, Ursula Weydin and Argula von Grumbach illustrate the massive resistance of public opinion to changing its views about the role of women. Indeed it probably regressed as a result of their initiatives. There will, however, have been some modest progress in the availability of books to women readers.

We have seen that Müntzer yoked together preaching, printing and singing, meaning by the latter, the liturgy.[54] Worship was to be the training ground for the new humanity. He interpreted dreams. He fostered a popular mysticism, and an exegesis which radically actualised the Biblical text. He had a communal understanding of the consecration of the sacraments. Karlstadt also saw the local congregation as having 'ears and eyes, and members ready for righteousness'. It is here, if anywhere in the sixteenth century, that public opinion was formed and transformed. We have learnt to conceive of the

[52]   Cf. Hans-Joachim Diekmannshenke, *Die Schlagwörter der Radikalen der Reformationszeit (1520–1536): Spuren utopischen Bewußtseins* (Peter Lang: Frankfurt a. Main, 1994), pp. 90–6, 189f.
[53]   A particularly repellent example is the poem by 'John of Landshut'; AvG, 160–8.
[54]   CW, 68.

pamphlet as a stylised conversation, intimately linked with sermon and classroom and social event. We need to be much more aware of its cultic bite, its confessional note, its blessings and imprecations, its exhortations and calls to discipleship, what we have called its doxological quality. As often as not it was addressed to God as much as to any hearer.

It may be, incidentally, that no one is less qualified to weigh the impact of this prophetic literature on public opinion than today's intellectual. Few academics have much first-hand experience of the upheavals in ordinary people's lives as a result of social change. They tend to range themselves among the opinion-makers. And while neither the authors nor the recipients of pamphlets can be described as 'the common people' – the Latin scribblings on many of the extant copies are eloquent evidence of that – yet the sermon, delivered to a remarkably inclusive congregation, became the model for this new literature. For the first time literature was designed at least to encompass the commoner, and leapt social and regional frontiers to do so. To sharpen the edge of anti-clerical polemic, but also to profile a lay-orientated Christianity a new image of the peasant/artisan/woman began to emerge, the village leader confronting the theologian, the spoon-maker taking on the cathedral canon. In turn this was in tune with a fresh reading of Scripture.

How profound was this outreach, this quest for a new public opinion? Köhler's figures make it clear that after the dizzy heights of 1524 the number of pamphlets, which had multiplied forty-fold in seven years, quickly receded and that by 1525 they were already fizzling out. The phenomenon had been as exciting, but also as transient as a sky-rocket. Certainly there was much superficial curiosity, lust for the sensational, which lined the pockets of the opportunist printers. Others at least understood the slogans about freedom and reform, as children recognise 'key words', and grasped that the Bible was 'their' book, the norm by which the powerful could be brought to account. The question of how 'their' Bible related to Luther's or that of the other Reformers is an important one. A further

group of lay people proceeded to a much profounder understanding.

Thus various communities of discourse were being formed.
Reformation public opinion cannot be measured by the
'literature of aspiration' of the leaders, without recording its
impact on the recipients. Their 'reception' or modification of
key themes for Luther such as justification by faith was
determined not just by the inevitable processes of vulgarisation
when sophisticated ideas are popularised but by the primacy of
their own concerns. If we can talk at all of 'mass media' in this
period, and those such as Thomas Müntzer did talk of reaching
out to 'the masses of the poor laity',[55] we may have to do much
more research on distinguishing between what the Reformers
wanted to say, how the media presented it, and what the very
diverse people of Germany wanted to hear and were able to
hear.

I conclude, then, that the coincidence of the spread of
Reformation ideas with the availability of the new technology
of printing led to the emergence for the first time in European
culture of a genuine public opinion. We can observe this
happening most clearly in the imperial cities, the councils
being nudged to offer support to the new preaching and ethos
in order to preserve social consensus and harmony. Occasionally
we can observe it happening in little market-towns such as
Allstedt. We also have abundant examples of how a determined
programme of repression, terror and torture can sweep public
opinion aside.

For a while, however, people certainly felt they had the right
to think for themselves. Giant-killers such as Luther provided
encouragement and models to emulate. Countless informal
groupings combined with more structured ones to provide a
safe environment to explore risky thoughts. Scripture provided
the critical norm. Printing enabled ideas to spread very fast,
very extensively and relatively secretly. Village convocation, civic

[55]   CW, 180.

disputation and Imperial Diet provided the necessary focus. The waggon of the word, in Luther's terms, carted the world of Scripture into people's lives, and dragged people back into the world of Scripture. The Reformation took hold because of a paradigm shift in the religious imagination. The public opinion which embraced it was, at least episodically, to be a mark of European society from that time on.

CHAPTER THREE

ANDREAS KARLSTADT:
A STUDY IN MOTIVATION

*In meinem Reich, sprach der Löwe, gibt es keine Zensur; bei mir
kann jeder sagen, was ich will.*

*In my kingdom, said the Lion, there is no censorship. Anyone can
say what I want them to.*

Gerhard Branstner, Der Esel als Amtmann.[1]

The importance of the Reformation pamphlet[2] in spreading
the ideas and ethos of the Reformation in the early 1520s is
not in doubt. Together with the illustrated broadsheet, the
book, and of course preaching itself, these cheap, smudgy
publications constituted the main bridge between the
Reformers' theology and grass-roots opinion. Their innovative technology, popular literary techniques, and back-pack
marketing enabled support to be mobilised with unprecedented speed. Literature became a medium not only for
information, devotion, and – increasingly – entertainment, but
for life-changing conversion. When Argula von Grumbach,
from the obscurity of Dietfurt in Bavaria, reported in 1523
that in her zeal to discover the truth she had read all the
German works of Luther and Melanchthon, she is far from

---

[1] Gerhard Branstner, *Der Esel als Amtmann* (Buchverlag der Morgen:
Berlin, 1976).
[2] This chapter was first given as a paper to the New Zealand Early
Modern Studies Association Symposium at Victoria University, Wellington
on 13 July 1991.

untypical.[3] It has been suggested that there were enough pamphlets in circulation for every literate German at the time to have possessed about twenty.[4]

The exceptional skills of Luther as a pamphleteer are, rightfully, a common-place of Reformation historiography. Much less known, however, is the role of his disciple, colleague, and later adversary, Karlstadt. In a most valuable study Zorzin has recently reminded us that next to Luther, he was by far the most prolific of the reforming writers in the German language.[5] Stylistically, too, he was far from the pedestrian clod-hopper which he has so often been portrayed as being, ever since Melanchthon dubbed him 'the Alphabet' in derisory reference to his name, Andreas Bodenstein von Carlstadt.[6] It is time that we began to take Karlstadt's skills as a communicator much more seriously. He illustrates well the motivations of such writers.

The Reformation pamphlet's charm and limitation is that it is an ephemeral creature. Many were little more than glorified letters, sometimes explicitly described as such: *Sendbriefe*. They frequently began and ended with personal greetings. Printing

---

[3]   *Ist doch warlich vil in Teutschen zungenn außgangen/habs gelesenn*; *Wye ein Christliche fraw des adels in Beyern . . . die hohenschul zu Ingoldstat . . . straffet.* [Augsburg, 1523] Bir; AvG, 86.

[4]   For a brief and excellent survey cf. Bernd Moeller, 'Flugschriften der Reformationszeit' in *Theologische Realenzyklopädie*, Vol. XI, pp. 240–46. Euan Cameron tends to limit the pamphlet to communicating 'memorable slogans'; *The European Reformation* (Clarendon Press: Oxford, 1991), p. 229.

[5]   Cf. the important study by Alejandro Zorzin: *Karlstadt als Flugschriftenautor* (Göttinger Theologische Arbeiten, Bd. 48; Göttingen, 1990), p. 217.

[6]   It lingers on in E. Cameron's description of his writings as 'pungent, laborious and inelegant' (*The European Reformation*, p. 176; for a more favourable view cf. Ronald J. Sider (ed.), *Karlstadt's Battle with Luther* (Fortress: Philadelphia, 1978); cf. also my analysis of *Von Abtuhung der Bilder* (On the Abolition of Images), 'Between Dialogue and Polemic', in *Religious Studies in Dialogue: Essays in Honour of Albert C. Moore*, ed. S. Rae etc. (Faculty of Theology: Dunedin, 1991), pp. 103–14.

was a very flexible, unpretentious business. A pamphlet served much the same function an an interview on a local radio station today. Without an efficient postal system, not to mention photocopiers and electronic mail, the printing-press was essential if one intended to communicate with people outside one's local circle.

Pamphlets were very close to oral culture, as their alliteration, rhythmic sequences and repetitions betray.[7] Effective pamphlets reflected the lively discussion of home, tavern, bathhouse and street, and in turn provoked it. They were a form of 'open lecture', 'open pulpit', the extended arm of teachers, preachers and activists such as Thomas Müntzer, who talked of 'singing, speaking, writing' against his adversaries. Clearly such writers saw their friends or opponents before them as they wrote. In mid-pamphlet Karlstadt will suddenly turn to the person to whom a tract is dedicated: 'Now note this, dear friend'; 'So see, my brother, how dangerous . . .'; or he will seek to anticipate his enemies' arguments, objections, and excuses (*flucht redt*).[8] Thus friend and opponent became the direct object of colloquy in this intimate form of literature. God, or Christ, were addressed too, and the dedications to God at the beginning and end of most pamphlets were far from being mere pious trimmings. From polemic and argument the reader can be abruptly plunged into prayer. There was always something splendidly uncalculating and direct about the good pamphlet! We should keep that in mind as we look at Karlstadt's motivations as a pamphleteer.

Remarkably, little attention has been paid to this question of motivation. Over-worked as they were – as teachers, preachers, pastors and administrators – why did the Reformers

    [7]   Cf. Walter Ong, *Orality and Literacy: The Technologizing of the Word* (Methuen: London, 1982.

    [8]   *Von beiden gestaldten der heyligen Messze* (Wittenberg, 1521 = B) Ciii; Dii; Ei'; *ich kan mich/ye nit endthalten/yr zukunfftige gedancken/an zugreyffen; Von geweychtem Wasser und saltz . . . wider den unvordienten Gardian Franciscus Syler* (Wittenberg, 1520 = WS) Bi'.

devote so much time to what they themselves often recognised as ephemeral literature? Were they simply caught up in the new passion for the printed word? Did they consciously see the pamphlet as a more effective sounding-board for their preaching? How did the authorship of pamphlets relate to their wider sense of vocation? What attitudes and expectations did they have of their readers?

On one level, the answer is relatively simple. The pamphlet was simply a new form of the 'tyranny of immediacy'. The occasion for a pamphlet could be the urgent request of a parishioner or pupil, relative or friend, for information, instruction or encouragement.[9] It could be a way of showing gratitude to a much needed patron. Some arose out of weekly exercises with university students. Pamphlets also grew out of sermons, or conversations or letters. It gave the latter a degree of authority and permanency, and certainly lent them wings. Not infrequently the author had never intended his manuscript to be circulated wider afield, still less printed. Copyright, in the modern sense, which would have exerted a brake on such dissemination, did not exist, and so, as Karlstadt said, 'my booklets went into print, and by print out into the whole wide world'.[10]

Who requested such publications? In Karlstadt's case, the requests came mainly from lay people, usually of some substance in the community: town clerks, teachers, provincial administrators, people such as Bartel Bach, Wolf Horteyler, Wolfgang Sturtz, and Heinrich von Könneritz, whose three sons were studying at Wittenberg.[11]

---

[9]   *Mich bat ein guter freund, ich solt yhm doch fur sein person solichen verstand schrifftilich stellen und leyhen, der selb bracht soliche lere vom Sacrament mit freuntlichen viel worten und anhebiger bit von mir*; the reference is probably to his pupil and relative Gerhard Westerburg; cf. *Erklärung wie Karlstadt seine Lehre von dem hochwurdigen Sakrament und andere achtet und geachtet haben will*, W 18, 459 Anm. 1; the *Missive von der aller hochste tugent gelassenheyt* (Wittenberg, 1521; = M), is dedicated to his 'dear mother and all his friends'; Air^r.

[10]   *und auß dem druck in die weite welt*; W 18, 459/17.

[11]   WS Aii; Cii^r.

Very often pamphlets were written to parry an assault on colleagues or on oneself: for example, when the Fransciscan, Seyler, contended that Karlstadt was a false prophet, a seducer of the people, a heretic.[12] The attack could either be in printed form, or a verbal one, often from the pulpit. Karlstadt then had to write to save his honour, *zu errettüng seins namens*; or to clear the name of the University of Wittenberg, whose zeal for teaching the word of God, he protested, was unequalled in Italy, Germany or France. A pamphlet could be the reluctant response to a challenge, since silence would be taken as an admission of defeat. One's peace was only as lasting as one's neighbour allowed it to be; Seyler should not blame Karlstadt if a 'drop of ink falls into his eyes', for he has provoked it in the first place.[13]

Sometimes a writing was prompted by an acute personal crisis, as at the stormy beginning of the Reformation, when Karlstadt published his poignant appeal for the support or understanding of his family, which could not understand why he risked such calumny for the reforming cause. Recantation of the true Gospel was an impossibility, Karlstadt insisted, beseeching those who loved him not to lose heart.[14] Similarly, in the desperate days after the Peasants' War, Karlstadt penned a vivid and dramatic denial that he had been a leader of the peasant insurrection.[15] The printing-press had became the doorkeeper of reputation. Without it one would be condemned unheard, *unverhört unnd unüberzeugt.*[16] Rumour-mongers and liars would be able to spread lies and excite hate against one

---

[12]   WS Aii.

[13]   *Ich kan nit lenger rwe und frid haben/dan/ßo lang mirs meyn nachbaur gönnet.* WS Aii.

[14]   *Darumb meynn mutter/bruder/schwester/öhmen/baßen/schweger/gesch weyhen und alle liebe freundt ynn Christo/Ich bitt yhr wollet euch nit vorseren/ und nit betrüben . . .* ; M Aiii^r.

[15]   *Entschuldigung des falschen Namens des Aufruhrs*; W 18, 438–45.

[16]   *des ferlichen und schweren gerüchts*; W 18, 438/4f.

with impunity, either out of malice, or with the ignorance of a miller's donkey.[17]

Printing was, of course, a weapon of particular importance when the university or the court or an influential pulpit were barred to one, when one had no access to patronage, or to the ear of prince and magistrate and administrator. Luther's resort to it while in the Wartburg, or Thomas Müntzer's while hiding in Nuremberg, are only two of the most obvious examples. It then became the weapon of the fugitive, or the exile, of those who could not reach supporters by their physical presence and charisma. As a way of reaching out to all nations and peoples, for gathering together the invisible Church of the elect, it could even take on eschatological dimensions. The universal audience is often adverted to. On the other hand, even in the chaos of jurisdictions that was sixteenth-century Germany, such copyright as existed was a contract between printer and prince or magistrate, and the 'hole-and-corner' printer, ready to risk the wrath of the magistrates by a clandestine publication, was a rare bird. Karlstadt was to suffer more than most from the suppression of his publications.

But why go to the trouble of having a pamphlet printed? There were no royalties to be gained, and venturing into print could lead to the loss of one's position, one's home, even of life itself; much too late, after the Peasants' War, Karlstadt reflected ruefully that his publications, especially on the Lord's Supper, had brought him nothing but poverty, insecurity and exile. It made him wish that his books were still 'in quill and ink', and that he had never gone into print, and addressed only those who could hear him personally.[18] If he had realised what risks he was running he would never have handed his books over – not even if someone had threatened him with an axe![19] There

---

[17]   *des müllers eseln . . . ; one ordenung und on grundt gehast, die allerley lügen auff mich erdacht und uber mich aus geworffen*; W 18, 464/27, 30f.

[18]   *noch yn der dinten und fedtern*; W 18, 459/13f.

[19]   *es solt keyner mein bucher von mir mit einer holtz axte gebracht haben*, W 18, 459/5, 11ff.

is a curious naivety about the animosity his polemic had excited, genuine surprise that it had given rise to such *neyd und hass*, envy and hate. Karlstadt noted that he had only learnt his lesson after suffering 'irretrievable loss'.[20]

Karlstadt wrote because he had no option. He simply could not keep silent any more, whatever the cost. This confessional imperative appears to have been for him, as for so many others, the primary motivation. He had to pour out his soul; one rather engaging admission of his own fear and anxiety depicts him nailed hand and foot to Christ's Cross, while his enemies poked out their tongues, and abused him.[21] One is reminded of the prophets of Israel.

In this time of emotional openness and moral introspection censorship, or the prohibition of resort to printing, was seen as a violation of the self as well as of the truth. The need to give an account of one's faith was acute: 'I cannot deny the truth, especially the one I have sworn to defend, though every devil join the Pope in oppressing me.'[22] On occasion this lofty motive could also excuse prolixity.[23]

By entering the public arena in print Karlstadt made solemn and, in principle, universal attestation to his faith: 'I, Andrew Bodenstein of Karlstadt, make known to everyone, and confess publicly by virtue of this writing. . . ."[24] The pamphleteer became the confessor, the potential martyr; he was a witness to the true faith, ready to risk persecution and death, whether at the hands of the secular princes or the Papal hierarchy, or,

[20]   *mit unverwindlichen schaden*; W 18, 464/25.

[21]   Yet the identification with Christ's suffering comforted him; such desolation (*betrubnüß*) washed away all sin. In a passage reminiscent of Ignatius of Antioch in the second century, he begged his family not to urge caution on him. M Aiii^r.

[22]   Lit. *quernen*, to grind; M Aiiii^r.

[23]   *So druckt mich mein gewissen weytter von der materien zusagen*; *Von Gelübden Unterrichtung* (Wittenberg, 1521 = G); Bi.

[24]   *Ein Frage ob auch jemand möge selig werden on die Fürbitt Marie* (Wittenberg, 1524 = F) Aii.

later, of Luther and the 'new Papacy' of Wittenberg. In his *Missive* Karlstadt prayed that God would release him from the lash and the scornful word, from the jaws of the lion and the horns of the unicorn, from the dangers of boiling and roasting, of breaking and tearing on the wheel.[25] He adjured his friends by their conscience, in the name of the living God, and taking 'heaven and earth, tree and grass, wood and stone as witnesses', to stand by him in this confession of his faith.[26]

Giving an account of one's faith could also mean, however, a willingness to enter into dialogue. The titles of many writings were framed as questions: 'Whether it is possible to reform gradually'?[27] The pamphlet was a new form of the scholastic *quaestio*, a problem seeking a resolution though submitting it to discussion. Here, at least in principle, was openness to critical engagement, and to a possible revision of his views: 'Let anyone who can teach us better, do so.'[28] He certainly wanted critical readers, who followed him not for his own sake but because he had a solid basis, *den rechten grund*, in Scripture; anyone who believed he had built up a false *gebew*, or structure, based on poor arguments, should reject it.[29] There always remained the hope of eventual agreement and reconciliation, *vertrags oder ferner gemeinschafft*, as Luther put it.[30]

Karlstadt's *Erklärung*, the 1525 apologia for his teaching on the Eucharist, was strongly coloured by his desperate plight at

---

[25]   M Aiii.

[26]   M Aiii[r]; the combination of Biblical and humanist elements is interesting; I am indebted to Dr Chris Ehrhardt for suggesting that the reference to the 'impersonal witnesses' may come from Plutarch's *Demosthenes* 9, 4; or *Moralia* 845 B.

[27]   *Ob man gemach faren/und des ergernissen der schwachen verschonen soll/in sachen so gottis willen angehen* ([Basel], 1524 = S).

[28]   *Wer uns besser weysen kan/der thu es; Dialogus oder ein gesprech büchlin. Von dem grewlichen und abgöttischen missbrauch/ des hochwirdigsten Sacraments Jesu Christi* (n.p.; 1525 = D) Giiiib.

[29]   W 18, 460/8, 11.

[30]   In his Preface to Karlstadt's apologia for his conduct during the Peasants' War; W 18, 436/20.

the end of the Peasants' War. Yet we can believe his claim that he only permitted his books to be printed because he believed his opinion was 'demonstrably true . . . and edifying',[31] and that he did not set himself up as an authority. Scripture alone filled that role. He lamented hypocrites and sensation-seekers latching onto him, seeking something to gossip about over a beer. His joy in writing disappeared when he saw this. He may have protested rather too much about the tentativeness of his views, and been somewhat disingenuous about those who misused his writings for their own ends, 'the pigs that wallow in the pearls'.[32] He was, however, quite consistent in denying any desire to innovate, to be trendy, to entertain.[33]

If Karlstadt's first motivation was this personal one, in which he saw himself as a confessor of the faith, and his primary emotion was that of trust, *gelassenheit*, self-abandonment to God, a second motivation was undoubtedly the pastoral one, where he saw himself as the shepherd, angrily and lovingly concerned for his sheep.

A mark of his writings was, of course, the emphasis on the laity. He reiterated constantly his desire to inform, instruct, and encourage the poor and the simple, the *gemeyn/ungelert hauff*.[34] His tracts were 'visiting cards' for their homes. He sought to instil in these honorary parishioners, reached only by the medium of print, his own passionate reverence for God's commands; the recurrence of such words as *hitzig* and *kreſſtig*, 'hot and strong', reminds us that we have to be cautious about labelling him a 'legalist'.[35] The laity were to be equipped to

---

[31]   W 18, 458/31ff.

[32]   *Aber das kan ich nicht leyden, das sawen ynn meyne lere portzeln . . .* ;
W 18, 458/21; 457/24ff., 29ff.

[33]   D Ai; a conscious distancing of himself from the promotion of many contemporary writings as *kurzweilig*, 'entertaining'.

[34]   B Aiiii; cf. Zorzin, *Karlstadt*, pp. 217ff.

[35]   Martin Brecht speaks of '*einer biblizistischen Gesetzlichkeit*': *Martin Luther; Bd.2; Ordnung und Abgrenzung der Reformation. 1521–1532* (Calwer Verlag: Stuttgart, 1986), p. 169; the question of his legalism is well

distinguish between the divine and the merely human, since the Pope, the 'devil's forerunner', had not only taught falsehood but strewn (*ein gepleut*) false words amongst the true ones; what looked like holiness could be the cunning work of the Devil.[36]

As a pastor his task was to free the bound consciences of the laity, whose necks were weighed down with unnecessary burdens, spiritual as well as economic, which caused gall, bitterness and despair.[37] We are idiots, he told his fellow-Germans, to gather money, cheese, oxen and such like, and send them to our supposed spiritual fathers in Rome.[38]

As a preacher, his task was to articulate people's inchoate worries and doubts, to voice the questions they hardly dared to ask, to liberate ordinary folk from their superstitious terror, and kindle in its place enthusiasm for the Gospel.[39] He noted that élitist scholarship always cohabits happily with popular ignorance. That is why he had to attack the false authorities of the Old Church, its hallowed traditions, the clergy's 'waggon-loads of lies';[40] it suited the cloistered intellectuals, the *hochgelarten*, to encourage simple folk's fantasies that holy water took sins away; in reality it only cleansed the body, not the conscience; the bath-master's water was as good.[41] The laity should hold on to the simple truth and let those with a high reputation, the *weltgeachten*, canter past.[42] If the scholastic

---

treated in Ronald J. Sider, *Andreas Bodenstein von Karlstadt* (Studies in Medieval and Reformation Thought, XI; Brill: Leiden, 1974), pp. 277–83.

[36]   B Biiir; the Devil has *sich maisterlich in die scheynliche hailigkait eingemischt*; F Cii; words like *eingemengkt, vermüscht* are frequently used to express this confusion; B Ai.

[37]   *die gepunden gewissen sich etlicher stricken entledigten*; D Ai[r].

[38]   G Biii[r].

[39]   Not with *unlust und grawen* but with *lust und begirden*; B Aii.

[40]   B Diiii[r].

[41]   WS Aiii[r].

[42]   *lautere worheyt*; D Ai.

authorities in Paris, for example, were to be believed then the writers of the Gospels must be heretics! [43]

Positively, like every pastor, he sought to lead the reader to good pastures (*speyss und wayd*), to the waters of life, eternal peace, the blessings of salvation.[44] Negatively – and much more time is spent on this – he wanted to protect the flock from what endangered their salvation: 'the abominable and idolatrous abuse' of the sacrament of Jesus Christ, for example. The urgency of correcting such errors as speedily as possible could even lead him to issue his books in serial form, as in the response to Luther's *Against the Heavenly Prophets.*[45]

For the weak have been deceived, seduced onto slippery ice, lured 'to join the chorus or the dance or the babbling of the same learned choir, and to say "Yea and Amen" to anything they propose'.[46] They should be freed from a false and outward piety, such as pilgrimages which led them to forsake wife, child and the responsibilities of family life. He ridiculed the veneration of the *Nothelfer*, specialised saints like St Otilie, St Sebastian, St Lawrence, responsible for diseases of the eye, for the plague, and for fire respectively.[47] God had to 'look through his fingers' at the absurdity of attributing recovery from poisoning to St Anne. How credulous, too, to think that putting a linen girdle around St Peter's throne in Rome would ensure one's wife a safe delivery for her next child.[48] Or to imagine we needed saints to 'introduce' us to God, like some marshal or key-bearer at a princely court;

[43]   B Biii.

[44]   D Ai^r.

[45]   *Erklerung des x. Capitels Cor. 1 Das Brot das wir brechen: Ist es nitt ein gemeinschaft des leybs Christi . . .* ([Augsburg, 1525] = E) Aii.

[46]   *gladt eis*; D Aiiii; *wenn sie den selben hochgelerten fürsingern nachsingen/ oder nachspringen/oder nachlallen/und zu allen irem rathe/ja sagen und amen.* D Ai^r.

[47]   G Aiii^r.

[48]   G Bii^r; Bi^r.

Christ has taught us that we already have intimate access to our Father.[49]

There is no mistaking, here, the centrality and seriousness of Karlstadt's pastoral concern. As their shepherd, he was also their servant, brother, and mother, and could tolerate no silly games (*keyn spil*) where sin was concerned.[50] 'I'm deadly serious about this business, it's no light matter', he said in reference to the taking of vows.[51]

Karlstadt's third motivation for venturing into print was a polemical one. Like the Apologists of the Early Church, Karlstadt argued his case as a counsel for the defence, refuting unfair or false accusations, and appealing to the reader's love of truth and sense of justice. He responded angrily to his opponents' 'wet and plaguey words', to false rumours about him, to threats and insults from the pulpit.[52] At times his primary concern was to provide accurate information: 'I will now give a brief report, so that it will be very clear just how much grace I found among the new lords and masters, the peasants; and that I was not their leader. . . .'[53] Witnesses could be called upon to testify to the truth of his statements. Very often the writing was a reaction to 'disinformation', to a misleading notice pinned up in a church, for example; or to the imprisonment of a lay person, whose sole offence had been to challenge a preacher, or *mutwilliger pfaff*, for Biblical proof of his arbitrary utterances.[54] These violators of the Gospel were monsters, who sought to devour the whole world; such silly oafs should preach to pigs, not to those hungry for salvation.[55]

---

[49]   *daß wir gott unnsern vatter so bloß und schlecht bitten möchten*; F Ci.
[50]   WS Biii[r]; the reference is to holy water.
[51]   *Mir ist disse sach nit lecherlich noch wenig zu hertzen gelegen*; *Byt und vermanung an Doctor Ochßenfart* (Wittenberg, 1522 = O) Aiii.
[52]   O Aii.
[53]   W 18, 441/9ff.
[54]   W 18, 439/33ff.
[55]   F Aii; Aii[r].

The aim of such polemic was to force the opponent to admit the falsity of his position, to 'knock the irons off the feet of Fritzhans', and thus liberate him as well.[56] 'Now, take thought, you dear Sophist', Karlstadt has a lay partner in dialogue say, to which the priest responded with a series of admissions, being steadily pushed onto the back foot. When he finally admitted: 'I don't know what to say', he is admonished: 'Just confess the truth', and finally abused for having no backbone, for being a new Proteus![57]

War-like images abound in this polemic; Karlstadt's arguments are likened to the sword of the Word; or to arrows shot from the Bible,[58] whether in self-defence (*wehre*) or to chastise (*straffen*) others. They are a snare to trap an opponent into an admission.[59] The Gospel itself becomes a missile to be slung at the Papists.[60]

Likewise the arguments of his opponent can be described as shields or ramparts, *schützworte*; the language is that of conquest, of overcoming an enemy, of throwing the opponent down on the ground – *bezwingen, niederwerfen, obsigen, überwinden*.[61] On occasion he tried to resist, however, the temptation to provoke his opponents unnecessarily, to 'pour cold water on boiling oil'.[62]

Sometimes Karlstadt used the image of the tournament, with its ritual challenge, and fight for honour and victory. He summoned his opponent to come out of the tent, and show if his actions were up to his boasts.[63] He taunted: 'Bring out the

---

[56]   *Antwort Andres von Carolstad Doctor: geweiht wasser belangend: wider einen bruder Johan, Fritzhans genant: holtzuger ordens* (Wittenberg, 1521 = Antwort) Biii^r.

[57]   D Ei.

[58]   M Bi^r; B Aiii.

[59]   D Giiii.

[60]   *Kurtzlich ich werffe dir das Evangelium inn bart*; B Eiiii^r.

[61]   D Cii^r.

[62]   *Antwort* Biii.

[63]   *ums leben disputiren; wolt ir unverspott/vom planh/gen haus kumen*; O Aiii.

sword of God, Luther; smite us with Scripture, not with fantasies.'[64] Or he likened an adversary to a mad bull: 'So, my dear bull, smash your horns against this question.'[65]

The term *straffen*, chastise, which he frequently used for his criticism of others, is also the word used for God's punishment of Israel. Karlstadt, it would seem, saw himself exercising punishment on behalf of God![66] Publications are certainly a way of exercising ecclesiastical discipline. Once he even threatened to send a *narrenfresser* to bind his foolish opponent, Seyler, hand and foot, and then, presumably, devour him.[67] The imaginary opponent might well cry out 'Why are you so hard on me?' But one *had* to be rigorous, because God's truth and justice were in the balance.[68] Closely allied with this concern for God's honour was Karlstadt's anti-clericalism. Priests were less interested in the truth than in defending their own power; they were sophists, tricksters, traitors.[69] The pamphlets constantly express anger at the ignorance, immorality, pomp, arrogance and abuse of power by Pope, cardinal, bishop, monk, priest, and especially the friars.

This was no mere mud-raking. Karlstadt saw himself as a sentry, hissing a public warning like the Capitoline geese. His aim was to 'take the lid off' corruption; to 'unmask' clerical hypocrisy, lies, and false worship; to remove the devilish *schalks mantell* or disguise, the pretence or *scheyn* of counterfeit holiness; to prevent the obscuring (*verdecken*) of Scripture and the inversion of reality which occurred when the language, the celebration, and the fruits of the Lord's Supper were distorted.[70]

---

[64]   *Bring her das schwerdt Gottes Luther/schlach mit schrifften und nit mit trowmen*; E Di[r].

[65]   O Aii.

[66]   D Cii[r].

[67]   WS Cii.

[68]   *Warheyt und gerechtigkeyt Gottes*; D Giii[r].

[69]   D Eiiii.

[70]   *außbloßen*; B Aii; *abconterfeyhung*; *schalcks mantell*; S Biii[r]; Ciii; *gleyssnerische glantze*; *In der summa ist alles umbkert/wort/weyß/werck/frucht/ und nutz*; B Aii[r].

All false claims to authority had to be undermined. Previously the truth had been gagged by a reference to tradition or authority; the laity had not been allowed to ask what Christ had done; they simply had to accept the arbitrary teachings of the Pope. Polemic, therefore, channelled frustration and anger into an effective pinpointing of abuse.

Polemic also empowered the reforming camp. By characterising the Roman theologians as 'heretics' Karlstadt turned the tables on them, and effectively disarmed them. Their threats, the 'fantastic, lying maledictions', of the Pope, which had made the laity timid and timorous, were rendered null and void when the authority of those who uttered them was subverted.[71] Karlstadt, the confessor, became Karlstadt, the inquisitor! As Pater observes, it became a form of 'counter-intimidation'.[72]

If the emotional note sounded here was primarily one of defiance and rage, it was almost always accompanied by a didactic dimension. A fourth motivation for writing his pamphlets was the pedagogical one. He saw himself as the spokesman for a new enlightened faith, for a Gospel which is alliteratively described as *liecht, klar und leycht*, full of light, clarity and simplicity. This 'message' came close to being identified with knowledge, with what could be remembered. He realised that many hesitated to be critical of the Mass, regarding it as a mystery which could not be plumbed, *als wer sie dunckell*; but we had to bring true piety to the light of day, *an tag tragen*.[73] For Karlstadt the key to the proper eating of the Lord's Supper lay in our remembering Christ, in a 'wondrous, passionate, heart-felt and loving knowledge'.[74]

---

[71]   *erdichte und erlogen vermaledyung*, B Ei.
[72]   Calvin A. Pater, *Karlstadt as the Father of the Baptist Movements: The Emergence of Lay Protestantism* (University of Toronto Press: Toronto, 1984), pp. 64f.
[73]   B Ai; Aiib.
[74]   *im/herrlichem/inbrünstigem/hertzlichem/und/liebreychem/erkenntnus*, E Aiii.

Hence the need for instruction. In his *Dialogue about the Abominable and Idolatrous Misuse of the Sacred Sacrament of Jesus Christ* Karlstadt emphasised that his aim was 'to be useful to you and to all Christendom and to do something for the glory of God. What I yearn for is that people should meditate with all earnestness on the truth.'[75]

The titles of some of his writings, such as the *Instruction on the Nature of Vows*, were explicitly educational. Their tone could be measured and patient. He showed considerable psychological understanding of how difficult it was to leave ancient customs behind, of the power of conditioning from early childhood.[76] He seldom hesitated to say the obvious, to spell out issues in very straightforward terms, with headings, illustrations, and summaries. For instance, he pointed out that in the institution of the Supper Christ did not say 'This is the *form* of the bread that is given for you' (my emphasis). Christ, in other words, was not talking about a 'baker's loaf', a mere sign, like the 'round white host' now used. Karlstadt seldom forgot that his readers were simple folk, who needed simple explanations.[77]

So he set about explaining the new Biblical scholarship: Hebrew terms, for example, or Old Testament history and theology.[78] The Vulgate's false translations had to be corrected, and the original Greek or Hebrew rendered *auf gut teutsch*, so that the ordinary person could understand. The lay person in his dialogues insisted on a comprehensible and clear German; whilst the priest wanted to keep 'the peasant', *der pawer*, in the dark.[79] Different names for the Word of God in Scripture – fire, water, hammer, wine, burden, sword, pure silver – were

[75]   *Das begere ich/das man die warheyt ernstlich ansehe*; D Ai[r].
[76]   D Bii[r]; B Bii.
[77]   B Aiiii; Bii[r].
[78]   The use of signs by the patriarchs and prophets, for example: B Biiii; Old Testament histories show no support for gradualism: *Disse historien zeigen klärlich an . . .* ; S Diii[r].
[79]   D Biii[r].

explained, as was the significance of Malachi's name: *Bote*, messenger.[80]

It is interesting to see that in this popular literature Karlstadt was more influenced by humanism than by mysticism. Scripture was the infallible base, the plumb-line, of truth. We are to handle it as if it were the body of the Lord.[81] The Erasmian image of moving up river to the pure source, *ursprunck, bron*, of Scripture was favoured.[82] In many ways he was the typical humanist teacher or exegete, moving from philology to piety to theology. He was quite self-conscious about his use of language, being prepared, like Thomas Müntzer, to use traditional terms to facilitate understanding, bearing with the 'weaker members' by continuing, in 1522, to use the term 'the Mass' in order to wean them from 'evil speaking into Evangelical language';[83] he was constantly commuting back and forward from Latin, Greek and Hebrew to German, though he lacks the dash of Luther and the elegance of Erasmus.

'I doubt, therefore I ask', he has one of his characters say.[84] His principle was that all Christians should understand their piety, not slurp up Scripture like some horse at the trough.[85] He was impatient with the *rodtwelsch*, the incoherent babbling, of the friars, which mingled the holy with the heathen, and ruined the bread of life with rough husks (*heckerling*) that not even a horse would stomach.[86]

His humanism wore a populist garb. He is at times an anti-intellectual intellectual, disdainful of the 'princes among the

---

[80] *Predig oder homilien uber dem propheten Malachiam gnant* (Wittenberg, 1522) Aiiii[r]; Aii[r].

[81] B Di[r].

[82] *die unbetriegliche gründe der warheyt*; D Ai[r], *richtschnur*; S Aii[r]; B Aii.

[83] *von böser rede yn Evangelische sprach*; B Bii.

[84] *Ich zweyfel/darumb frag ich*; D Bi.

[85] *das keyn vornunfft hat*; WS Aiiii[r].

[86] *Bedingung: Andreas Bodenstein von Carolstat: Doctor und Archidiacon zu Wittemberg* (Wittenberg: n.d.); Aiii.

scholars', of Luther and his colleagues in Wittenberg.[87] In his pamphlets the layman tended to win all the arguments;[88] anyone with an ounce of brain and wit had the right to 'judge', or interpret Scripture.[89] His logic could be crude common-sense. After its consecration in the Mass, the bread remained unchanged: 'For the shape of the bread remains as small, or as large, or as thick; in every way the same as it was before the priests breathed or blew over it and cackled like geese. So I ask whether Christ's body, arm, breast, thigh, legs, crown of thorns, nails, and spear are in the bread, which is smaller than Christ's little finger was.'[90]

To catch the attention of the ordinary reader – and despite his protestations that he is not out to entertain – he could introduce a folksy, Falstaffian touch. One person promised to be as 'quiet as a water-mill'; the layman, Peter, was told 'You're dashing around like a startled hare leaping over a bush'; later he retorted to the cleric: 'Get wise! Let's clear our throats; or we'll die of laughing'; to the claim that priests will always be around, he rejoined: 'Sure, like butter lying in the sun; or a thief on the gallows'.[91]

Yet, for all his didactic interest, he was aware that God's word is bitter and alien; that the prophets were always reluctant to speak it. Our mouth was but an instrument for the word, as the pipes of an organ for music. We have no authority, or *macht*, to add to or substract from God's word; we simply have to accept it in trust, in *vorlassenheyt*, like Christ, forsaken on the Cross. 'I have to submerge my will entirely in the divine one, and drown my own will in all matters.'[92] Karlstadt's mysticism set boundaries both to his humanism and to his populism.

---

[87]   *die fürsten der hochgelerten und schrifftweysen*; D Ai[r].
[88]   D Bii[r].
[89]   *ein lot hirns und vorstands*, B Bi.
[90]   D Bi.
[91]   D Bii[r]; Dii; Fiii; Giii.
[92]   M Biii.

Karlstadt's final motivation for writing was to move people to action, in line with the old rhetorical precept: *docere, suadere, movere* – to teach, to convince, to motivate. Writing a pamphlet, of course, was itself an action. It was a way to fight ignorance and fatalism, to enable and encourage people to do something. On the question of iconoclasm, to cite but one instance, Karlstadt saw himself confronting a veritable Babel of voices shouting: 'The weak, the weak; the infirm, the infirm; not too quick; softly, softly.'[93] His reaction was to call for decisive action: 'You have to confess', he said in his *Instruction about Vows*, that only the one true God is to be worshipped, not the saints.[94] Understanding led to decision, which in turn led to action.

Simple folk, it was true, could be scandalised when one abolished long-standing practices.[95] It was a false pity, however, a false love and prudence, to delay action because of this, to confuse brotherly love with *schad und ergernus*, with tolerating an idolatry which caused harm and scandal and flew in the face of God's revealed will.[96]

So he had to raise his voice, to insist that the reform of abuses was urgent; that one could not wait for the consent of everyone. Christ's instantaneous action in the Temple showed the way.[97] This was no mere human programme. God covenanted with one and all; in a striking phrase God was described as the 'husband of the created spirit'. If sexual adultery should be punished, how much more spiritual! Whenever we perceived God's will, we had to follow it at once. We would fall under a curse if we failed to act for the reform (*besserung*) of our neighbours' lot.[98] Any dichotomy of the inward and the outward was excluded.

[93]   *Schwachen schwachen/krancken krancken/nit zu schnell/gemach gemach*; S Ai.
[94]   G Biiii[r].
[95]   D Aii.
[96]   S Ciii.
[97]   S Diiii.
[98]   S Biiii[r]; *eeman des geschaffen geistes*; Aiii; *Die that sol dem verstand bald und allzeit folgen* (a heading); Aiii[r].

Among Karlstadt's most interesting emphases is that on the right and duty of the individual and the local group to respond to God's covenant. The parish, or congregation, was not a lifeless corpse; it had 'ears and eyes, and members ready for righteousness, as each family head (*hauss vatter*) does'.[99] The note of empowerment is unmistakeable. The laity should feel free to interpret Scripture.[100] They should not be patronised by the clergy; indeed their understanding of the Gospel often exceeded that of the most celebrated masters and doctors. Lay people had every right to ask preachers for a Scriptural basis for their statements, and to take the place of the speaker if they were given a revelation from God.[101] Preus comments that Karlstadt seeks to cultivate the formation of the laity as 'responsible subjects, whereas in most contemporary texts (including Luther's) they are the objects of learned and uncomplimentary judgments by the authorities'.[102]

They also had a right to take action against the clergy. Under the old Law (Deuteronomy 13) people could lay hands on a false prophet and throw the first stone, showing neither mercy or compassion. As Moses said: 'Spare them not, slay them; let your hand be the first.'[103] Scant wonder, reading these words, that Karlstadt was understood to be an advocate of violence!

To list Karlstadt's motivations is not to rank them. Most of Karlstadt's pamphlets manifest a complex battery of motivations; he was concerned to honour God, to confess his own faith, but also to give pastoral advice, to bring the authorities to their senses, to refute an opponent, to inform all

---

[99]   *Nicht das die ganze menge oder commun/ein solicher todter leib sein solt* . . . ; it has *glidmaß zu der gerechtigkeit bereit*; S Bii.

[100]   *frey und dapffer richten und urteyln*; P Ai[r].

[101]   *So aber ain sitzender oder zuhörer ain eröffnung hatt soll der oberst/das ist der Redner und Prediger/still schweigen*; F Ciii[r].

[102]   James S. Preus, *Carlstadt's Ordinaciones and Luther's Liberty: A Study of the Wittenberg Movement 1521–2* (Harvard Theological Studies XXVI: Cambridge, Mass., 1974), p. 49.

[103]   S Ciiii.

good Christians, to galvanise people to action. The range of his arguments is great: Biblical, legal, logical, historical. The range of emotions found in the pamphlets is also considerable, and may afford the best clue to his motivation. Karlstadt was all too aware that he could be swept completely off his feet by the depth of his rage, and for a while this led him to put a halt to any more publications.[104]

Anger, with its close allies, disgust and loathing, is perhaps the greatest of all human motivators, after love. Karlstadt's language frequently ran out into the sand in the face of the 'unspeakable' pride and presumption of the abominations he witnessed. His pamphlets then became graffiti, scrawled, as it were, on the ramparts of the enemy. The exclamations which peppered them: 'Shame on you, who devastate the Scriptures and tyrannise souls'; 'You would devour the world itself!'[105] remind us of his outrage. In one particularly memorable phrase, a subtle, but devastating modification of the Scriptural 'blood on your hands', he cried out against clerics who exploited the poor: 'Is there not blood on your prayers!'[106]

All this, however, was but the shadow side to Karlstadt's commitment to reform, to serving his neighbour, to honouring his God. For all these he was ready, he declared, to die, preferring the death of the body to the eternal, hellish death of the soul which would be his lot if he obeyed that Florentine lion, the Pope.[107] Even today, reading his writings, one catches a whiff of his passion, and understands why it captivated his readers. For the whole drama of the Reformation was mirrored in their urgent, personal message. Confessor, preacher, pastor, teacher and reformer, he used these rough, impulsive tracts, to step before a new, extended congregation. He pled with them in the language of workshop, home and street, and challenged

[104]   *Ursachen, daß Andreas Karlstadt eine Zeit stillschwieg.* Jena, 1523.

[105]   *Es ist nit zu sagen . . .* ; *Pfui euch, verwuster der schrifften und selen herschern*; *O weldt fresser!*; S Ciiii^r; iiii.

[106]   *Ist es nit blueth in deynem gebeth?* G Fiii^r.

[107]   M Aiii^r.

them to respond to his transparent commitment with one of their own.[108] A new form of literature had been forged to meet the needs of a new lay readership. A covenant had been forged between professor and people. If his attitudes are similar to those of the other Reformers, and I believe they are, this personal relationship needs to be taken into account when we look at the so-called Reformation dialogues.

---

[108] Cf. Pater's observations on Karlstadt's concern to use the language of the common people for preaching and theology; *Karlstadt as the Father of the Baptist Movements*, pp. 67f.

CHAPTER FOUR

REFORMATION DIALOGUES

Song to the Lord God on a Spring Morning
The light of a new morning is bright on the grass
And the voices of the poor are welcoming the day
When the cloud of night will be lifted and Pharoah's kingdom gone.

James K. Baxter[1]

In the end of the day the Reformation spread because the ordinary person could identify with its concerns. The merchant, artisan, village headman as well as the cleric, teacher or lawyer had to be convinced that its cause was theirs. Their reception of reforming ideas would determine how the in-talk of Church leaders, reformers and theologians could become converted into common currency. Linguistically and culturally, as well as socially, politically and theologically the Reformation was to change the face of Germany.

Yet how did this happen? In one of the most popular dialogues of the early 1520s, *A Conversation between a Fox and a Wolf*, the wolf, representing the predatory noble, asks rhetorically: 'Who can ever abandon their familiar ways?'[2] Who, indeed? It is as hard, Brother Henry says to the 'old mother' of

[1]   James K. Baxter, *Collected Poems* (Oxford University Press: Oxford, 1979), p. 592.
[2]   *Wer kan aber die art und gewonheyt lassen? Eyn Gesprech eynes Fuchs und Wolffs/ so die andern Füchs und Wölff auff den Stayger wald zusammen geschickt/ sich zu unterreden/ wo und wie die beyde partheyen/ den winter sich halten und neren wollen* (henceforth FW) Aii^r.

Ulm, as stopping an epileptic from falling into the water or the fire; yet times must, and do change.[3] And as even a cursory look, say, at Hans Sachs' famous *Ode to the Wittenberg Nightingale* shows, the transformation of attitudes and lifestyle for the citizens of Nuremberg was, in fact, breathtakingly comprehensive.

The literary expression of this revolution – enacted in the lives of hundreds of thousands of people, as they moved from the Old Church to reforming ways – was the conversion with which so many of the Reformation dialogues culminate. One of the most famous of these, *A Fine Dialogue and Conversation between a Pastor and a Village Mayor,* ends with the pastor deciding, after all, to follow Luther, and begging his parishioners' pardon for his past mistakes.[4] Typically, however, it is not a conversion 'experience' which is portrayed, certainly not in the modern sense of that word, but a change of mind after weighing up the arguments for and against. For even the early years of the Reformation, certainly in its magisterial form, bore few of the marks of a revivalist movement. It was much more a considered, though remarkably sudden, shift in basic convictions, a jettisoning of ancient loyalties, an embracing of a cluster of new images around which life and thought came to gravitate.

[3]   *Eyn gesprech bruder Hainrichs von Kettenbach mit aim frommen altmüterlin von Ulm von etlichen zufeln und anfechtung des altmütterlin/ auf welche antwort gegeben von bruder Hainrich* (henceforth A); Aii; Aiiii[i]; interesting is the additional note under the title saying that the written account of the answers to her questions requested by the widow had circulated from hand to hand, *Darnach weytter komen in annder menschen hend zulesen,* until it came finally 'into print'.

[4]   *Eyn schoner Dialogus und gesprech Zwischen eym Pfarrer und eym Schultheyss, betreffend allen übelstand der geystlichen/ und boßhandlung der weltlicheit. Alles mit geytzigkeyt beladen* (henceforth S); Ci; few of the 'conversions' are convincing; an exception is that of the 'carder' in the very sprightly dialogue: *Eyn gesprech/ von dem gemaynen Schwabacher Kasten/ als durch brüder Hainrich/ Knecht Ruprecht/ Kemerin/ Spüler/ und jrem Maister des Handtwercks der Wullen Tüchmacher* (henceforth SK).

The Reformation dialogues – brief, pungent, folksy summaries of the grievances and hopes of ordinary people – had an important role in bringing this process about so speedily. They constitute an important new literary form, brought into existence by the Reformation crisis. They were generally headed by a symbolic wood-cut, and by a preface, sometimes with a rhyme or poem attached, to catch the attention of the reader, much as the publisher's blurb on the dustcover of modern books does today. The prospective reader is often addressed personally: 'My dear reader'; 'Elect brothers and sisters'.[5]

The dialogues, however, were themselves symbolic. They brought together, within the compass of a few pages, the issues being discussed up and down the land, and they personalised them in the form of readily identifiable, idealised figures. The blunt, honest peasant, primed perhaps by a student son, challenges the representative of the Old Church, whether theologian or pastor. Or a nobleman, a monk, and a Roman courtier trade insults about who is the most heinous exploiter of the poor, while the reader is steered to the conclusion that there is nothing to choose between *reüterey* and *münchwerck*, highway robbery and monkish practices.[6] Or the 'old mother' of Ulm, nurtured in the traditional ceremonies of the Old Church, has her worries about the attack on them answered by an evangelical preacher.[7] These dialogues, which would often have been read out aloud, are in fact, with their characterisations, humour and dramatic tension, quite close to being small dramatic pieces. While the main focus is on priest and peasant, father and son, others, such as the Pope and Luther,

---

[5]   FW Ai[r]; *Der gestryfft Schwitzer Baur. Diß büchlin hat gemacht ein Baur auß dem Entlibuch/ Wem es nit gefall der küss jm die bruch* (henceforth SB) Aii.

[6]   *Ein newer Dialog oder gespräch /zwischen ainem verprenten/ vertribnem/ Edelman und ainen Münch welichen am unrechsten geschech wann die selben bayd vertriben/ und die Münch Clöster auch verbrannt würden* (henceforth EMC), B.

[7]   A Aii ff.

hover menacingly in the wings, and sometimes appear in person. As literature they both reflect, and themselves helped to precipitate the drama of the Reformation itself. This is literature at its most engaged.

The word 'dialogue' is in some ways misplaced. They could not be more removed from dialogues in the sense of a patient listening process. At times there is more of the knock-down flavour of a Punch and Judy show. Even if we replace the term 'dialogue' with 'conversation', which accurately translates the word *Gespräch*, which is often found in their titles, it frequently tends to be a very one-sided conversation. For most of its length, for example, one of the dialogues, between the pastor and the village mayor, is much more of a monologue, with the pastor tossing in the occasional, conventional defence of the old ways. The monk in *A New Dialogue* even admits straight away that the Reformers have the Word of God on their side; while the Roman courtier says that if he were to get his deserts he'd be hanged on the highest gallows going.[8] This is fairly typical. The representative of the Old Church, as the anti-hero, gets none of the good lines. The *Scourged Swiss Peasant* abruptly halts the dialogue about three-quarters of the way through.[9] There is little genuine dialogue, and still less in the way of character development. The repartee can be quite wooden or crude.

Nor are these anonymous dialogues written, as they claim to be, by the poor man, or peasant. That, too, is a literary convention. They were a product of the clergy or the humanists, sometimes in co-operation with artisan or commoner, as in

[8]   EMC Aii[r]; Bii[r].

[9]   The striped or brindled appearance of the faith of the Old Church, an admixture of divine truth with merely human laws and wisdom, is reminiscent of the unrecognisable nature of Christ's face after his scourging; SB Biii[r]; cf. also *Ein brüderliche warnung an meister Mathis Pfarrherren zu sanct Lorentzen im Münster zu Strassburg* . . . Steffan of Büllheim; 1522(?), Strassburg; ed. Marc Lienhard, 'Mentalité populaire', pp. 37–62; it ceases to be a dialogue and becomes a warning to Zell, as the title suggests.

the case of Zwingli's *The Divine Mill, Die göttliche Mühle,* and ironically, of the urban clergy.[10] They cannot even be said to be particularly well crafted. They frequently drift off into an excursus, and seldom achieve a satisfactory dramatic climax.

Literary criticism has demonstrated, then, that the dialogues are not folk culture, the product of 'the people', but of the learned humanist and Reformer. Yet the illusion they conjured up – a dialogue between peasant and priest, folk wisdom and clerical folly – reflected a repressed reality, and helped in turn to create a new reality. The alternative – literary creation or social documentary – may well be a false one. Charles Dickens, Emile Zola, and a host of contemporary film-makers, novelists, or dramatists such as Dennis Potter are all, in their way, depicting reality in an unforgettably vivid way. Similarly, the dialogues created a mirror in which people believed they could recognise themselves, and were spurred to become subjects of their own history. The way in which they are drawn upon by marginalised readers, by women such as Argula von Grumbach, for example, suggests that they provided encouragement for the latter to become writers themselves, to engage in their own dialogue with the powerful, to champion the use of German for religious debate, to criticise the defective knowledge of society's gate-holders. Argula von Grumbach, for example, frequently couples the cause of the peasant and of women.[11] The dialogues certainly idealised peasant realities, and caricatured priest, monk, friar and scholastic, but their shrewd polemic and humour indicate that they frequently hit a raw nerve.

What accounts, then, for the popularity of these writings? For popular they undoubtedly were. Winkler computes that the *Schultheiss,* or the dialogue between the pastor and the

---

[10]   Jørgensen, *Bauer, Narr und Pfaffe,* pp. 77, 173–5; there is a useful analysis of the dialogues in Werner Lenk, *Die Reformation im zeitgenössischen Dialog. 12 Texte aus den Jahren 1520 bis 1525* (Akademie Verlag: Berlin, 1965).

[11]   'Are peasants or women excluded here?' AvG, 177/5.

village mayor, with thirteen different editions, would have had a minimum circulation of some 13,000 copies. *Karsthans*, undoubtedly the most famous of them all, went into ten editions; the *Dialogue of the Fox and the Wolf* had seven.[12]

This chapter will examine this question. It will explore the themes chosen, and the manner in which they were presented. It will look at the way in which they seek to reflect ordinary life. It will examine the emotional tone, the images used, the language and style employed. It will be less concerned with the religious or social ideas of the pamphlets than with the way in which they are presented.

Of the themes, three stand out: a robust new role for the laity, a fierce anti-clericalism, and the primacy of a vernacular Scripture.

First of all, a composite 'identikit' picture of the liberated lay person begins to appear. He – it is almost always a he[13] – is simple, *einfältig*. This can mean simple-minded, and so open to exploitation. The greedy clergy used the cult of the saints to milk the simple people of money;[14] they duped them by tricks, for example, a monk speaking through a tube, to think a divine voice is speaking.[15] The poor, blind people have allowed the devil to set up his kingdom under the appearance of godliness.[16] Luther is portrayed as talking in this way of the *einfalt des tütschen volcks*, the German people's credulity.[17]

Generally, however, 'simple' is used in the sense of single-minded, or straightforward; 'I would like to know if there is

[12]   Hannelore Winkler, *Der Wortbestand von Flugschriften aus den Jahren der Reformation und des Bauernkrieges* (Akademie Verlag: Berlin, 1975), pp. 58f.

[13]   Though not always; cf. the reference to *der from ley es sy man oder frow*; and the explicit address: 'my dear brothers and sisters' in SB Biii[r]; Diii f.

[14]   S Aii[r].

[15]   A Ci[r].

[16]   FA Aii[r] f.

[17]   *Karsthanns mit vier Personen/ so vnder jnen selbs ain gesprech und Red halten/ Mercurius/ Murnar/ Studens/ Karsthans* (henceforth K).

any greater love than a natural, simple one.'[18] Christ established
a simple, uncomplicated faith, Karsthans (*Karst* = hoe) declares,
and he wants to 'abide by his old peasant faith'.[19] The first
disciples of Jesus, the fishermen, were simple, and so are today's
peasants.[20] On occasion the peasants of the dialogues flirt
with their simplicity, asking to be excused as *dorfflüten*, folk
from the sticks; when the angry Thomas Murner, representing
traditional theology, threatens to plague Karsthans like a devil,
he replies: 'How can a spiritual man like you be a devil: God
forbid.'[21]

In fact, the 'peasant' in the dialogues proves to be remarkably
well informed. He knows about recent and contemporary
events, such as the treatment of Hus at the Council of Constance, the Reuchlin controversy, the debate between Luther
and Eck at Leipzig, or the events at the Diet of Worms.[22] He
knows many of the religious and political personalities involved.
There are innumerable references to other writings of the
period, especially of the Reformers' 1520 polemic, but also to
Murner and other secular literature such as the *Eulenspiegel*.[23]
He can quote Scripture freely, and sometimes interminably;
even the Fathers are sometimes quoted.[24] On occasion the
literary conceit of the simple peasant can wear very thin indeed,
as when Karsthans takes Murner's Latin to task! [25]

The peasant is also described as 'poor'; he has to work hard
for his living. Much of the moral outrage at 'idolatrous'
ceremonies is that while the lifeless images in the churches are
elaborately dressed the poor Christians walk around naked and
hungry; that the laity leave money to the Church while their

---

[18] SB Di[r].
[19] *will by mym alten puren glouben bliben*; K Cii[r].
[20] *die einfältigen fyscher sine lieben apostlen*; SB Aii[r].
[21] K Aiii.
[22] K Aiiii.
[23] Cf. the list of Murner's writings; K Aiiii[r].
[24] K Dii[r]; SB passim.
[25] K Dii f.

poor relatives are in dire need.[26] Concern for the provision of funds for the poor, on the other hand, is taken as a mark of the Reformation.[27]

The peasants who take part in the dialogues are portrayed as relatively fortunate. Yet it gives us pause that, despite the overwhelmingly negative picture of the peasant in so many contemporary wood-cuts, and in humanist writings, the figure of the peasant is chosen as the standard-bearer of the Reformation.[28] Is it to sharpen the contrast with the hierarchy and clergy of the Church?[29] Is it to find a symbol of earthy 'Germanness'? Is it to promote, at least subliminally, the idea of Adamic innocence, compared with the corruptions of the present world? An unspoilt, 'noble peasant'? On occasions the dialogues do emphasise that humanity was created with a natural love of God, and for the understanding of God.[30] It may have been easier to identify with this idealised 'peasant' than with a lay nobleman or patrician or artisan. Undoubtedly, too, there is an echo of the emphasis of the medieval radicals and of Erasmus on true discipleship as simplicity, innocence and poverty of spirit. The poor, simple, down-trodden peasant, not least the poor widow, *die alten müterlein*,[31] symbolises oppressed humanity; oppressed by the secular authorities, but above all by friars, monks, clerics, prelates, by the Pope. Echoes of the Psalms and prophets such as Amos are unmistakeable. The apocalyptic note is not absent, either; in a time when all normal conventions are turned upside down, at a time when a young son instructs his old father, for example, it is natural

---

[26]   A Aiii; Bi.

[27]   SK passim.

[28]   Keith Moxey, *Peasants, Warriors, and Wives: Popular Imagery in the Reformation* (University of Chicago Press: Chicago, 1989).

[29]   If the Church is defined in terms of the Pope and his following, 'we poor Christians have no chance'; *So het wir armen Cristen ain verloren spyl*; S Aii.

[30]   SB Biiii[r].

[31]   EMC Aiiii.

that the traditional simpleton triumphs over the wise of this world.

And now, as the poor begin to find champions for their cause, who speak, both literally and metaphorically, their language, they are denied access to them by the gate-keepers of spiritual power. The dialogue, *Der gestryfft Schwitzer Baur, The Scourged Swiss Peasant,* was occasioned by the denunciation of a 'good simple Swiss peasant' for requesting access to German books, primarily Luther's translation of the New Testament.[32] Given the inadequacy of so many preachers, he argues, access to these was quite vital: 'What can pious country folk do, whose priest can scarcely read out the Gospel in German, far less expound it?'[33] Many a lay person can recite his Scripture by heart better than the pastor can stumble through his reading of it on Sundays![34] 'Nowadays the lay people take the priests and the scholars to task for their blindness and ignorance.'[35]

The dialogues, then, would have been read as charters of human rights for the 'ordinary man or woman', who previously have been treated, not like creatures of God, but like 'dirt'; like the 'old mother' of Ulm they have a right to understand what is going on at worship.[36] They have a right to knowledge, above all to divine knowledge, to books, to Scripture, and to discuss religious issues with those who in the past saw such discussions as their prerogative alone. For how else was the paterfamilias to instruct his household and his neighbour as he was in duty bound to do?[37] He is quite able to decide for himself whether Luther and his ilk are heretics. Even the public hangman at Mainz, ordered to burn Luther's books, is

---

[32]   SB Ai.

[33]   SB Bi[r].

[34]   SB C iiii[r].

[35]   SB Biii.

[36]   *dreck und laymen* (Lehm = clay) *des Bapsts und Endchrists*; A Bii; Bi[r].

[37]   *Dann ein jetlicher huß vatter ist schuldig sin gesind zu behalten in christelicher übung mit allem flyß*; SB Biiii.

depicted as judiciously inquiring about the authorisation for this.[38] This literary portrayal of the peasant jousting intellectually with the spiritual authorities of the day, who regarded him as a *purren klotz*, a cloddish peasant,[39] was itself intended to be symbolic of the new era that was dawning. The lay community, *gemain*, would take control of its own destiny.[40]

Undergirding this new self-image was a theological emphasis on the equal status of all Christians, however simple they may be: '. . . any Christian who reads the words of the holy Gospel in true faith, love and confidence in God, simply following the text, will understand everything . . . necessary for salvation'. There is a variety of gifts, as Paul says, and the gift of love has been given especially to the poor and the humble.[41] References abound to Luther's *Appeal to the German Nobility*, and especially to his teaching on the priesthood of all believers.[42] Again, to have a peasant citing such writings as this, in the course of complaints to his religious betters, is meant to adumbrate a new age.

We have to ask how contemporary readers of the dialogues would have reacted to a peasant instructing, and reproving the clergy, even, on occasion, forgiving and 'converting' them. Truly an inversion of all the conventional values! 'You peasants have no competence (*vernunfft*) in such matters', Karsthans is told.[43] Yet it was the contention of the dialogues that it was to and through such 'simplicity' that the Holy Spirit speaks, in the German language as in Latin; the bread of heaven, Holy Scripture, will nourish all who reverently seek it.[44]

---

[38]   K Bii.
[39]   Karsthans is warned by his Student: 'O Father, you should not talk with such important people; you just anger them.' K Aiii f.
[40]   SK Aiiif.
[41]   SB Aii[r]; Diiii.
[42]   S Bii[r].
[43]   K Cii[r].
[44]   SB D i.

The dialogues painted a crass contrast between the sophisticated and privileged monks, scholars and prelates and their humble interlocutors. Salt was rubbed into the wounds of the representatives of the Old Church by the plebeian nature of their conquerors. 'I can neither read nor write', the mayor in the *Schultheiss* says, but he has been brought up to date by his son, who does have some education.[45] In the figures of the 'pupil', or student son of the peasant we glimpse another important intermediary figure. The new learning is not insulated from the ordinary person in an academic or religious ghetto. It trickles down to the illiterate and semi-literate from the universities, schools and printing-presses through the discussions in the wine shops, the bath houses, the market place.

Interestingly, too, it is suggested that the ideas are not necessarily watered down as they reach the less-educated, as contemporary Reformation historiography is beginning to realise. Karsthans, having invested much money in his son's university education in Cologne, had expected him to perceive the justice of Luther's case, and is disappointed at his conservatism.[46] Likewise the village mayor is much more radical than his cautious 'student'. His way of 'reading' Murner's pamphlet attacking Luther – spluttering rage which hardly got beyond the first page – may in fact give us quite an accurate insight into how books and pamphlets were, in fact, 'read' in this period: with explosive indignation and a highly selective focus! Karsthans repeatedly calls out during the dialogue for a flail by which he can clean up Church and society once and for all![47] The Reformation is portrayed as a grass-roots movement with its own dynamics.

The 'docta rusticitas',[48] or earthy wisdom, of our utopian peasant combines book knowledge with peasant guile won from

---

[45] S Aiiii^r.
[46] K Bi^r.
[47] *Wo ist myn pflegel*; K Aii^r; Bii^r.
[48] K Bii^r.

personal experience.[49] His *buren regel*, or peasant ways, lead Karsthans to the common-sense view that both sides, Luther's as well as that of the Pope, should be heard before he is condemned,[50] and this indeed is one of the most pervasive themes of the dialogues. Karsthans is indignant that Murner will not engage in an open disputation with Luther.[51] The village mayor angrily warns the clergy that condemning Luther as a heretic is no substitute for engaging in disputation with him, and that they will be in trouble if they continue down this path.[52] Their authoritarian theology covers up their desire for power and wealth. The 'Swiss peasant' dismisses the accusation of heresy against the German books as a *sin verkerung*, a distortion of the truth.[53]

Imperceptibly, then, the emphasis on the rights of the ordinary man leads to anti-clericalism. The poor and the simple reprove (*straffen*) the clergy when their teaching is of no value, just as Paul criticised Peter in Galatians 1.[54] 'Ach', says a servant, 'all [our preacher] can talk about is what is written in the first chapter, the second chapter'; we need a preacher of the Gospel.[55] The furious reaction of Murner: 'What do you think you're doing, correcting me?' only confirms Karsthans in his view that 'I understand all right; it's the cowl which makes a monk, though the man himself be a rascal.'[56] The ordinary man is being made a fool of by the clergy, who load heavy

[49]   Dieter Seitz characterises Karsthans as the 'very personification of common sense' (*der verkörperte gesunde Menschenverstand*); he is seen as a projection of humanist reform ideals, legitimising them with his peasant guile and directness; 'Flugschriftenliteratur der Reformation und des Bauernkriegs', in Horst Glaser (ed.), *Deutsche Literatur: Eine Sozialgeschichte* 2 (Reinbek bei Hamburg, 1991), p. 350.

[50]   K Bi[r].

[51]   K Aiii[r] f.; Bi[r].

[52]   S Ci; cf. also Ai[r].

[53]   SB Biii[r].

[54]   S Aiii[r].

[55]   A Bii.

[56]   K Aiii.

burdens of fasting, for example, on the laity, but flout them themselves.[57]

Some of the dialogues are, at first sight at least, little more than long lists of anti-clerical complaints, the traditional *gravamina*, with a particular focus on the Papacy and Rome. This is true, for example, of the *Schultheiss*. It is largely a call for reform, with a minimum of theology, no emphasis on justification by faith, and almost no traces of the mystical or apocalyptic notes one comes across in so many of the Reformers' writings, though the Pope is seen as 'the king in the realm of Antichrist'.[58] Often, as in the *Scourged Swiss Peasant*, an anti-humanist strain comes through. The emphasis is severely practical, with interest deriving mainly from the colourfulness and energy of the critique, and from the sharp and simplistic polarisation of clergy and laity, Pope and Luther, Rome and the Empire. Orthopraxis is the main concern, loving care for one another: 'Yes, one often finds in Holy Scripture that all things were held in common by those who truly believed.'[59]

The fierce determination to demolish the entire clerical system is apparent in all the pamphlets. This comes close at times to propaganda; it is certainly not carefully qualified writing.[60] The clergy are seen, first of all, as driven by mercenary considerations. They devour the substance of the poor. Their appetites for tithes, fees, and dues of every conceivable kind is so insatiable that the poor would find 'more mercy in Hell' than from the clergy.[61] Salvation has become a commodity, sold at a flea-market: 'When our Lord Jesus gave Peter the keys to bind and to release, he did not instruct him

[57] S iii[r].
[58] FA Aiii; the *Altmütterlin* refers frequently to Antichrist and the synagogue of Satan.
[59] SK Aiii[r].
[60] The 'Swiss peasant' admits that there are a few pious shepherds; SB Biii.
[61] K Di.

to sell them.'[62] They flay (*schinden*) the poor; they live off their backs. The sole motive for so many church ceremonies is their abominable greed; at the church fairs (*kirweych*) you can see the priest prowling around, like a falconer with his hawk, looking for victims; if he gets some money he rushes over to the church and, crouching like a bagpiper, rattles through a Mass or two.[63] Of course, the poor are oppressed by the nobility and the civic authorities, too, but the clergy, who should give a good example, are the worst of all; the greed of all the others stems from them. As Christ drove the learned (*gelerten*) of his day, the money-changers(!), out of the Temple, so reform today must begin with the clergy, a medicine (*ertzney*) must be found to bring them to their senses.[64]

Secondly, the clergy use this wealth to live a life of luxury which is quite contrary to the Gospel. They glory in rich costumes, adorned with glittering diamonds and gold; they try to ape the secular princes. They surround themselves with servants, and women of dubious reputation; they live for the hunt.[65] They are masters, not of theology, but of the wine glass.[66] They fail to reside in their parishes, they pile up pluralities, they are often minors, quite incapable of carrying out their office. The *Schultheiss* piles up the accusations in almost incoherent rage: the clergy's evil deeds and words are legion; they roam through the streeets at night, licentious, noisy, strangely attired (*mit verkerten klaydung*).[67] When the monk in *A New Dialogue* says the monks have to abstain from women, the noble throws back the usual accusation: 'But nuns, Beguins and peasant women are allowed'; 'you're allowed to talk to a whore in your cell'.[68]

[62]   SB Cii.
[63]   *allayn von des schendlichen geytz willen*; S Aii[r] f.
[64]   *Ydoch ist die geyzigkayt von erst bey euch auff gestanden*; S Biiii; Bi[r]D.
[65]   S Aii.
[66]   *Magister jm weinglaß*; S Bii.
[67]   S Bii f.
[68]   EMC Aiii; Bii.

Thirdly, the abuse of their power has made them a real plague; they use excommunication and interdict to intimidate the laity, while their vows, their status as ordained people, give them immunity from the secular courts. For four hundred years now this evil system (*böse ordnung*) has prevailed; almost everything that our ancestors have scraped together by their bloody sweat has wandered into the pockets of the clergy. 'So we poor fools have . . . been compelled to be your servants, been held captive all this time.'[69]

Village analogies are used to make the critique explicit. When a community entrusts one of its lay members with its cattle he becomes accountable to the community for their care.[70] But as the shepherds entrusted by Christ with the care of his sheep the clergy have scandalously abused their office for their own gain. That is why they oppose Luther so violently: '. . . if the teaching of Martin Luther had not threatened their power, honour, their food stores, cellars and kitchens, they would not be so opposed to him'.[71] The only answer is to have the dumbwits (*Stocknarren*) removed if they are incapable of carrying out their pastoral tasks. 'I know the right medicine; anyone who is incompetent, and lacks the skills for the priestly office, should lose his benefice and be chased out of the land, or forced to go to work.'[72] Those who do stay should be given a fair stipend.

The present incumbents are hypocrites and Pharisees, loading burdens on others which they have no intention of bearing themselves. It is not the Swiss peasant, with his appetite for foreign books, who is scourged or 'striped', that is, of divided loyalties, but the scholastics who disfigure the holy Gospel with their heathen 'stripes'.[73] Worst of all is their murder of people's souls.[74] The tone of the dialogues is consistently aggressive,

[69] S Cii.
[70] SB Cii f.
[71] SB Ciiii.
[72] S Bi^r f.
[73] SB Bii^r f.
[74] EMC Aiiii.

96   THE RHETORIC OF THE REFORMATION

turning the attack back on those who launched it. It is the clergy of the Old Church, not the Reformers, who are heretics, false prophets, false shepherds, idolators.[75] The village mayor declares: 'So I say that you – the majority of you – are heretics, and that's a fact, for what you preach to us is nothing but human chit-chat.'[76] Like a court jester, the priests make the most elaborate, pompous preparations for the Mass: 'dress up and decorate the wooden and painted idols on the altar'.[77] The sermon is turned into a great dramatic show, as if the Holy Spirit were active only 'when they yelled and thumped on the pulpit and thundered out denunciations'.[78]

All these departures from good evangelical simplicity are accompanied by contempt for the lay people, and a pretence that the higher mysteries of the faith are beyond them.[79] As Murner is made to say: 'No good will come from challenging some portions of our faith'; this requires the great subtlety of the theologians, who can weave, as it were, through the eye of a needle. And often miss it, retorts Karsthans, by a mile.[80] The contempt of the clergy for the laity, and for their German language, is returned with interest. A weird Church it has become, with strange spiritual leaders, 'doing nothing but cursing, denouncing, raging, wishing the people ill', always scrapping with one another, like pike devouring one another in a pond.[81] They may have the title and appearance of spiritual authority, but it is counterfeit and valueless in reality.[82]

The arguments put in the mouth of the defenders of the old order are two-fold. First of all, to raise such questions and

---

[75]   . . . *falsche propheten/ lügenhafftig maister/ und eyn furent falscher leer der verdamnuß/ und haben geirt etc* . . . ; S Biiii[r].

[76]   S Bii[r].

[77]   S A ii[r].

[78]   SB Aiiii[r].

[79]   *sie weren mit gespöt den frummen leyen in zu gon*; SB Diii; *vitium est indignis secreta vulgare*, put in Murner's mouth; S Aiii[r].

[80]   Lit., 'by as far as a peasant can leap'; K Ci[r] f.

[81]   K Aiiii[r]; Biiii[r].

[82]   *ein schin und kunterfee*; K Ciii.

challenges is to endanger all authority in Church and state. This, of course, is far from being a specious argument. In the *Dialogue of the Fox and the Wolf* it is suggested that, in their revolt of 1522–3, the Imperial Knights under Franz von Sickingen did precisely this. They overstepped the mark, *der sachen weyt zu vil gethan*; instead of gathering the support of the princes and the nobility, the lions and eagles, falcons and hawks, they set out on their own; they 'wanted to reform the world, but without any authorisation'.[83] The result of such *vermessenheyt*, or head-strong audacity, was that they alienated not only the princes, but the city-dwellers and the peasants too, who saw them as simply pursuing their old aggressive ways; as a result they were now being visited by the deserved punishment of God.[84]

The question of *aufruhr*, then, of fomenting rebellion, was anything but an idle one, and was much discussed in the literature of this period. It was important for the dialogues to deal with it convincingly. As far as spiritual authority was concerned, *Kursthans* leans heavily on Luther's *Appeal to the German Nobility* and on the idea of the stewardship of power. In the face of the absolutist claims of the Papacy, he asks: 'tell me, has a steward more power than his lord has given him? For me as a peasant – O no! When a prince bestows power on his administrator – power over the community – it is the intention of the prince that such power should only be used to advance the honour of the prince and the welfare of the land'; it must not be abused to fleece his subjects. Similarly Christ told his disciples how they should exercise their office; but the current Pope and bishops do the very opposite of this. Look at the militaristic exploits of recent Popes![85] In similar vein the *Schultheiss* calls on the princes to cut the hierarchy down to size, and to reform the Church. Confrontation cannot be

---

[83]   *wolten die welt reformiren/war uns doch noch nit befolhen*; FW Aii, Aiiii.

[84]   FW Aiii.

[85]   K Bii^r f.

avoided, as Christ told his disciples; and the ordinary man is willing to play his part in assisting the nobility.[86]

Karsthans goes further. He adduces the Classical precedent of the Roman tyrant Tarquin. Warned that one should leave things well alone if this leads to *uffrür* against the authorities, he quickly disclaims any such intention: 'But it can happen that an authority abuses its power so crudely and shamelessly . . . that it brings itself into discredit'. In our own times, he continues, king, emperor, bishop and Pope have often been prevented by their councils or parliaments, or by the opposition of the common people, *widersprechung der gemeinen,* from launching bloody wars. Citing the example of the Duke of Württemberg he asks whether one is to allow a ruler to become 'ever more sick and crazed (*wütig*), to have the innocent murdered, to slay them with his own hand'.[87] The 'Swiss peasant' agrees: '. . . unjust power is not so firmly established as just power, and all temporal power comes to an end'.[88]

This critique of secular authority is, however, exceptional. The *Schultheiss* is much more typical; he excuses the secular powers for any exactions they lay on the poor. They have to carry the expense of defending them, and do show flexibility if, say, the weather prevents the peasants paying their full dues.[89]

The clerical abuse of power, however, must be resisted: 'Yes, and to strike a defiant note, neither pope nor bishop has any power apart from and beyond Holy Scripture, any more than a stone does.' The plumb-line (*richtschit*) of all authority is Scripture, the real testimony (*der recht houpt brieff*) which Christ has left behind him as to how Christendom should be governed.[90] The trouble about the Knights' Revolt is that its leaders treated Scripture as 'a lot of gossip in an old book'.[91]

---

[86]   S Biiii[r].
[87]   K Cii ff.
[88]   SB Cii[r].
[89]   S Biii[r].
[90]   K Ciii f.
[91]   FW Aii.

No arguments for the monarchical principle in church government can be adduced from secular politics for these are 'silly human precedents'.[92] It is no insurrection, but a necessary duty to withdraw obedience from those who are opposed to the Gospel. They have to be brought to reason (*vernunfft*).[93] Until they show knowledge and righteousness (*kunst und gerechtikeit*) they have to be resisted, just as Paul resisted the High Priest Ananias.[94]

The second main argument attributed to the Old Church's defenders is the need to show deference to tradition. But the dialogues argue that neither Canon Law nor medieval history are acceptable as criteria. Canon Law is subject to the law of God.[95] Karsthans protests that if the teachings of the scholastics were to be followed one would end up having to believe in 'whatever some mad monk has dreamed up'.[96] Scripture alone is the criterion, especially the New Testament: 'the holy Gospels and St Paul's teaching'.[97] Over against Murner's 'useless prattle', his 'subtle arguments in the new fashion', the good, simple (*einfaltigen*) Luther is seen as the true exegete of Scripture, especially when he expounds the priesthood of all believers.[98] The Papist reading of Scripture, on the other hand, circles selectively around the four lines which are always adduced as the basis of Papal authority: 'You are Peter . . .' etc.[99] But Christ as the living head of the Church is the principle on which the Church rests, not any bodily head such as the Pope.[100] For all office in the Church is for ministry. 'And the pope is the servant and bondsman of God and the Church. Likewise all priests are

---

[92]   K Di[r].
[93]   S Biiii.
[94]   K Cii[r].
[95]   S Ai.
[96]   K Cii[r].
[97]   S Ai.
[98]   K Dii[r] f.; *ein hochspitziger man . . . uff die nüw manier*; A iiii[r].
[99]   K Biii.
[100] K Di[r].

our servants.'[101] Tradition has been used too often to protect the abuses of the clergy and to deny the common folk their due rights. One has to get back behind it to the practice of the Early Church and of Scripture: '[The offerings] belong to the poor, as was the case in the Early Church, not to you [clergy].'[102]

A close connection is drawn between the Church being of and for the humble and the poor and the emphasis on the supremacy of Scripture. For Scripture is accessible to all. 'For it is the glorious river of the delightful paradise of the high heavens, which flows through and waters the noble paradise of holy Christendom and the believers in Christ in our vale of sorrows'; by learning from it daily the simple can be strengthened in the works of love and the ways of reason (*vernunfft*).[103] It is love which is central, the practice of divine knowledge (*götliche kunst zu üben*),[104] not clever speculations. Word and deed should be one.[105] 'Love God and your neighbour': that is 'the highest doctorate'; 'what need have we of other lofty doctors, who have wasted their time with human ordinances, quoting whole sacks of canon law'.[106]

Having the Scriptures in the vernacular enables lay people to free themselves from the many snares set them by their spiritual masters.[107] Ignorance and immorality are the enemies of faith, not reformers such as Luther who open up the Scriptures.

Thus there are two types of learning. The Holy Spirit leads one to an understanding of Scripture, to the true learning, which is championed by Erasmus, Karlstadt, Oecolampadius, Luther, who understand the ancient languages – Greek, Hebrew, Latin – and interpret Scripture simply and piously.[108]

[101]   S Aiiii[r].
[102]   S Aiiii.
[103]   SB Aii f.
[104]   SB Cii[r].
[105]   SB Diii.
[106]   SB Diii[r].
[107]   SB Dii; S Ai[r].
[108]   S Ci[r].

'Now tell me! What can there be that is more certain than the holy Gospel?' But our preachers desert it to speculate about heaven and hell and purgatory.[109]

On the other hand, the subtle, false learning of many famous doctors has led people into the abyss of hell.[110] It is full of speculation, driven by arrogance, based on the heathen philosophers, and relies on scholastic theologians who are always disagreeing and disputing with one another.[111] It inverts all values; what normal folk regard as sin is taken to be wisdom and courage.[112] Controversial theologians, such as Eck and Murner, have been led astray by their own vanity; Murner is described as an 'ignorant painted theologian': all surface and no depth.[113] None of them can offer a faith with any certainty to it.

Sometimes an anti-humanist strain emerges, as has been noted, a sweeping critique of the Classical poets and philosophers such as Aristotle, and of Origen (and latterly Murner) who are seen as following in their footsteps.[114] All this is dismissed as 'heathen', in exactly the same way as 'idolatrous' ceremonies are.[115]

More consistent is the nationalist emphasis, the resentment of foreign, namely Italian, oppression, and of foreign teachings. At times all these flow together. Irrational foreign, heathen teachings are seen as legitimising papal oppression.[116] The simple Gospel, on the other hand, suits the simple, honest Germans; Luther should have no anxiety. Let him write the divine truth in Karsthans' own language, and the Germans will defend him; from the earliest times the tough-skulled

[109]   SB Bi.
[110]   SB Ci.
[111]   SB Aiii ff.; Bi.
[112]   K Bii^r.
[113]   S Ci; K Ai^r.
[114]   SB Aiii; K Aiiii^r.
[115]   S Bii^r; A Aiii.
[116]   ... *vast ußlendig dorecht leren geben/ in beschirmung bäpstlicher oberkeit/die durch zu viel ... heidnisch anzeigen zu grund keren*; K Ai^r.

Germans have always borne off the prize, whether against the French or the Italians.[117]

A hostility to Latin often surfaces. 'You and your mate think yourselves so clever, always blethering away in Latin', Karsthans explodes.[118] The Latin language was such a deceptive one that the Scripture should never have been translated into it; it was just a way of keeping 'us poor, simple lay people so ignorant';[119] '. . . one finds many Latin-speaking donkeys, too'.[120] The clerics' contempt for German, as if it were irrational, ignores the natural, rational, God-created character of vernacular language, as in the first man, Adam.[121] Our own language is always the closest to our heart; just as David used his own tongue in the Psalms, so should we.[122]

Yet many of the dialogues betray their humanist origins by their use of Latin tags and proverbs.[123] In *Karsthans* Mercurius plays the role of the rather ironic, detached observer. His comments are all in Latin, and, rather like a stage whisper, point up issues for the initiated Latin reader, and introduce a word-play between the languages which can be highly amusing. When Murner seeks to intimidate Karsthans, for example, Mercurius interjects: *Opera spiritus patent* – the works of the spirit are revealed.[124] Eck (in German = corner) is dubbed *Eck von spitzen*, a dig at the subtle distinctions of his thought. Mercurius comments, in Latin, 'mischief seeks a dark corner'

---

[117]   *Tütschland hat von alter har noch . . . den priß gmeinlich behalten*; K Biii^r.

[118]   K Ciiii^r; the same term *plapast* (blether) is, interestingly, used by Karsthans' student son of his father's talk, hinting at the cultural tension between the Latin-speaking and the vernacular world.

[119]   K Di.

[120]   SB Dii^r.

[121]   SB Biiii^r.

[122]   SB Ciii^r f.

[123]   E.g., *latet anguis in herba* (there's a snake in the grass); K Ai^r.

[124]   K Aii^r; some of the marginal notes in the *Altmütterlin* – though not all are in Latin – function in a similar way, as sub-headings, which emphasise a particular point.

(*angulum*), to which Karsthans responds, 'Yes, he certainly has a poisoned hook' (*angel*).[125] The constant stream of minor misunderstandings adds a dash of Falstaffian humour, and, of course, allow the humanist reader a cultivated snigger at the expense of the peasant hero, or indeed at Thomas Aquinas, misheard by the 'old mother of Ulm' as Thomas of *kackwin* (shit-wine).[126]

The language of the dialogues is conversational, sometimes slangy. They catch the attention immediately with direct, lively dialogue.[127] Often they begin with chatty remarks about recent events: *was sagt jr newer mer*, What's the latest?[128] They may end with a drink or a meal together and a blessing as they go their different ways.[129] There is considerable humour and word-play or punning; for example, with Luther's name; in German *lauter* means 'pure'. Cardinal becomes Karnöffel, Kamel, Katzanal (carnival, camel, catanal(?)).[130] The text is full of interjections: ' Ho Ho Ho!' 'Ha ha ha he!' 'Just listen to that!' 'Note this, Pastor!' Or exclamations and ejaculations: *Ey wo sein sie jetz* (Yeah, where are they now?); *der teufel hol sie all* (the devil take them all)[131] 'Oh, you thieves, how terribly you have betrayed the common man!'[132] Folk wisdom and proverbs are frequent: 'It's hard to paint white over black' (to change one's ways).[133] At times the dialogue breaks into a prayer or a curse.

In clever persiflage of the catechetical manner, the text is often an apparently endless succession of questions, frequently

[125] K Diii^r.
[126] A Ci^r.
[127] EMC Aii^r; SK Ai^r.
[128] S Ai^r; a very good example is the beginning of *Ein Frag und Antwort von zweyen brüdern /was für ein seltzames Thier zu Nürmberg gewesen im Reychstag nechst vergangen/ geschickt von Rom zu beschawen das Teutsch landt* (= FA).
[129] S Cii; SB Biii.
[130] K Biii; FA Ai^r.
[131] FW Aiii; Aiiii.
[132] EMC Bi^r.
[133] A Bii^r.

rhetorical or sarcastic ones. Who constitutes the Christian Church? Are all the poor lay folk damned, and only the clergy saved?[134] Why should Luther be seen as a heretic? What is the justification for so many clerical exactions? Who gave the Pope such power? What use are the monasteries, anyway? Is heaven so dark that the saints need us to burn candles to them?[135]

Thus the dialogues are designed to open up the discussion of taboo areas, to offer a hearing to those denied it elsewhere. Christ himself is portrayed as a questioner of the religious authorities of his day.[136] Luther is presented as calling for both sides to be heard without prejudice, so that truth and reason alone may decide.[137] After a lengthy trading of insults the nobleman, monk and Roman courtier in *A New Dialogue* accept that the common man has tumbled to the rascality of all three of them, and covenant together to a life of crime which will bring them wine, women and fine horses to ride. The lid will be taken off all these abuses, the leaf turned over (*kers pletlein umb*).[138] The prelates hate lay people precisely because they fear being shown up in this way.[139]

The dialogue can have a sharp edge: 'Dear Murner, you better get a grip on yourself (literally: on your nose).'[140] Or the firm ring of command: 'Take all this to heart, dear Pastor.'[141] The rhythms of oral language are often in evidence: *grund und boeden/ türn und thor schlemmen/ demmen/ prassen davon.*[142] Long lists of substantives often roll out for additional effect, the following all on one page: Pope, cardinals, bishops, prelates and pastors; tithes, confession fees, baptism fees, sacrament fees; so much bread and wine, lard, meal, eggs and money;

---

[134] A Cii.
[135] A Aiii^r.
[136] K Ciii.
[137] K Bi^r.
[138] EMC Bii^r f.; Biiii.
[139] *emblöst und uffthust dz laster der oberkeit*; SB Cii.
[140] K Diii.
[141] S Biii.
[142] A Aiii^r; S Aiiii^r.

corn, grain of all kinds, calves, sheep or lambs, fruit.[143] Alliteration is frequent; contrasts are almost always stark and absolute: God and the devil, Luther and the Pope, faith and the world, sheep and wolves.[144] Arguments are often taken *ad absurdum*: Instead of endowing Masses for the dead why not leave money for a bagpiper or a lute-player?[145] The clergy exact so much from us, why not our new-born children, too? Why doesn't the Pope set up a pillar and worship a calf on it?[146]

At times there is a definite element of carnival, or clowning. *Karsthans* begins with an elaborate and rather droll entrance of the mewing cat (*murmaw*) which is gradually transmogrified into Murner: 'O God, it is a man of the cloth!'[147] There is an extended, and quite clever description of two brothers pondering on the 'monster' sent from Rome to the Reichstag at Nuremberg; the 'strange devil' looked like a carnival figure, rode on a donkey, wore long, flowing red womanish garments, and had a red basin on its head, in which were a calf's head and a donkey's head. From its canopy and long train of costumed followers the brothers concluded it must be a masquerade. Onlookers thought it was the red whore of Babylon or the apostle of Antichrist, or a Papal Legate.[148] There is much humour at the expense of the clerics, learning to walk on their heads, but also of the peasant: 'Your peasant logic would have stools hopping up onto the bench.'[149] There is black humour, too, at the expense of relics: the clergy of Trier, exercising their usual form of pastoral oversight, mulct the people of thousands of gulden to mend Christ's robe.[150]

---

[143]   S Aiiii.
[144]   K Ciiii.
[145]   A Bi.
[146]   S Aiiii; K Ciiii.
[147]   K Aii f.
[148]   FA Aii ff.
[149]   S Ci^r; K Cii^r.
[150]   A Aiiii.

The language can be quite crude or vulgar: 'That's why we've all shat ourselves; may the devil wash us clean'; 'I shit into his wolfish gob'.[151] The Roman courtier and the German monk quarrel about who has shat upon the Germans more.[152] The Roman Legate uses the Germans' petitions to wipe his arse.[153] The title page of the *Scourged Swiss Peasant* invites anyone who doesn't like the book to kiss his arse. To the student's comment that Murner has 'a lot of arrows in his quiver', Karsthans responds: 'Yes, and lets them off in his habit.'[154]

The folksy character of the dialogues is emphasised by their rich imagery, drawn from daily life. There are countless animal images: the deceptive cat, a creature of the darkness, with its soft paws and sharp claws, licking you from the front, but scratching when your back is turned, pretending friendship but about to infect one with a toad's poison.[155] It represents, of course, the clergy, who play blind mice with the Germans (think they can deceive them).[156] There are references to dogs barking, to crows swarming together, to pike in a pond, to swans and snakes, to sheep, foxes, wolves; to hawks, eagles, lions. The muttered Masses for the dead are like frogs croaking.[157] At times, as in the *Dialogue of the Fox and the Wolf*, the animals talk to one another. In one scene, reminiscent of a fairy-tale, the predatory animals are forced to disgorge their victims.[158]

There are countless Biblical images: Israel in the desert; Balaam and his ass; the Babylonian captivity; Christ as shepherd and spouse.[159] The image of the fool, so prevalent at this time

---

[151]   FW Aiii[r] f.; or into the bishop's throat; FA Aiii.
[152]   EMC Aiii[r].
[153]   FA Aiii[r] f.
[154]   K Diii.
[155]   K Aii; Diii.
[156]   FA Aiii[r]; A Aiii[r].
[157]   A Bi.
[158]   FW Aiiii[r].
[159]   A study of the use of Scripture in the dialogues would be most worthwhile.

– in Brant and Erasmus and Murner – keeps recurring. But is it the thick peasant or the wise doctor who is the real fool, the *narr*, the *gouchmeister*?[160] The endless varieties and habits of the monastic orders are likened to the court fools with their different costumes.[161] There are many images of captivity, of being caught in snares, and one prolonged, unintentionally hilarious one of the poor lay person, lying frozen in bed, having been robbed of nearly all the bed-clothes by the clergy, but still desperately hanging on to one corner of the coverlet.[162]

Similes and metaphors abound: 'ill-fortune plays fiddle to our dance'; 'the heat of our stomachs drives us'. 'Our hearts sank to our pants.'[163] A monk says: 'the peasants . . . would drown us in a spoon if they could'; as for Luther, in their wild enthusiasm: 'they gobble him up, skin, hair and all (*hawt und har*); and they pay as much attention to our excommunications as to a goose honking'.[164] The clergy eat so well that they look like pregnant women; their teeth must be aching to judge by the swollen cheeks of their buttocks.[165]

For all their rational arguments the dialogues are full of emotions, too. Alliteration and repetition hammer home the message. A long list of the objects of devotion – a silver cross, agnus dei, heart, candle, gold images, gilded paintings – heightens the sense of outrage.[166] Terms of abuse are frequent. The word *Rölling* seems to have been specially coined to fit Murner; the prelates are surrounded by pimps and buffoons.[167] The priests feed their fat faces; they stink of the shit-house.[168]

---

[160] K Dii[r].
[161] EMC Aiii.
[162] S Cii.
[163] FW Aii ff.
[164] EMC Aii[r] f.
[165] A Cii[r].
[166] A Aiii.
[167] *kuppler und schalckßnarren*; K Aii.
[168] Lit. their fat masks (*bolster mumen*); K Aiiii; *Ja warlich stincken yr vom secret*; K Aiii[r].

They are *seelmörder*, murderers of souls; *des Teüffels mastschweyn*, the devil's fatted pigs.[169] Karsthans with his flail symbolises the rage at the arbitrary violence of the Papacy. 'Is violence to be the only law?'[170] Dark fears are raised about what the priests are up to in the peasants' homes when they are absent.[171] Sexual accusations are never far absent: 'It seems that daughter (doctor) Murner has been more often whoring on the fools' meadow than studying Holy Scripture.'[172] As the mockery and derision of clerics shades into disgust there are frequent threats, too, of direct action: to drive them out of the village, for example.[173] 'To the gallows with the cat! [Murner]!'[174] Yet there are also warnings against any resort to weapons, an emphasis on the need for prayer and patience.[175] There is a call to confession and defiance, to boast of the Gospel whatever the cost.

A by-product of the dialogues' concern to reach ordinary people is that they depict village and civic life vividly: the young girls' hearts thumping as the drums give the signal for the dance to begin;[176] the gossip in the market-place, or in the wine house with its games of dice and cards, or in the baths, where the priest's feeble sermon is torn to pieces and the reputation of his cook further traduced;[177] the cheating in the market: watered wine, impure spices, rotten hay, bad eggs, bruised fruit, false weights.[178] We hear of books being read out, or the main points written up with chalk on the wall for the peasants.[179] We read about the lisping German of a Jew; the stable-boy

---

[169]   EMC Aiiii^r.

[170]   K Bii^r.

[171]   S Biii.

[172]   K Ci^r; similarly *Ein brüderliche Warnung*, 50–4.

[173]   K Aii f.; *Volgen aber mir die bawren ayn mal so woll wir sie zum dorff auß jagen*; Biii.

[174]   K Diii^r.

[175]   A lively and genuine dialogue about these issues in SK Bi^r.

[176]   A Aiiii^r.

[177]   S Bi.

[178]   S Biii^r f.

[179]   S Ai^r f.

taking off the guests' boots and seeing to the horses as they settle down to a Lenten meal of cold peas and roast herring;[180] the scrapings and leavings of 'charitable' food given by the monks to the poor: 'I wouldn't insult my dog with them . . . only bitter hunger forces it into the poor folk.'[181] We learn that in winter time poor women in Ulm have to weave by the light of the moon because they cannot afford candles.[182] We are reminded of the insecurity of life, with the constant threat of illness, robbery and kidnapping: 'No one has a guarantee against poverty.'[183]

The message, then, of the dialogues is clear enough. Perhaps a considerable part of their success lies in their ability to package the reform programme attractively in a home-spun way, with a minimum of explicit theological reflection. They are full of confidence that a new era is at hand. In Strassburg, for example, where bishops are treasured as little as German wisdom in Rome, ten thousand people gather in the cathedral to hear the Gospel preached.[184] *Ein brüderliche Warnung*, which shows so many similarities to *Karsthans*, is little more than a catalogue of anti-clerical delicts, at first sight. But it soon becomes clear that what attracts the 'Father' in the dialogue to the reforming camp is the positive image, the personal credibility of Matthew Zell, the preacher. It is when the 'Son' personalises the issues in the honest, learned, Bible-based preaching of Zell, who is ready to face death for his views, that the 'Father' is converted, and he joins Luther's 'side'.[185] The choice for the dialogue is

---

[180]   *Ein gesprech auff das kurtzt zwuschen eynem Christen und Juden/ auch eynem Wyrtße sampt seynem Haußknecht/ den Eckstein Christum betreffendt/ so noch Götlicher schrifft abkunterfeyt ist/ wie alhie bey gedruckt figur auß weyßet* (both the reference to brevity and to the wood-cut in the title are of interest) Aii.

[181]   EMC B i[r].

[182]   A Aiii[r].

[183]   SK Aii[r].

[184]   FA Aiii[r].

[185]   *Ich kenn in wol, ist ein gilerter mann/ das ist mir von hertzen leyd. . . . Ich käm schier uffs Luthers seyten. Ein brüderliche Warnung*, 47, 50.

not so much between two systems of belief, but two sets of personalities, one led by Luther and identified with Scripture, and the other the immoral, law-wielding, persecuting 'clerics'. Where the dialogues do become preachy, moralise, dogmatise, and lose the humorous touch –as in the *Scourged Swiss Peasant* or the *Dialogue between a Christian and a Jew* – they are markedly less successful.

In humanist literature they have their counterpart in, say, Erasmus' *Colloquies*, or the *Letters of Obscure Men*.[186] Lucian's satirical dialogues, such as *The Fisherman*, so popular at this time, offer an obvious Classical model. The literature of folly has already been mentioned. Brant, a conservative humanist, used the wood-cut, the rhyme, and the vernacular to portray contemporary mores in his *Ship of Fools* in a way remarkably similar to the later dialogues. Hutten's *Vadiscus* is in many ways the immediate model for them. So it will not do to see them purely as 'popular' literature. Yet their stock characterisation, with the good, pious Luther emerging as the father figure, the peasant as society's good conscience, and the Pope as the arch-villain is reminiscent of the traditional chap-books. The crude humour of the *Schwänke*, or farces, and Hans Sachs, with his solid, commonsense world, but fine feeling for personality and language, is never very far away either. The literary evaluation of the dialogues may have scarcely begun. Like Luther himself, their genius is that they bridge two worlds.

---

[186]   Ed. Francis G. Stokes, *Epistolae Obscurorum Virorum* (Chatto & Windus: London, 1909).

CHAPTER FIVE

REFORMATION LANGUAGE

Meine Sprache

Ich spreche im Slang aller Tage derer
noch nicht Abend ist
in der verachteten und verbissenen der
Sprache die jedermann entspricht.

My Language

I speak the slang of every day
whose sun has yet to set;
in the despised and gritty
language everyone is at home with.

Günter Kunert[1]

The innovatory form of the Reformation pamphlet, highlighted by the Reformation dialogues, was complemented by a vigorous new language. This will be illustrated primarily by reference to Luther himself, to Argula von Grumbach, and to Thomas Müntzer.

Martin Luther

Luther may have been remarkably conventional in the literary genres which he chose to use, abiding on the whole by the traditional church forms such as the commentary, tract, letter

[1]   Günter Kunert, *Unruhiger Schlaf. Gedichte,* 1979, pp. 95f.

and sermon, and avoiding the trendy humanist encomia, dialogues and declamations, as well as the popular ballads and folk songs.[2] Within these forms, however, he was remarkably innovative.[3] We are coming to understand his considerable debt to humanist rhetoric, as crucial for our understanding of Scripture, as well as to much of the best of the humanist ethos. He believed not only that learning was all important, since the Holy Spirit is no fool, *der heylige geyst ist keyn narre*, but that education should be entertaining, and that it is not only children who gain their knowledge best by enjoyment, *mit lust und spiel*.[4] His theology itself was playful, structured by that innate sense for language which is rhetoric at its best, alluring the audience, weaving together literature and life, text with context.

Home, school, university study at Erfurt and Wittenberg, and travel further afield made Luther aware of the variety of German dialects. His own German was based on that of the Saxon chancellery, which was gradually becoming increasingly influential, and his own impact markedly accelerated that process. It had considerable advantages in transcending the frontiers of other dialects, since waves of settlers moving eastwards had brought with them elements of lower and upper German and fused them with the local dialect to form *ostmitteldeutsch*, East Middle German. His preference for the latter in his vocabulary certainly helped to promote it and

[2]   Heinrich Bornkamm, 'Luther als Schriftsteller', *Sitzungsberichte der Heidelberger Akademie der Wissenschaften* (Philosophisch-historische Klasse 1965, 1; Heidelberg, 1965), p. 17; it can, however, no longer be argued that Luther did not use the dialogue form; it quite frequently occurs within his writings; cf. Hans-Gert Roloff, 'Reformationsliteratur' in *Reallexikon der deutschen Literaturgeschichte*, 3, 377.

[3]   Similarly Martin Brecht, *Doctor Luther's Bulla and Reformation: A Look at Luther the Writer* (Valparaiso, Indiana, 1991), p. 2; this is a shorter version of his fine study: *Luther als Schriftsteller: Zeugnisse seines dichterischen Gestaltens* (Calwer Verlag: Stuttgart, 1990).

[4]   W 15, 39/19, 46/5.

marginalise the upper German variants.[5] By 1517 he was already writing in German, though of course his ease in Latin and familiarity with Greek and some Hebrew sharpened his awareness of language. 'I have no time for those who restrict themselves to the one tongue and are contemptuous of all others.'[6]

He also was convinced that truth was best presented in the most straightforward way possible, without too much fuss about form and ornamentation. He avoided unusual foreign terms, explaining them wherever he does with the use of synonyms. His pamphlets were vernacular in presentation as well as in language. They could never be described as folksy, but the conversation within them is not based on literary models, but leans on the grammar of reality.[7] His language and style, while borrowing many features from the great classical models, was exercised in freedom. The rhetorical conventions of the humanists were as alien to him as the constraints of the scholastics.

Rhetoric, for Luther, is a tool for the exercise of human judgement in much the same way as dialectic is. In itself it is neutral, and can be used for good or evil, both by the Holy Spirit and by the Devil.[8] Dialectic teaches, documents and proves a case; it is a serious, belligerent business; it deals in iron. Rhetoric, on the other hand, draws, entices and persuades us, it is playful, and fights its battles with a wooden sword.[9]

[5]   Joachim Schildt notes the influence on Luther's language of German mysticism and the popular sermons of the time: 'Die Sprache Luthers – ihre Bedeutung für die Entwicklung der deutschen Schriftsprache', in Günter Vogler (ed.), with S. Hoyer and A. Laube, *Martin Luther. Leben – Werk-Wirkung* (Akademie Verlag: Berlin, 1986), pp. 307–24.

[6]   W 19, 74, quoted by Schildt; ibid., 310.

[7]   'Es sind Zwiegespräche von nacker Realität.' Bornkamm, 'Luther als Schriftsteller', p. 31.

[8]   W 43, 120/1, 124/3; LW 3, 341, 347.

[9]   *Rhetorica . . . ludit saepe, saepe praetendit lignum, quod tu putes gladium esse. Dialectica autem belligeratur, et agit res serias . . .* ; W 43, 12/3–6, 274/1f.; LW 3, 191; LW 4, 192.

Dialectic is more precise: it defines, distinguishes and compares.[10] Rhetoric is illustrative. It 'enlarges' issues, repeats and even exaggerates in order to reach the emotions.[11]

Paul, as Luther sees him, can be 'amazingly rhetorical', appealing to the emotions, using overflowing, gentle and soothing words to gain the favour of his correspondents.[12] Such 'divine rhetoric' is wonderful and lovable.[13] Rhetoric has its limitations, however, and Paul in his high flights of fervour transcends its rules.[14] For rhetoric can be rather superficial, exhibiting ingenuity rather than wisdom and sincerity, as in Agricola's alleged defence of antinomianism.[15] Jacob uses simple dialectic when speaking with his father, while the proud, hypocritical Esau deploys elaborate, elegant and fine-sounding rhetoric.[16] Potiphar's wife used a most winsome rhetoric to embroil Joseph in trouble, but it was an inversion of the truth.[17]

Generally, however, dialectic and rhetoric complement one another, the former conceiving, like faith, what is to be believed, while the latter, like hope, develops it, urges, persuades and exhorts. They are really inseparable. 'A rhetorician without dialectics is a gas-bag, and a mere dialectician cannot reach the heart. But a rhetorician with dialectical skills can really make things hum.'[18] In the last sentence Luther might have been talking about himself! Even theoretically, then, Luther was quite self-conscious about the need to make use of good rhetoric. In practice his writings, especially his exegetical ones,

---

[10]   W 40², 38/14–17; LW 27, 31.
[11]   W 44, 31/29, 61/30; LW 6/43, 83.
[12]   W 40¹, 649/1–4, 625/26–8; LW 26, 430, 413.
[13]   W 43, 122/1; W 44, 128/10; LW 3, 243; LW 6, 171.
[14]   W 40¹, 170, 10f.; LW 26, 92.
[15]   W 44, 154/25f; LW 6, 208; WBr. 4, 558/8; LW 49, 212.
[16]   *verbis ad ornatum, elegantiam et splendorem accommodatis*; W 43, 529/37–530/5; LW 5/147.
[17]   W 44, 365/19; LW 7, 89.
[18]   *Si rethor non habet dialecticam, tum est wesscher. Si simplex dialecticus, nihil monet. Sed rethor habens dialecticam der kans treiben, das lebt*; note the shift to German to make the key points; W 40², 27/8–12; LW 27/23f.

are littered with references to simile, metaphor, allegory, hyperbole, confutation, understatement, interpretation, anthypo-
phora, ellipsis and similar technical terms. He uses rhetoric,
however, in freedom. It is not just that he is disdainful, at times,
of Quintilian's proprieties.[19] There is a seriousness of intent
about his language, a coinherence of form and content, which
gives it a rigorous edge. It is never flowery, and is seldom
elegant, although it can be tender, racy, coarse, entertaining,
absorbing. Language is very much a means to a confessional
end, a tool for the preacher and pastor, not an ornament for
the poet.

Luther's German pamphlets are vernacular not only in
language, but in form and style. He wrote as he preached,
relationally and contextually, usually in response to a particular
situation or crisis or challenge.[20] This did not mean, however,
that his pamphlets were reactive. He refused to let his
opponents determine the form of the argument, and frequently
slipped the noose of their accusations, leap-frogging their
plodding points to explore quite new ideas. The development
of his understanding of Indulgences from 1517 to 1520 is a
good example. The objections of Tetzel, Sylvester Prierias, or
Eck, became springboards from which he bounded off into
ever deeper waters![21] There is, of course, a transparent delight
in disputation here, which can have its less attractive sides.

One undoubted fascination of Luther's writings is that they
combine or interweave close exegesis, argument and docu-

[19]   It is well to remember, however, that Quintilian saw oratory not
primarily as a technical accomplishment, but as *vir bonus dicendi peritus*, a
good man with skills of speech: *Institutio Oratoria* VI. 4.

[20]   As he said of preaching: *Occasio facit predicatorem. Ego me ipsum non
possum assequi; quin potius una persona aut privata aliqua causa mihi praebet.*
WTr 1, 488/965.

[21]   The famous opening words of the Preface to the *Babylonian Captivity*
about being taught willy-nilly by his opponents what the real issues were
are followed by other sniping comments: *beneficio Sylvestri et fratrum adiutus
. . . Post haec Eccius et Emser cum coniuratis suis de primatu Papae me erudire
coeperunt*; W 6, 497/16, 24f.

mentation with breathtaking conceptual shifts. For all the tightness of his logic, compared, say, with Müntzer, he also thinks associatively, or, as we would say today, laterally, making daring connections between hitherto disparate areas, and then clothing the whole in a master-image. The theme of the three walls with which the 'Romanists' fence off the hierarchy from accountability is repeated with constant variations in the *Appeal to the German Nobility*. He uses the language of a walled fortress to describe the apparent invulnerability of the Roman Church, then encourages and empowers the dismayed reader by describing its walls as made of mere paper or straw, as dreamed up, imaginary, phantasmagoric barriers. He calls for the siege trumpet to be sounded against the walls, as if the Reformers were Joshua and the whole edifice Jericho, doomed shortly to come tumbling down. Countless subordinate images supplement this main one. The nobility, who bear the sword, are pictured as stern dominies, or schoolmasters, who have to wield the rod on the corrupt clergy, using the term *straffen* in its double meaning of correction and bodily chastisement.[22] Though he calls for this to be done prayerfully and without violence the militant language is what the reader will have heard. Not for the last time, the apparently pacific content is overlaid by an aggressive rhetoric. Behind the image lurks a new vision of the Church, a paradigmatic shift in ecclesiology. It is the breathtakingly bold brush-strokes which ravish the onlooker.

Yet his writings also keep diving back into detail. One mark of Luther's writings is the abrupt transitions. The reader is kept on tenterhooks, propelled from initial prologue right into the nub of the matter, from exegesis to polemic, from general to specific, from historical illustration to passionate pronouncement, from theological principle to demands for particular reforms. The reader is swept along, diverted, informed, fired up by passionate denunciation and appeal,

[22]   W 6, 409.

wooed by arguments, offered a host of references to Scripture, to the Fathers or to the history of the Church.

Thus the *Appeal to the German Nobility* begins with a riveting new vision of the Church, or as Luther would say, a return to the original apostolic one, and follows this up with a muckraking documentation of contemporary abuses, and a bulging shopping-bag of projected reforms. A mere list of gravamina, the now traditional complaints and grievances of the German nation, of which there had already been a multitude, would have made far less impact. We tend to forget what a fine investigative journalist Luther was, with an eye for a good story, a phenomenal memory, the patience to accumulate a devastating body of evidence, and, above all, a convincing interpretive framework.[23]

His genius lies precisely in his ability to control the material, to reduce it to a few salient issues, to encapsulate them in punchy formulations, to drive to the heart of the matter. The *Babylonian Captivity* virtually reinvents the sacraments, so fundamental to the mission as well as the piety of the Church, by redefining them as a personal response to the promises of God. The whole is wrapped in another image of surpassing power, the terrible rootlessness and alienation of exile. For all the whirl of new perspectives, ideas and language in such seminal writings as these Luther retains the eye of the pruner, relentlessly trimming away the redundant. Often a passage of fierce polemic will be followed by a key Biblical passage which sets out the positive invitation to discipleship. The way forward for the future determines the pattern and progress of the tract.

Luther's writings usually begin with a brief dedication, so that the reader leans over his shoulder as he writes, say to his

[23] Cf. his numbered list of the sharp practices of merchants, such as hoarding, storing in a damp place to add weight, displaying one's best goods and hiding the others, in *von Kaufhandlung und Wucher, On Selling and Usury*, W 15, 304–11; or the enumeration of the prohibited relationships which were obstacles to marriage or his close analysis of the allegations raised against Hans Schönitz by Albrecht von Mainz.

father, explaining the personal background to his tract *On Monastic Vows*, or to his spiritual father, Pope Leo X, in *The Freedom of a Christian*. As in the latter he will then wade straight into the heart of the subject-matter. There is no beating about the bush. The use of short, snappy, and easily memorable theses captivates and provokes the reader: 'A Christian is free to lord it over everything, and is subject to no one. A Christian is at the beck and call of everything, and is subject to everyone.'[24]

The interpretation of 1 Corinthians 9:19 is linked with a drastic distinction between the spiritual and the temporal, the realm of faith and the realm of love. This may have been what an impatient anti-clericalism wanted to hear, but it also met the hunger of the age for a genuine spiritual challenge. Or take his *Sermon on Good Works*: 'The first thing to note, then, is that the only good works are those commanded by God. . . .'[25] As a preacher Luther knows that the attention of the listener has to be caught straight away. He has the genial communicator's gift for a sharp, compressed, gnomic utterance, either to introduce or to conclude an argument, or for a smart throwaway line: 'Maybe I owe the world and my God just one more act of folly.'[26] His writings leap from the page as his sermons or lectures from pulpit and lectern. He writes dialogically, in interrogatives and imperatives, in the first and second persons: 'So we have to distinguish between good works on the basis of God's commandments. . . .'[27]

This is engaging literature, on the verge of oral culture, not ponderous, impersonal prose.[28] It is relentlessly concrete, piling

---

[24]   W 7, 21; LW 31, 344.

[25]   W 6, 204/13f.

[26]   W 6, 404/23.

[27]   W 6, 204/12f; LW 44, 23.

[28]   Johannes Schwitalla offers a brief but very fine analysis of the differences between verbal and literary polemic in Luther; the former adheres closely to the words of the opponent, ironically affirming, twisting, contradicting them, often in recurring, stereotypical forms, the latter, given Luther's linguistic creativity, can appear livelier than actual direct speech;

up illustrations and examples. He does not talk abstractly about the priority of grace; he paints a word-picture of a tiny child 'crawling out of baptism'. He did not write the usual monologues found in theological tomes, but addressed himself to real and imaginary partners. He needed these colleagues, parishioners, opponents to bring out the best (and the worst) in him. 'Even when he was writing, Luther was always speaking.'[29] In *On Monastic Vows* he beckons the reader forward: 'Come on, let's get to the nub of the matter', and uses direct speech in a most effective manner to satirise vows: 'Dear God, I promise not to subject myself to all, as the Gospel insists, but only to my superior . . .', and then, in performative language parodying the confessional, he absolves monks and nuns throughout the world, at one stroke, from their vows.[30] The black humour does not cloak the serious intent.

This is why it is so unhelpful to characterise such writings as propaganda. Propaganda plays on the fears and weaknesses and prejudices of the reader. It is consciously manipulative, moulding the audience like clay, feeding off it, as Hitler loved to do, reducing it to a mass mind, a mob. In the *Appeal to the Christian Nobility*, on the other hand, the audience is the Christian congregation, in the first instance the Emperor and the nobility, secondarily the whole German nation, and they are addressed by a preacher and pastor, from a base of passionate concern for the Church, a clear vision for Church and theology, a concern for Paul and the rest of Scripture. Luther speaks, for

---

polemic is not a matter of coarse language, it can use subtle techniques of repetition, of bracketing what the opponent says with pejorative comments or descriptions; verbs can be as important as adjectives or nouns to express ridicule; 'Martin Luthers argumentative Polemik; mündlich und schriftlich', in Albrecht Schöne (ed.), *Akten des VII Internationalen Germanisten-Kongresses* (Göttingen, 1985), pp. 541–4.

[29]   Bornkamm, 'Luther als Schriftsteller', p. 23.

[30]   W 8, 584/1f.; 586/34; two other examples in LW 293, 4; W 8 597/; a more heavy-handed example in W 53, 231–60.

all his dazzling rhetoric and glorious cheek, as one who is himself under authority. And his concern is to empower all the baptised. It is a category mistake to see this as propaganda.

The weakness of this interactive approach, however, is that his writings can frequently be misshapen. Luther wrote far too much and far too quickly, some portions of his writings often already being at the printer while he completed the rest. He seems seldom to have revised what he wrote. The result, as he himself frequently confessed, is that, as in *Kaufhandlung und Wucher*, there is a 'scissors and paste' feel about the pamphlets. They can be ill-organised, repetitious, and prolix rather than, in the good rhetorical sense of the word, copious.[31] Good communication, of course, is never curt. The orator has always required room to elaborate ideas, to evoke emotion, to entice and motivate as well as to instruct. Repetitiveness, as every concert-goer knows, is far from negative if imaginatively varied. The considerable length of *On Monastic Vows* may well have been necessary because of the huge emotional freight it had to carry. At his controlled best Luther has the gift of sharing his own yearnings, frustration or rage with the reader. When, however, he loses control over his own emotions, and loses sight of his audience he can all too easily become, as he himself confesses, a *Wäscher*, splashing and foaming around like someone washing clothes, but to no great effect. What he is not is a cynical manipulator, a propagandist.

At his brilliant best, as in the *Appeal to the German Nobility*, his writings have the flair of grand theatre. The dedication and introduction read like the prologue to a play, setting out his intentions, and whetting our appetite. His *captatio benevolentiae*, with its mockery of himself as a court fool, and its quite genuine humility, is in lively counterpoint to his equally breathtaking audacity. He may only be a poor monk addressing the worldly wise, but God's

[31]   As he said, in his Table Talk, comparing himself and Melanchthon: *Philippus ist enger gespant denn ich, pugnat et docet; ich bin ein wescher, bin magis rhetoricus*; WTr. 5, 204, 5511.

overflowing wisdom, he believes, relativises all normal human categories.

The foolery turns quickly to deep earnestness, however, as he focuses on the *iamer und not*, the urgent distress of the German people, to whose cry he has to respond. His writing itself constitutes this response: it is one, long, stylised cry of pain. He is *zwungen*, forced, impelled, compelled, to go public. This prophetic sense of 'having to speak', of prophetic reluctance and yet relish, is characteristic of all the Reformers' writings, and again differentiates it from propaganda. 'The time for silence is gone, the time has come to speak' are the very first words of the *Appeal to the German Nobility* after the formal greeting. It is a note which will be echoed again and again in the pamphlets of the next three or four years. Luther feels constrained to, as he says, *durchleuchten*, bring to the light of day, the clerical wickedness which has frustrated up to now the hopes embodied in the Councils. Perhaps God will grant his Spirit to the Empire's lay leaders. It is on God's power and wisdom alone, however, not on themselves, that they will have to rely. These religious reflections are immediately followed by slashing polemic. It contrasts the German princes, under the young blood, the Emperor Charles V, with the Romans, the Popes, and especially the blood-sucking Julius II. The devil, and the forces of Hell, are already on stage, and Antichrist is in the wings. Scarcely embarked on reading the pamphlet, the reader is swept headlong into a cosmic struggle. Humour, seriousness, piety and polemic follow one another at breakneck speed, until Luther plunges into his dramatic evocation of the three walls, goes on to outline the abuses, and suggests necessary reforms.

Much of Luther's most effective writing evokes the patterns of oral discourse. He briefly outlines his argument in advance, and sums up after each section, as all effective speakers must. He hooks his reader's attention with questions, sometimes whole chains of them: 'How many penances are there; how many prisons? How many penalties? How many pains for those

who fail to perform them? How great the load on the conscience at not having kept one's Rule?'[32] Frequently these are
rhetorical questions, or he provides a speedy reply to his own
question: 'If a priest is murdered a whole land is put under
interdict, why not when a peasant is murdered as well? Where
does the great difference come from, when all of us are
Christians? From human laws and fantasies, nothing else!'[33]
One can imagine his lay readers thumping their fists on the
table in agreement!

Luther also can use a truly Rabelaisian flood of terms to
extol or to ridicule something, the scholastic definitions of
faith, for example: 'For they have all sorts of faith: general,
special, acquired, infused, unformed and formed, catholic and
particular, implicit and explicit, in a word, the most confused
Babel of errors and opinions.'[34] Such accumulative lists of
substantives or predicates can have a mantra-like effect,
reinforcing the message, the impact, the elation, the outrage.
Luther is a past master at this, often reinforcing their musical
ring with alliteration and rhyme.[35] They have to be read out

[32] W 8, 603/32–4.
[33] W 6, 410/16–19.
[34] W 8, 591.
[35] One of the best examples of this satirical use of an avalanche of
terms is to be found in Hans Sachs' *Wittenberg Nightingale*, as cited by
Bernd Balzer, *Bürgerliche Reformationspropaganda. Die Flugschriften des Hans
Sachs in den Jahren 1523–1525* (Germanistische Abhandlungen 42;
Stuttgart, 1973), p. 68:

> By becoming monks, nuns, and priests
> By wearing the cowl, and shaving the head
> Mumbling away day and night in the churches.
> Matins, Prime, Terce, Vespers, Compline
> By vigils, fasting, abasing oneself in the form of a cross
> By kneeling, inclining, bowing, bending,
> By ringing bells and thumping at the organ,
> By carrying relics, candles and fans
> By making incense and baptising with bells
> By trimming lamps and selling grace
> By consecrating churches, wax, salt, and water.

aloud for their full force to be appreciated. Sometimes these long freight trains of words carry the liturgical *gravitas* of a hymn or chant or creed: one baptism, one Gospel, one Faith![36] Sometimes the weight is that of condemnation. Popes seldom occur alone, but are linked with Romanists, bishops, priests, monks in a long clinking chain-gang of corruption. 'We may have the name of Empire', the *Appeal to the German Nobility* concludes, 'but the Pope has our wealth, our honour, our lives, bodies and souls, indeed all we possess'. A recurring negative qualifier can heighten the effect: 'Christendom has no discipline, no punishment, no control, no order.'[37]

Another common borrowing from oral language is the delight in dwelling upon the obvious: 'Christ does not have two bodies . . . one secular, one spiritual.'[38] A similar, very wide-spread topos in south German pamphlets was: 'Christ did not say "I am tradition", but "I am the truth".' Instead of a careful structural analysis of the relationship between lay and cleric or of the complementarity of Scripture and tradition a dramatic personalised image is presented. This is an imaginative deconstruction of a whole universe of interlocking authorities of quite awesome proportions, yet it is the positive emphasis on the headship of Christ which lingers in the mind. Of course, the pious reader agrees, this has to be correct! Closely related to the statement of the obvious are arguments which are taken to absurd lengths: if Papal authority is emphasised at every turn we will end up with a new creed, and instead of saying 'I believe in the catholic Church' we will say 'I believe in the Pope at Rome, thus reducing the Christian Church to one person. . .'.[39] Note how the alternative to Christ's headship is also expressed in personal terms: the Pope.

Drastic contrasts are another indication of the closeness to oral culture. Just as Luther had physically 'fronted up' to

[36]   W 6, 407.
[37]   W 6, 463/36–8; 429/24f.; LW 44, 209, 159.
[38]   W 6, 408/33–5.
[39]   W 6, 412/17f.; LW 44, 135.

Cardinal Cajetan at Augsburg, to the theological gladiator Eck at Leipzig, and was soon to appear before the whole Imperial Diet at Worms, his writings partake of this drastic, no holds barred, confrontational character. Part of the unparalleled effectiveness of his *Appeal to the German Nobility* was its running comparison of the corruption and tyranny of the hierarchy of the Church (the few) with the demand of ordinary people for reform and justice (the many). Externals such as dress or anointing are contrasted, in good Erasmian style, with the internal consecration of the Spirit. The power or authority which pertains to all Christians, to the community as a whole, has been monopolised by a few,[40] while the universalist reach of the Gospel is underlined by the recurrent use of 'all', 'every'. This is true of countless writings of Luther, in which quotable one-liners tumble out, apparently effortlessly, one after the other. Money, he complains, is wrenched from the needy and squandered on the adoration of the saints.[41] 'Papal consecration creates a hypocrite, not a Christian.' 'Government by the apostles and by the Pope are as compatible, as Christ and Lucifer, heaven and hell, night and day. . . .'[42] Today's profiteering merchants live like kings, while we are beggars.[43]

Closely related to this is his penchant for the extreme statement. The application of the merchants' principle that one can charge whatever the market will bear is, he curtly declares, simply theft; and princes who hang petty thieves, but negotiate with large ones, become themselves the accomplices of thieves.[44] Such revelling in hyperbole is deployed, of course, for rhetorical effect, but it goes far beyond this. His predilection for the frontiers of language reflects the audacity and polarising quality of his thought itself, his determination to push issues to their logical conclusion. No doubt it is in part an inheritance

[40]   W 6, 407.
[41]   W 6, 46/20–2; LW 45, 288.
[42]   W 6, 430/2–4; LW 44, 159f.
[43]   W 15, 313/1f.; LW 45, 271f.
[44]   W 15, 313/1f.; LW 45, 271f.

from the tradition of the academic disputation. 'There is no option to marriage but sin', he declares in his tract *On Married Life*. If they lacked faith, all the nuns and monks of the world together would not be worthy to prepare the gruel for a whore's child.[45] He loves the extreme case, such as a group of Christians stranded in a desert place, with no access to a priest. Clearly they would choose a priest from among themselves, whether married or not.[46] Truth is found at the extremities of discourse and reality. If the Pope is not answerable to anyone, he argues, he could lead great multitudes to the devil and still not be deposed![47]

One form of the extreme statement is the insult, and insults, of course, are part of the common coin of oral discourse, as children's playgrounds and parliamentary debating chambers may remind us. They are often as harmless as flirting or fencing, and have the same ritual function, to test boundaries. But they can also be deadly serious. Vividly descriptive, and consciously caricaturing, they intrude into the territory of the other. At their best, they are often rapier thrusts, which draw blood the more effectively for being rapidly withdrawn. Though apparently indicative in quality they have imperative or performative force; abuse, after all, is characterisation on the way to becoming a curse.

The *Appeal to the German Nobility* wraps up the scornful description of priests as 'oily idols', *olgotzen* (from their consecration with holy oil) in precise argument about the nature of baptism and the priesthood of all believers.[48] Such sparing use of invective is a powerful tool, spicing the more solid discursive sections of the discourse. Sarcastic comments about the first wall protecting the clergy are immediately followed by a Biblically based affirmation that all Christians are members

[45] W 10/2, 277; LW 41.
[46] W 6, 407.
[47] W 6, 410.
[48] W 6, 407.

of the spiritual estate. It is this combination of swingeing criticism and visionary statement which empowers the laity, and frees them from being *schuchter*, intimidated.[49]

Martin Brecht has drawn attention to Luther's resort to 'buffoonery' in dealing with opponents such as Tetzel, and Alfeld and Emser, as he realised that the traditional form of rebuttal had outrun its usefulness.[50] At the early stage of his reforming career, he used little satire, but gradually freed himself from the normal literary conventions of scholarly literature. His very popular defence, which ran to eleven editions, of his *Sermon on Indulgence and Grace*, for example, breaks repeatedly into direct speech, into snorts of disbelief and derision. He mocks the Indulgence-seller Tetzel's interpretations of Scripture: 'He yanks so hard at the hair of Scripture, that he is scalping it.' To Tetzel's argument that money should be used for Indulgences and not for alms unless someone is *in extremis*, he explodes 'Just look at this, and may God have mercy on you. And these are supposed to be teachers of the Christian people.' Such lousy teachers don't even know what *hereticus* means in Latin.[51] He treats feeble opponents such as Alfeld at the beginning of the *Babylonian Captivity* of 1520, much as an angler plays fish on a line. He offers a mock recantation of his previous writings, but only to move on to still more radical positions about Indulgences and the Papacy.[52] This 'buffoonery', however, is episodic, offering light relief to an original, sustained and well-documented argument.

Luther also loves to describe himself as a fool.[53] This picks up a quite prevalent leitmotif in contemporary literature, from Erasmus' *Praise of Folly* to Sebastian Brant's *Ship of Fools*, but

[49]   W 6, 407.

[50]   Brecht, *Luther als Schriftsteller*, p. 16.

[51]   W 1, 383–8, esp. 386/1f., 387/21, 391/16.

[52]   Cf. also his mock recantation at the end of the writing; W 6, 497–501; 573/14; LW 36, 11–18; 125.

[53]   Bornkamm, 'Luther als Schriftsteller', p. 32; cf. E. W. Gritsch, *Martin – God's Court Jester: Luther in Retrospect* (Fortress: Philadelphia, 1983).

as folk-stories, wood-cuts and street carnivals show, this is a motif from popular, proverbial and Scriptural wisdom rather than a literary construct. In Luther's case, as at the beginning of the *Appeal to the German Nobility*, it expresses his awareness of the rich absurdity of his position, an obscure monk from a distant corner of Germany, standing before Germany's assembled pomp and power, and daring them to renew and reform the Church. At the same time he is conscious of Paul's dictum that true wisdom will always be folly in the world's eyes. Luther plays cleverly with his dual authority: he is a fool for Christ, and yet is a Doctor of Holy Scripture, under oath to defend the truth.[54] This combination cruelly undermines the ponderous pretensions and defences of the theological establishment.

Luther also was fond of the fable. Part of the attractiveness of the fable for him was that the author, in the carnival gear of an animal, had the freedom to speak without giving offence, rather like a court-jester.[55] No one likes the truth, when it relates to themselves, so if one can 'laugh people into it', as Aesop did in his fables, where wisdom is put in the mouth of an animal, this is a formidable advantage. As Brecht has pointed out, Luther uses the device quite brilliantly in a late writing of 1539, *Against the Bishop of Magdeburg, Cardinal Albrecht*. Luther had been criticised by others, notably by Duke Albrecht of Prussia, for the intemperateness of his attacks on Catholic princes. This time, therefore, he launches a trenchant attack on Albrecht's judicial murder of one of his administrators, Hans Schönitz, apparently for crimes which he himself had committed. Luther writes not in his own name, but in that of the courier, or 'postie', who just happened to be there when the most high judge, God, made his judgement on the case. It begins with God's word in Job 31:13–15, about those who deal unjustly with

---

[54]   W 6, 404f.

[55]   *Ja alle Welt hasset die Warheit, wenn sie einen trifft ... Denn die Warheit ist das unleidlichste ding auff Erden.* W 50, 452–5, esp. 453/23f., 454/7; cf. Brecht, *Doctor Luther's Bulla*, p. 8.

their servants. How dare the Cardinal appoint himself judge
in his own case! Anyone else who did that would be called a
tyrant, but if it is a Cardinal he is praised as a good, pious
prince! A Roman priest can do no wrong, in any case. Since
the lawyers, whose task it is to crusade for justice, are idle
drones and cowards the postman has to act in their stead. The
writing documents, inter alia, the dangers of basing a judgement on evidence extracted by torture.[56] A 'postie' takes on a
prince!

A much less successful, indeed rather lumbering, satire is a
late work defending his appointment of a reforming bishop of
Naumburg in January 1542. He pretends to confess his sins
against 'the hellish un-Christian Church of the most hellish
Father the Pope' for conducting this ordination without holy
oil, butter or lard, but he doubts if he can be forgiven. The
heavy sarcasm about *Bapst, Mentz, Heintz* (Pope, Cardinal
Albrecht, and the persecuting Catholic Duke, Henry of
Brunswick) these 'chaste and delicate saints', mirrors Luther's
own gloom, rage and weariness at this time.[57] Satire requires a
lighter touch to be effective. There is a loss of interactive quality
in these later writings, a growing absorption in self.

Frequently the emotion boils over into ejaculations of
disbelief and anger. 'O what inconceivable blindness! O what
a grave, terrible reckoning the bishops will have to give. . . !'[58]
It is astonishing that the world is allowed to continue, given
the abuses of usury.[59] Here he is addressing his God as well as
the reader and the over-spilling emotion often slips into prayer:
'O Christ, my Lord, arise, let your Last Day break in and
destroy the devil's lair at Rome.'[60]

[56]   W 50, 395–431, esp. 399, 431/2f., 411–13; cf. Brecht, *Luther als
Schriftsteller*, pp. 118–22.
[57]   *Exempel, einen rechten christlichen Bischof zu weihen.* W 53, 230–60;
a less critical assessment in Brecht, *Luther als Schriftsteller*, pp. 107f.
[58]   W 8, 579/17f.; W 6, 44 4/20; LW 44, 185.
[59]   W 6, 58/2f.
[60]   W 6, 453/22f.; LW 44, 194.

At other times it moves into exaggerated defiance: 'My very greatest fear and anxiety is that my case might fail to be condemned by Rome, because then I would definitely know that it is not pleasing to God.'[61] Such passages frequently culminate in a call to action. The outrageous exploitation of the poor by the merchants, sucking up their blood and sweat, must lead the princes to action.[62]

Demonstrative, interrogative and imperative language conspires to force the readers to a decision, though it frequently seems something of a Hobson's choice: 'There you have it, you monks! What's your reply? Either deny that the counsel of the Gospel is a counsel, or admit that your vow is not an evangelical one.'[63] Towards the end of *Von beider Gestalt des Sakraments zu nehmen*, written in 1522, he warns against those who seek to mark out a neutral position for themselves, being neither for Luther nor for Rome. While he shudders at the thought of people describing themselves as 'Lutherans' they must distinguish between his person and his teaching and stand by the evangelical position.[64]

At their best, then, Luther's pamphlets are interactive. He is concerned not just to instruct, and to refute, but to persuade, to enter into the readers' minds and nudge them to challenge old thoughts and think out new ones. He frequently anticipates possible objections, and suggests Biblical, rational or historical answers to them. There is often, as in Augustine, a remarkable degree of psychological insight into the problems with which people are wrestling as well as much robust common sense. It is impressive that he frequently draws the line, declining to deal with issues, such as the sexuality of marriage, on which he

---

[61]   W 6, 469/11–13; LW 44, 217.
[62]   W 15, 322/5f.
[63]   W 8, 584/12f.; LW 44, 262.
[64]   Some, alas, driven by Satan, who had noticed that 'the body of the Papacy had taken such a thumping from me', had taken up a too evangelical position; decisiveness should not be confused with impetuosity and failing to pray for those who persecute one; W 10², 39/26–40/4; cf. 12/2, 21f.

is ignorant.[65] Perhaps this is one reason why Luther and the Wittenberg reformers generally wrote no dialogues, while they were pouring out of places such as Augsburg, for example. Or is it that they seek the direct contact with the reader, rather like the preacher with the congregation?

One wonders, in the light of all this, at Brecht's contention that Luther's writings demonstrate that he 'dealt with his subject matters [sic] as the professional theologian that he was. . .'.[66] No small part of Luther's success was that he skipped over the walls of the professional ghetto, and engaged with his public in their language, and on their 'turf'. Although he was of course proud to be a doctor of theology, and used this vocational authority to fend off attacks,[67] his vernacular eye and ear meant that he stood on the frontier between high and low culture. He had as little time for Ciceronianism as for the caste discipline of scholasticism. One might almost say that his abiding merit was to deprofessionalise theology, though admittedly one would hardly think this when labouring through the works of some of his most ardent disciples of yesterday and today.

When he was attacked, for example, for spending so much time producing apparently ephemeral booklets for the simple-minded, he retorted that he would leave it to others to judge whether the production of weighty tomes benefited Christendom. His main concern was for the *eynfeltig mensch*, the ordinary guy; if his books had helped one of them he would be contented.[68] Ironically enough, it was to be some of these simple folk, such as Valentin Ickelsamer, the follower of Karlstadt, who were to accuse him of using his scholarly and rhetorical skill, his 'murderous and tyrannical rhetoric', to

---

[65]   'lest someone stop my mouth and say I'm speaking of something I have no experience in, and that there is more gall than honey to it'; W 10², 299/5–10; LW 45, 43.

[66]   Brecht, *Doctor Luther's Bulla*, p. 4.

[67]   E.g. W 7, 162/8.

[68]   W 6, 203/7–9; LW 44/22.

silence any who disagreed with him, and to incite the princes against simple folk.[69]

It may be helpful now to monitor what has been said about the way in which the language of Luther crosses the boundaries between high and popular culture by reference to Thomas Müntzer and to Argula von Grumbach's first pamphlet, which went through a remarkable fourteen editions within a couple of months.[70]

Argula von Grumbach

Unlike the male Reformers, of course, Argula von Grumbach had no Latin, no university education, still less a theological training. She may well have preached or taught informally, but she certainly had no licence to do so. She had, however, been brought up in a cultured household, learned to read Scripture extensively in the vernacular, and spent her teenage years at the Bavarian court. Proud of her descent from the von Stauff family, she had no inhibitions about corresponding with the Reformers, or lobbying the princes at Imperial Diets. Scripture functions as her plumb-line, almost as her code of law. Her Christian conscience, her vows of baptism, are where she finds her authority to speak.

There is evidence in her writings of a thorough knowledge of Scripture, and some acquaintance with popular German literature and several of Luther's writings. Occasionally one notices phrases which are reminiscent of *Karsthans* or the pamphlets of Matthew Zell and others. She was aware, no doubt from the prefaces to her German Bible, of Jerome's willingness to engage in scholarly dialogue with women.[71]

[69] *Clag ettlicher brieder* (Tübingen?, Ulrich Morhart? 1525; Fiche 991/ 2513) Bii'.

[70] *Wye ein Christliche fraw des adels/ in //Beyern durch iren/ in Gotlicher schrifft/wolgegrund//tenn Sendbrieffe/die hohenshul zu Ingoldstat/ // umb das sie eynen Euangelischen Jungling/zu widersprechung des wort gottes betrang// haben/straffet.* AvG, 72–91.

[71] AvG, 88.

She writes, then, with limited knowledge, very much as an ordinary 'Christian'. She is conscious of being a representative of a new articulate breed of non-clerical Christians, not a professional, not a scholar, not a religious. She is introduced on the title page by her printer as a 'Christian woman of the Bavarian nobility'. Her language is that of common sense and personal experience, the straightforward talk of conversation or letters; factual, descriptive, down-to-earth, not at all flowery. Her as yet unpublished household correspondence reinforces the impression of a practical, down-to-earth person, at home in the detailed administration of domestic and estate life.

There is much less overt revelling in images than we find in Luther or Müntzer, with the exception of dramatic Biblical images such as the raging lions and bears who symbolise God's wrath, or Jeremiah's flaming cauldron.[72] Her apocalyptic world-view does break through at times. Her writings suggest a deeply religious individual 'speaking her mind' about a wide range of moral and spiritual issues. And yet there is nothing pedestrian about her discourse. One understands why it ignited imaginations all through Germany. It has an authentic, even prophetic quality which catches the reader by the throat. There was, of course, the sensational novelty underlined by the Preface that here a member of the 'female sex' was admonishing the 'biblical scholars' of the University.[73]

Although all her writings, with the exception of the poem, are in letter form, they are written *coram Deo*, in the presence of God, as a form of confession or proclamation of her faith. They have a three-fold orientation. The first letter, for example, was addressed to her opponents in the Ingolstadt University, but its appearance in print, after circulating in manuscript copies for a while, meant that it was envisaged for a wider public, and in particular, no doubt, for the supporters of reform. Finally, it was peppered with 'arrow' prayers to God,

[72] AvG, 77.
[73] AvG, 73f.; the term of abuse *schrifftgelerten* is favoured by radicals such as Müntzer.

brief petitions for God's light, grace or protection: 'May God forfend'; 'may God be their reward.' The language is intensely Biblical, and prayerful, bracketed by her own religious devotion.

The language was exceedingly personal. Argula von Grumbach frequently speaks in the first person. Her little tract has the peculiar fascination of the intimate made public. She is quite open about her initial hesitations as a woman about speaking out, but goes on to explain why in the end she decided to write: the evangelical compulsion under which all Christians, including women, stand to confess their faith. To be silent would not just be to deny Luther, it would be a sin against the Holy Spirit, denying God and his Word.[74] The theologians are not her superiors in the faith, to whom she must defer. They are her Christian 'brothers', in need of her sisterly reproof. The medium of print is used to give an account of her actions, as if the readership were a high court of appeal.

It is unguarded, deeply emotional language. She describes how her heart goes out to the princes, who are being so misled. 'Yes, when I reflect on this my heart and all my limbs tremble.'[75] There may, too, well be something of a motherly, protective attitude to the young eighteen-year-old student, Arsacius Seehofer, who has been forced to deny his beliefs by the coercive alliance of Church and University. The emotional tone, however, is far from the expected one of womanly 'weakness'. She has no fears for herself. Her language expresses astonishment, outrage and indignation, not only that the young student Arsacius is being so inhumanely pressured, but that the clergy are duping the people.

Aren't they ashamed of themselves, she asks the Ingolstadt theologians, for bringing the University into such discredit?[76] Aren't they ashamed to use violence against the word of God?

---

[74] AvG, 75f., 79f., 77.
[75] AvG, 76, 81; she repeats twice her sympathy for the princes.
[76] AvG, 85, 82.

'A disputation is easily won when one argues with force, not Scripture. As far as I can see that means that the hangman is accounted the most learned', she says scornfully, paraphrasing Luther.[77] How can the University prevail if it goes on like this? How can lawyers make up the laws 'out of their own heads' as they go along?[78] Of course, this makes for good, interactive prose, but one also notes that her emotional openness allows all manner of unaskable questions to be asked, all manner of taboos to be infringed. Only the 'innocent' can write like this.

Her emotional energy is manifested in statements of lyrical abandon: 'Ah, but what a joy it is when the spirit of God teaches us and gives us understanding, flitting from one text to the next. . . .'[79] Equally, however, it generates profound outrage: God will punish the Ingolstadt theologians. They will become notorious, 'the laughing-stock of the whole world', derided for their cheap victory over a young student.[80] They will suffer the woes which the Old Testament reserves for all false prophets.[81]

Mockery is the domain of the confident, the self-assured. Argula von Grumbach does not hesitate to resort to it. Her opponents, she frequently says, have made themselves a laughing-stock. Professor Hauer's abuse from the pulpit, quite possibly directed at her, does not rattle her. She suggests that it was hardly evidence of great Latin, or deep thought. It takes no great intelligence, after all, to accuse people of heresy. She hadn't been to university, but could have made a much better job of it herself.[82] One can imagine the reader chuckling at this come-uppance for the distinguished academic.

At a much more profound level, however, she goes on to deride the pretensions of the Ingolstadt theologians, and to attack their credibility as leaders of the Christian Church. With

[77] AvG, 84, n. 89.
[78] AvG, 76, 81.
[79] AvG, 86.
[80] AvG, 82.
[81] AvG, 78.
[82] AvG, 79.

the disquieting insouciance of the non-professional she goes right to the heart of the matter: Do the theologians understand the basic point that knowledge comes from God? Do they imagine there is no limit to their power?: 'You may imagine that you can defy God, cast down his prophets and apostles from heaven, and banish them from the world. This shall not happen.'[83] The hyperbole is effective because of the passionate indignation which launches it.

There is a direct, unflinching quality about her denunciation of the University. One has to remember that here a lay person, and a woman to boot, is admonishing the professional custodians of Christian truth! Yet she uses the pamphlet to put them in the public dock, cross-examining them, the experts, on Scripture, firing off question after question. Haven't you read this, she asks, in astonishment? She scolds them as if they were her own children or servants, caught out in some misdemeanour: 'Show me! Hear what the Lord says! There is no doubt about this at all!' On moral issues, too, her language is straight and unguarded, and cuts to the bone. Wealth has been torn by the clergy from princes and poor alike. Canon Law costs have become outrageously expensive. 'Greed has possessed you. . . .'[84]

Her language is not just direct. It is simple, spare, at times almost bald. The adjectives have a predictable, 'ballad-like' quality. Luther is 'loyal', Argula's heart is 'heavy', the parents of the princes are 'good and godly'. The flip side to this predictability, however, is that she calls a spade a spade. What is required is human integrity and God's light and truth. Her lack of Latin is no hindrance. The issues can perfectly well be discussed in German. She doesn't depend on Luther, or 'Martin' as she prefers to call him. He is as fallible as young Arsacius and it is not impossible that he could recant his views, too! It is very clear that she had thought out her own position: 'I do not

[83]   AvG, 77.
[84]   AvG, 78.

build on his, mine, or any person's understanding, but on the true rock, Christ himself. . . .'[85]

One can hear her speaking as she writes. This is oral discourse, and will reflect countless spirited conversations and disagreements and debates with friends and family members as well as her own reflections. The systematic study of Scripture to which she refers complements this. Indeed one of her achievements is to recover the oral quality of Scripture itself.[86] Her writing is often in direct speech, in the vocative: 'You lofty experts', she says sarcastically, to the University teachers.[87] She pleads and exhorts in a direct, undiplomatic manner. 'I beseech you for the sake of God. I exhort you.' Or she sums up like a judge: 'What I hear is this.' 'What I find is this.'

There is little rhetorical sophistication. There is the odd piece of repetition, or dramatic contrast, or effective hyperbole: to condemn Luther as the University is doing 'means that the holy Gospel and the Epistles and the story of the Apostles . . . are all dismissed by you as heresy'. It would be easier to come to terms with a Jew than with the Ingolstadt theologians.[88] She lapses into colloquialisms at times, angrily denouncing the dismissal of her words as 'womanly chit-chat'.[89] The writing begins rather abruptly, and ends with something of a skid and a rush. The thread of argument is seldom hard to follow but it is rather over-freighted with Biblical quotations. Her identification with Biblical figures, however, can be quite striking: 'I cry out with Jeremiah.' 'With Paul, I say this.' On

[85]   AvG, 89.
[86]   On her use of Scripture cf. Silke Halbach, *Argula von Grumbach als Verfasserin reformatorischer Flugschriften* (Peter Lang: Frankfurt a. Main, 1992), pp. 195–204; AvG, 27–39, and Peter Matheson, 'A Reformation for Women'.
[87]   'Did Christ teach you so, or his apostles, prophets, or evangelists?' AvG, 76.
[88]   AvG, 85; this may be more than sharing the prejudices of the age; she had many dealings, as her household correspondence shows, with Jewish money-lenders.
[89]   Reminiscent here of Karsthans.

occasion she coins some very striking phrases indeed: 'The Word of God is a Yes which excludes any No.'[90]

It is certainly polemical language, but without any abusive 'edge' to it. She is quite abrupt and challenging, and has no illusions about securing any positive response from the University. Yet for all its bluntness, she is also curiously vulnerable: 'It is my desire', she says, 'to be instructed by everyone.'[91] This, as her other writings show, is more than a polite formula. She is very conscious of being a woman, a non-expert, of doing something quite unprecedented. She expects Christians to counsel and correct one another. She will also have been sharply aware of the risks she was taking: of contumely, threats, physical violence, prison, or even the stake. Yet she was quite uncompromising. Her language points beyond her, and her own views, to her prophetic role. She speaks, as it were, with authority, with charismatic finality. 'Philosophy can avail nothing.' 'Jurisprudence cannot harm me.'[92] Her language has an apodictic ring. The cumulative weight of the Biblical quotations would have persuaded many contemporary readers, exegeted, as it was, by her own credibility. She had written 'God's graffiti' on the public wall for all to read.

How then should her language be characterised? Hardly as 'womanly chit-chat'. On the contrary it is her opponents' discourse at times which is redolent of the gossip-column. One senses that the author has been surprised into speech. She does not take the public stage of her own volition. Certainly straight-speaking, for Argula von Grumbach, is a mark of every true Christian. Hers goes beyond this, however. It is the language of distress and of ecstasy. It is a primal cry. Combined with her sharp analysis of the situation and her evident mastery of Scripture, it is this confessional 'innocence' which makes her

[90]   AvG, 88.
[91]   AvG, 89.
[92]   AvG, 89f.

writing such engaging reading, and provides an interesting comparison to the writings of professional scholars such as Karlstadt and Luther, and even to preachers such as Müntzer.

Yet she knew very well what she was doing. This was a new form of public theology. Her consciousness of belonging to the von Stauff family with its long record of public service combined with excitement at the potential of the new medium of printing to launch her new initiative. One could scarcely find a better example, however, of the inappropriateness of the term 'propaganda' to characterise such literature. Here, if anywhere, we see an individual conscience compelled to seek the public stage. Here, if anywhere, the language of the heart reaches out to the reader.

Thomas Müntzer

Another pioneer in opening up theological language to ordinary people was the radical reformer, Thomas Müntzer. This may seem a surprising claim, because attention tends to have been focused in the past on the creativity, plasticity and range of Luther's language.[93] His opponents, whether Catholic controversialists like Cochlaeus or radicals like Karlstadt, tend to be regarded, at best, as worthy plodders when compared with the vivid images, the merciless wit, the clarity of line of Luther's writings. By throwing a bridge between high and popular culture, between the university and the city, and between court and countryside Luther's works constituted a new linguistic event. He communicated, it is said, with equal flair to prince, artisan and even – in catechism and hymns – to the peasant. And, of course, there is much truth to this view. To read Luther at his lithe, ebullient, persuasive best is always to appreciate afresh the winsomeness of his gospel, with its rare coinherence of language, thought and life.

[93] This treatment of Müntzer's language was first published in the *Sixteenth Century Journal*, XX.4 (1989), pp. 603–15. Reprinted by permission.

Yet the claims about the uniqueness of Luther's language and communication skills may need some modification. We need to be aware of the academic and social vantage-point from which such judgements have been made, and look again at some of the radical reformers. A careful comparison, for example, of Luther's famous *Letter to the Princes of Saxony* with Thomas Müntzer's retort to it, the *Vindication and Refutation*,[94] both written in 1524 on the eve of the Peasants' War, suggests that caution is in place.

For the startling content of Müntzer's last published writing is echoed by its language. It is very rich and varied, more than 1,500 terms being used, and it is characterised by exceptionally powerful imagery. In patches at least, its verbal caricature is reminiscent of Rabelais, or of the pitiless realism of Jörg Ratgeb's contemporary art. It employs the language of popular culture, of the upside-down world of carnival, *die verkehrte Welt*, in a spectacular parade of impressions, sketches, masques which uncover the lies, tyrannies and self-indulgence of a hypocritical world.

It operates on three levels, as a colloquy with Christ,[95] with Müntzer's Christian brothers, and with his arch enemy, Luther.[96] Both Christ and Luther are addressed in the second person singular. Like Augustine's *Confessions*, the language is

---

[94] *Hoch verursachte Schutzrede und antwwort wider das Gaistloße Sanfft lebende fleysch zu Wittenberg . . . ; Thomas Müntzer: Schriften und Briefe.* In collaboration with Paul Kirn edited by Günther Franz (Gütersloh, 1968); henceforth MSB, 321–43; the translation is taken from my English edition (CW); the assistance of the Computer Studies Department of Otago University was invaluable; cf. the analysis of the two writings, which incorporates reflections by Ulrich Bubenheimer on their rhetorical structure, by Siegfried Bräuer, 'Selbstverständnis und Feindbild bei Martin Luther und Thomas Müntzer: Ihre Flugschriftenkontroverse von 1524', in Günter Vogler (ed.), *Wegscheiden der Reformation. Alternatives Denken vom 16. bis zum 18. Jahrhundert* (Verlag Hermann Böhlaus Nachfolger: Weimar, 1994), pp. 57–84.

[95] CW, 327/11ff., 338/5.

[96] CW, 338/8.

partly that of prayer. In part, however, it is polemic: the refutation of Luther, and the vindication of Müntzer's own cause. And finally it is an appeal to his 'dear', 'very dearest', 'most beloved' brothers in Christ. He had long been pleading for an impartial hearing of his case; this had been refused him. So now, by courtesy of the printing press, he presents his case before the forum of public opinion, the elect throughout the world acting as judges.

As such it incorporates a form of personal stocktaking, a reflection on his whole life so far, and on the progress of the Reformation. In addition to all this, the *Vindication* is an exposition of John 8.[97] Its intensely interactive and existential nature is a good example of the inappropriateness of the term 'propaganda' to describe such pamphlets. It is also a mistake to dismiss it as mere reactive polemic. Müntzer does, of course, meet many of Luther's criticisms of him, and some of the language reflects this. About forty of Luther's terms or concepts find an echo in the *Vindication*, quite apart from the initial dedication, which is a parody of Luther's opening address to the princes of Saxony. Among the most significant terms are 'spirit' (the bold, lofty, world-devouring, Pharisaical, Allstedt spirit), devil, Satan, false prophets, heavenly voice, insurrection, violence, fist, lies, tricks, poor sinners; phrases echoed include: 'dreading the soup', 'smelling the roast', 'crawling into a corner', enjoying the 'shield and shelter' of Luther, 'indulging the weak'.

At no point, however, is Müntzer's language mere rebuttal. Indeed one has the impression that Müntzer read Luther's writing once and once only, and then proceeded to write a

---

[97] Virtually every verse, every significant passage and term in John 8 is echoed in the *Vindication*: the welcome of the people to Jesus compared with the wiles of the doctors of the law and the Pharisees, the story of the woman caught in adultery, the theme of true testimony, the contrast between the godly and the worldly, the promise of a truth which will set people free, the devil's kingdom of lies and murder, false claims to nobility of birth, the genuine fame and glory of those glorified by God, the accusation that Jesus is 'possessed'.

vindication of his own position, making no attempt at a systematic answer to Luther's provocative questions and arguments. It is certainly more vindication, *Schutzrede*, than refutation, but even as such, Müntzer is seldom 'on the back foot'. Luther's powerful critique of iconoclasm, for example, is not taken up; nor are some of his patent mistakes corrected, for example the accusation that Müntzer wanted to abolish Scripture and preaching.[98] Many of the gibes and taunts, on the other hand, stuck in Müntzer's gullet, and are countered at length, especially those relating to his claims to revelation, and to his alleged cowardice. Clearly he saw no value in a point for point refutation. He went on, rather, to develop his own theological ideas, and above all his 'political' views on the power of princes and people. The term 'godless', for example, is used eighteen times, and almost always refers to the abuse of political power; 'hypocrisy' and 'indulgence' likewise denote flattery of the powerful.[99]

The structural weakness of the *Vindication* has to be acknowledged. It presents neither a coherent refutation of the *Letter to the Princes* nor a systematic exposition of John 8.[100] Its main strength may lie elsewhere – and help to explain its determined suppression by censorship. After producing a new and highly popular liturgy in Allstedt, Müntzer began to forge a new language for the common people,[101] which can speak in startling, unheard-of collocations, of a 'justified uprising' of

[98] *Er will die schrifft und das mündlich Gottes wort auff heben und die sacrament der tauff und alltars austilgen.* . . . WA 15, 216/29f.

[99] Note, however, the interesting marginal note on Tertullian's *Adversus Marcionem: omnes heretici obtentu lenitatis deceperunt ecclesiam Dei*; CW, 411/23

[100] As U. Bubenheimer makes clear, however, much more attention needs to be given to the rhetorical form of Müntzer's writings as well as Luther's.

[101] Note Luther's criticism of Müntzer's language, apparently fearless, but only because he knew he was secure: *Und treybt doch die weyl ynn seym nest die aller unerschröckeneste wort.* . . . WA 15, 213/27f.

the poor, for example.[102] Part of its strength is that it defies definition; it is neither 'simply' a political language nor 'predominantly' a religious one.

Our aim is to draw attention to the originality of this language, from which the traditional jargon of courtier and jurist and theologian[103] has disappeared, and to make a first attempt at examining its vocabulary, style and imagery. It is certainly on the verge of oral discourse. Its analogies are taken from the life of the kitchen, the farmyard and the workshop. It is language on the quest for directness, integrity, and authenticity, language launched against the *verkehrte Welt*, the perverse, upside-down, hypocritical world of prince and priest, scholar and theologian. It is one long parody of the obscene carnival which Müntzer sees prancing before his eyes in Church and society, the mad Fasching or Mardi Gras capers which have usurped the place of true Christian penitence.

Müntzer's first task is to restore the integrity of Scriptural language. For the genial, devilish trick of Luther and his allies, the Biblical scholars, has been to make a fool of Scripture. They have turned it upside down, have misunderstood, perverted, distorted and twisted the language of revelation.[104] Their language is like that of the Pharisees; wearing biblical masks,[105] they condemn Müntzer and his allies as deluded spirits just as the Pharisees condemned Christ, and deceive the common people in the same way, shitting on them with their

---

[102]   *füglicher empörung*; MSB, 335/26.

[103]   Müntzer had long been critical, as in his marginal notes on Tertullian's *De carne Christi*, of the approach of the theologians: *In littera versantur omnes doctores palpant ubique tenebras*; CW, 414/14.

[104]   Distortion is mentioned in the title: *mit verkärter weyße*; Luther's judgement, and that of the authorities, is *verkert*; he distorts (*gezerret*) Deuteronomy and Isaiah: *auß dem text Esaie one allen verstandt Got machest zur ursach des pösens*; MSB, 322/2, 323/16, 329/6f., 324/8, 339/12.

[105]   A favourite image of Müntzer: in his marginal comments on Beatus Rhenanus' *Admonitio ad lectorem de quibusdam Tertulliani dogmatis* he speaks of the *Theologi larvati pessimi pessimi*; CW, 410/27.

new logic.[106] They invert all values, praising the wicked, and scolding the good.[107] They sing at the top of the scale that the laity are at the bottom of the scale.[108] They are liars and lampooners. Above all they confuse their own fancies with the Word of God, and denounce the true Spirit as satanic.[109]

Hence a new language of the heart has to be found, which embraces the truth, to replace that of the clever head, the learned fool, who merely parrots Scripture.[110] It is the language of those outside the gate, of the prophetic dweller in the cave, symbolised at the very beginning of the writing by Elijah, and of the oft-exiled, tireless warrior[111] such as Müntzer himself. The similarity to the language at the beginning of Müntzer's Prague Manifesto is not accidental;[112] here, too, the prophetic and apocalyptic notes are primary. Scripture is mined typo-logically – Esau and Jacob, David and Saul, Christ and the Pharisees – to illustrate the message that a new world is at hand. Today's outsiders, the lowly and the despised, will soon be turning the tables. The language of deference, usually addressed to prince and magistrate, is stripped from them and

[106]   *mit einer newen logiken bescheischen mit teüscherey des wort Gotes*; MSB, 334/16f.

[107]   'since he does not despise the godless, but denounces many God-fearing men'; CW, 333/20f.

[108]   CW, 331/23ff; MSB, 326/5ff.

[109]   Luther begins his writing by referring to the fate, or ill-fortune (*das glück*) of the Word of God, that whenever it appears, Satan resists it with all his might; WA, 210/8ff.; Müntzer, addressing Christ, responds that 'Your holy spirit has always suffered the fate (*sölich glück*) of being treated by these merciless lions, the Biblical scholars, as the worst of devils'; CW, 327/17f.

[110]   The very mention of 'Spirit' makes Luther *den klugen kopff schütteln*; MSB, 326/3; Müntzer was particularly irritated by Luther's claims to interpret Scripture better than all 'sophists and Papists'; WA 15, 216/3f.; 'He still wants to be the wisest man on earth, and boasts, that there is none to equal him'; CW, 331/17f.

[111]   Müntzer sees himself as Christ's *unverdrossen landtßknecht*; MSB, 323/23.

[112]   Note the reference to the 'dear and saintly warrior, John Hus', and the appeal to the elect throughout the world; CW, 362/5.

applied to Christ alone.[113] The carnival-like farce in Church and state, the hypocritical alliance of the court fool,[114] Luther, and his godless princes, is coming under attack. The apocalyptic final section of the *Vindication,* also reminiscent of the Prague Manifesto and perhaps written in Latin to mock the anathemas of Church authorities and councils, prophesies the imminent end of Luther, while the common people will go free,[115] being answerable to God alone. Today's hunters will become tomorrow's quarry.

The polemical character of much of the language is clear. It borrows heavily from John 8 for its dualistic categories: light and darkness, truth and lies,[116] deeds and words. Müntzer and Allstedt confront Luther and Wittenberg as absolute, polar opposites of simplicity and deviousness,[117] frankness and hypocrisy[118] service and domination. The City of God confronts that of the world.[119] While Müntzer openly confesses the spirit of God, Luther calls the spirit of God a devil.[120] While Müntzer sings and writes for the people in his liturgy, Luther plays the carnival fool, and cavorts and

---

[113]   Especially in the dedication of the book to Christ, CW, 327/11ff., mocking Luther's rather conventional dedication to the noble Saxon princes; the term *hochgebornen* will have been particularly offensive to Müntzer, with John 8:41 in mind.

[114]   Luther is developing more and more *zum hochfertigen narren* MSB, 323/5f.; he is a *stocknarr,* a 'numskull' MSB, 326/11, while making a fool of the 'good brothers' ET 347/18f.; the actual term 'court fool' is not used, but Luther's antics in dancing and singing for the mighty would indicate that this is meant; cf. n.121, n. 139 below.

[115]   John 8:36.

[116]   Cf. the personification of Luther as 'Dr Liar', the word-play Luther/ Lügner being closer in the German.

[117]   The term *ainfeltig* (simple) and its cognates occur six times, as does *tückisch.*

[118]   'Hypocritical' (*heuchlerisch*) and its cognates occur seven times.

[119]   Augustine's concept of the two cities may have been in Müntzer's mind; certainly John 8:23

[120]   CW, 329/11ff., 24f.

dances around for the princes.[121] The poor thirst for the truth, the Biblical scholars thirst for the death of those who speak the truth.[122]

Almost literally, everything is in black and white. Luther, the black fox, the black crow, the black monk, is contrasted with Müntzer, the pure, innocent, silver-winged dove from the Ark. Terms pile up to express the extent and dreadfulness of the corruption in Church and world: it is pollution, filth, poison, an abomination.[123] Since it is cunningly concealed and blotted over[124] (fascinating in view of Müntzer's later use of blots to erase parts of his own correspondence), and made to look pretty[125] the covering must be snatched away from this *verkehrte Welt*, this upside-down world, this carnival playground for rascals and fools. Luther is Dr Liar, Dr Lampooner, Dr Pussyfoot.[126] The term 'Dr Liar', used ten times, sums up his character as a charlatan.

On the personal level Wittenberg is condemned for its ambition and pride, its lust for glory and an easy life, its hypocrisy and permissiveness. Socially it has encouraged an arrogant contempt for the poor and humble, and fostered the assumption that land and animals and property, even people themselves, belong to the privileged few. Politically, tyranny reigns unchecked, the innocent are persecuted, the ruthless

---

[121] The devil plays bagpipes for Luther, who dances, winning the admiration of the godless; CW, 345/4f.; he sings and dances and the whole world falls at his feet; CW, 342/5ff.

[122] Müntzer compares *das arme dürstige volck* who pour along the streets to his services, and longed for (*begerte*) the truth, with the Pharisees: *Ire begyre waren zu eytel todtschlahen dürstig*; MSB, 332/23.

[123] Terms that are used include *gifft* (poison), *unfladt* (filth), *greuel* (abomination), *besudeln* (pollute), which are contrasted with frequent references to *rainigkeyt* (purity), and its cognates.

[124] *klicken alle bücher vol*; MSB, 325/8f.; everything is covered up *im gedichten glauben und in iren phariseischen tücken*; MSB, 323/6.

[125] *dich schöne brennen*; MSB, 332/15.

[126] Note the alliteration in German: *Dr Lügner, Dr Ludibrii, vatter leisendritt.*

flattered, the weak fleeced and flayed by corrupt judges,[127] and all under the pretext of religion. Religiously it has led to Luther arrogating to himself the role of a new pope. As a princely pretender,[128] even as a mock Christ,[129] he leads the blasphemous dance of the scholarly fools, who utterly distort Scripture.

The language is direct, provocative, uncompromising: the secular rulers are robbers, hangmen and tyrants; the cultural or spiritual leaders are liars and false prophets. The structural injustice meted out by law courts is contrasted with God's righteousness in the Last Judgement[130] (it is worth noting that the term, 'distort', *verkehren*, is used for the perversion of both Scripture and justice);[131] the cautious observance of legal oaths and duties by the minions of the rulers with bold obedience to God's word,[132] the stifling exercise of censorship and Luther's abdication from a prophetic role with the call to the whole world to prophesy,[133] the abuse of privilege and power with the true order of creation.[134]

Yet only about half of the terms used in the *Vindication and Refutation* are pejorative. Negative polemic by no means swamps the writing. The only substantives of any significance used more than twenty times are God, Christ, spirit, law, people. The joy and delight of the elect, the friends of God, Christ's ransomed members, who find the full treasure and

---

[127]   *schinden und schaben*; MSB, 329/24

[128]   'Under your shield and shelter you say. Oho! how you give yourself away! I take it you're a prince too?' CW, 343/19ff.

[129]   Luther 'now makes himself out to be a new Christ, one who has purchased so many good things for the Christian people by his blood . . .' CW, 341/28ff.

[130]   CW, 349/1ff.

[131]   *Ob die oberkait das urteyl wolte verkeren*; *vil genaygter, verkerter richter*; MSB, 329/6f., 332/3; cf. also *sein verderbliche gerechtigkayt*; MSB, 331/3f.; cf. n. 104 above.

[132]   CW, 349/11f.

[133]   '. . . *es muß dye gantz welt prophetisch sein* . . . MSB 341/6.

[134]   CW, 335/15ff.

consolation of the Gospel, and plumb the mystery of the divine Word, is pictured in lyrical terms. The common people, the good brothers, the farmworkers, the poor, humble folk, are portrayed flocking towards Allstedt, hastening towards the truth, living witnesses to the success of Müntzer's liturgies. The Trinity is praised: the Father's gracious covenant and stern mercy, Christ's fame and glory as our only saviour, prince, duke, master, protector, the infallible, irrefutable testimony of the Spirit.[135] There is much positive emphasis on simple, straightforward obedience to the stern commands of God, about the harmony of Law and Gospel while distinguishing accurately between them, about free will, displaying accountability for one's life and faith, and about the imminent vindication of reason, justice and truth. Virtues such as frankness, honesty, innocence, justice, simplicity, zeal are commended.

Words used between ten and nineteen times include devil, godless, princes, world, Doctor, Liar, Biblical (scholars), all of which are overwhelmingly pejorative, but they are outnumbered by positive terms such as good, just, holy, poor, teaching, way, faith, Paul, Scripture. There are whole constellations of words relating to prophecy, fulfilment,[136] preaching, judgement, purity, suffering, understanding, God's law, truth, the order of creation. The linguistic evidence is against the Wittenberg contention, followed by much subsequent research, that Müntzer's language was one long outpouring of 'slaughter and blood'.[137]

The reason why the *Vindication* impresses us as being so overwhelmingly polemical is the power of the figures of speech it uses, almost all of which are polemical in intent.

---

[135] The term *beschirmer*, interestingly, was a title often given Müntzer during the Peasants' War; cf. MSB, 465/16f., 466/20f.

[136] *die erfüllung des geysts der forcht Gotes, Ich setzte Christum mit allen seinen gelidern zum erfüller des gesetzs, denn es muß der wille Gottes volfüret werden*; MSB, p. 327/3, 11ff.

[137] CW, 30/9.

Puns,[138] similes, metaphors, metonyms (noble blood), and synecdoches (clever head, coarse mouth) cascade on top of one another. I counted some ninety different images. Many are drawn from daily life: from patching garments, sleeping, waking, even defecating; or from the workshop of the tanner, the cobbler, the butcher, the refiner; many refer to cooking or eating: to roasting or stewing food, to tasty dishes, tough meat, to fake sausages made of fox meat, to drinking, wining and dining, gobbling, smearing the mouth with honey; many of the parts of the body figure: the eyes, the ears, the nose, the mouth, the beard, the cheeks, the fists; fighting, crime and war provide many analogies; a whole menagerie of animals is presented as actors in the carnival: domestic farmyard hens, roosters, and pigs; wild, and predatory animals such as lion, wolf and bear, and mythical creatures like the dragon. Such animal images are, of course, normal enough in apocalyptic writings. There are – unusually for Müntzer – few mentions of plants.

Some of the more striking analogies, however, are drawn from the higher ranks of society, from hunting and court life, with references to advocates, arch-chancellors, flatterers and heralds, court clowns; the importance of the carnival theme is emphasised by the repeated references to games, to music, singing, piping, dancing, the Punch and Judy show.[139] One derisory vignette follows the other; the dancing monk, the carnation-toting hero at Leipzig,[140] the soft-living, sweetly sleeping flesh of Luther.

[138]   *krümmer/richter* (crook, not a judge); *prandtfuchs* (black-brushed fox, but also burning, raging, fox which is *hayßer* (hoarser, but also hotter) every day); there may also be another reference here to *sich schöne brennen*, Luther's superficial refinement and purity; MSB, 339/25, 30f.; *schrifftsteler* (both author, and thief of Scripture).

[139]   Cf. *affenspil* (monkey-play); *poppenspill* (Punch and Judy show); the theme of the painted puppet, an idolatrous image of Christ, is a recurrent one in Müntzer's writings; MSB, 325/5, 29; MSB, 326/6ff, 336/8ff., 339/1ff.

[140]   MSB, 340/23.

There is humour here, then, but no playful humour. It is grim, bleak and black, directed at the blasphemous abominations in high places, countering the hurt the mockery of Müntzer's opponents has inflicted on the 'friends of God'. The number of terms used to describe this derision – abuse, show contempt for, denounce, deride, despise, insult, jeer, laugh, libel, scoff, scorn[141] – emphasises the importance of this motif. Since the days of Egranus and Agricola Müntzer had been ultra-sensitive to criticism. Luther's derision of Muntzer's 'lofty spirit' and 'heavenly voice' are now met, tit for tat, with references to Luther's soft-living flesh, singing at the top of the scale, and playing the bagpipes. As in Luther's writing heavy irony abounds: references to the 'truly pious' Pharisees, the onion-like 'simplicity' of Luther, the fine 'protection' a wolf offers to sheep.[142]

Again and again undertones of rage and indignation break through, most vividly in a striking cannibalistic fantasy about Luther's tough flesh being dished up to his mealy-mouthed friends,[143] though there is nothing comparable to the stream of anal and obscene references in Luther's later writings. Luther is a vulture-like crow, living off carrion, pecking out the eyes of the wealthy to blind them to the truth.[144] He is Doctor Liar and Doctor Lampooner. He is a wily fox, luring others into trouble, raiding hen-coops, but getting his come-uppance in the end. He is Esau, Goliath, Saul, Caiaphas: the personifications of greed, violence, envy and hypocrisy. He is a new pope, a new Christ, the arch-chancellor of the devil, who in turn acts as his 'angel'. He is the advocate and herald of the powerful, a fool, numskull, thief, hound of hell, wolf, merciless lion, a poisonous worm, a snake slithering over the rock, a

---

[141] Terms used include *bespotten, verspotten* (deride), *lestern* (abuse, blaspheme), *verachten* (show contempt), *zu narren machen* (make a fool of).

[142] CW, 335/14; 339/39; 337/12ff.

[143] CW, 348/16ff.; the reference to *milchmeulern* recalls 1 Corinthians 3:2.

[144] CW, 333/21ff.

puffed-up dragon. In the end the very profusion of images becomes somewhat confusing, for none really prevails, unless it be that of Brother Soft-Life, which caricatures Luther as symbolising and justifying a corrupt, self-indulgent society. By apostrophising him as 'godless flesh' he hits back, of course, at Luther's attack on him, in the *Letter to the Princes*, as a deluded spirit.[145] The names one is called are significant; Christ, too, was abused and called a Samaritan, or Beelzebub.[146] The inversion of truth leads naturally to an inversion of language.[147]

Linguistically, perhaps the most notable feature of the writing is the stream of associations which flow around the three main images of Luther as crow, as soft-living flesh, as fox. The wily crow of Genesis 8, which, unlike the innocent dove, does not return to the Ark to inform Noah, is transmuted by Müntzer into a black carrion crow. It is contrasted with the gleaming silver and gold dove of Psalm 68, which symbolises the joy of the righteous as God scatters his enemies. In a rapid scene change Müntzer then presents Luther in black robes as the scholar crow, Dr Liar, who cannot dwell in the house of God, for, as in Psalm 15, he speaks ill of the innocent, and kow-tows to the godless. And then, in a splendidly mixed metaphor, Luther becomes the courtier crow, who flatters the mighty, self-indulgent pigs that they are, and pecks out their eyes, thus blinding them to the Word of God, so that he can gobble up their wealth and honours with impunity.[148] Later in

---

145   *diser schwymmel geyst*; WA 15, 216/1 9f.; Müntzer's marginal notes on Tertullian's *de carne Christi*, and *de Resurrectione carnis* remind us of the importance of the flesh for Müntzer: *Deus diligit carnem nostram; caro templum dei* and, above all, *Carni mortificatae prodest spiritus*; CW, 422/3, 11f., 427/7f.; the flesh, as our 'glory and ignominy', must be kept pure and virgin, if the New Adam, the son of the virgin, is to be born in us; hence his strange views on marriage and propagation, and the force of his attack on the 'Virgin Martin', *die keusche Babilonische fraw*; MSB, 335/20f.

146   MSB, 323/21ff., 332/16ff.

147   The very first of Müntzer's marginal notes on Cyprian reads: *Christus innocens imo innocentia ipsa inter facinorosos deputatur*; CW, 408/1f.

148   CW, 333/13ff.

the writing the crow even becomes a thieving magpie, stealing the title 'son of God' for himself.[149] Müntzer also draws attention to the ugly, denunciatory cry of the crow, as it opens its great, coarse mouth, but is unable, ironically, to draw attention to anything but itself: 'Craw, craw!'[150] This is verbal caricature at its best.

Secondly, Luther is presented as the fox, known to folk wisdom as wily and devious. The fox's blackness is stressed (perhaps with a double pun on the theme of a fiery, pretended purity),[151] and its hoarse barking, just before dawn, picks up the eschatological theme. For the truth about Luther is about to be revealed. Then Müntzer slips into the tale of Reynard the Fox, Luther being the fox who entices the princes into the well with false promises. The fox theme suggests, in turn, that the nobility be described as roosters. Then along comes the fox as the false prophet of Ezekiel 13, as the predator of Ezekiel 34, as the scatterer of the sheep (actually a wolf) in John 10. A reference to Psalm 72 follows, which appears to combine a reference to the theme of soft-living flesh (v. 7) with the sudden end of the ungodly (v. 18), who are not actually identified as foxes in the Psalm. The most remarkable association now follows: the dogs mentioned by the Canaanite woman in Matthew 15, as picking up the crumbs from under the master's table, become the humble people of contemporary Germany, little terriers[152] aroused by the Gospel to track down the false fox in its den and put an end to it. This vivid image is blurred by yet another, the smell of a roasting sausage, made of fox-meat, a cannibalistic reference to Luther. Luther even becomes Esau, the fox's fur perhaps suggesting a reference to Esau, the

---

[149]   CW, 342/11f.

[150]   CW, 344/4f.

[151]   CW, 46/3ff.; *prandtfuchs*, MSB, 339/30, takes up the theme of 'blackness', and is immediately followed by a reference to *hayßer* (hoarser, hotter) which suggests that the idea of a raging, burning fox is also meant; cf. n. 138 above.

[152]   *die klaynen hündleyn; Der fryschhundt;* MSB, 340/9, 11.

hairy man, who will be supplanted by Jacob / Müntzer.[153] The very last words of the *Vindication* revert again to the theme of the wily fox / Dr Liar, who has grieved the righteous and given comfort to the godless and who will, as God enters into his Kingdom and his people go free, be hunted down and killed.[154] As a sustained metaphor it is quite remarkable and unforgettable. The accumulation of images does leave one somewhat dazed, however, and the exegetical liberties taken are extraordinary.

The third theme, that of Luther as the soft-living flesh in Wittenberg, is adumbrated by the first words of the title. It is a riposte to the repeated accusation of Müntzer as the Allstedt 'spirit' in the *Letter to the Princes of Saxony*. Popular themes from traditional anti-clerical polemic are turned on the Reformation's father figure. His easy life encourages an unspiritual outlook, and a 'robbery' of Scripture, leading to the total pollution of the Church.[155] With this is contrasted the pure zeal of Elijah in his cave. John 8:15, 'You judge according to the flesh', is the key text for Müntzer here, leading to an association of Luther with the world and the devil. The actual term is taken from the Vulgate version of Job 28:13, where wisdom is said to be absent from the land of the *suaviter viventium*, those living a life of ease. Such godless flesh is always opposed to the purity of the Law, to the whole order of creation and to Christ's grieving bride, the Church.[156] The image of the carrion crow continues the theme of greed, as does Luther's self-serving clemency to the powerful, so contrary to the friendly severity of the Holy Spirit. In a damaging aside Luther is represented chanting a liturgical 'Amen' to the exploitation

---

[153]   CW, 346/21ff.

[154]   CW, 349/22ff.

[155]   Note the collocation of *gaistloße* (unspiritual) with *sanfftlebende* (soft-living), the crowding together of the metaphors of distortion, theft, pollution; MSB, 322/1ff.

[156]   CW, 336/17ff.; the desires of the flesh (*begyre*) lead not only to self-indulgence, but to hate and murder, *zu eytel todtschlahen*; MSB, 332/24.

of the poor.[157] His claims to have suffered persecution lack credibility in view of his fleshly love of 'good malmsey and whorish fare'.[158] Ironic references to 'our virgin Martin'[159] conclude this rather unconvincing *ad hominem* attack.

Behind it, however, lies the conviction that the easy life of the scholar distorts Scripture, reflecting a very widespread topos, *die Verkehrten die Gelehrten*. In a virtuoso carnival performance Luther dances to the bagpipes, played by the devil! His fleshly understanding opposes the unerring spirit of God, like the false apostles of 2 Corinthians 11.[160] He sleeps comfortably himself, but accuses Müntzer of cowardice, alleging that he had 'smelt the roast' of martyrdom. But soon it will be Luther's arrogant flesh that will be roasted, or rather stewed in a cauldron.[161] This repetition of the cannibalistic theme is supported by an alarming reference to Jeremiah 1's cauldron, and to Jerusalem as the bloody city, to be burnt in the great pot of God's wrath (Ezekiel 24). Abruptly Luther's soft-living flesh becomes as tough as that of an ass, unpalatable to his mealy-mouthed, fleshly followers, fobbed off with the milk, rather than the meat of the faith, 1 Corinthians 3.[162] The coherence of the image collapses in the end, over-weighted by too many associations and diversions. Behind it may well lie the burlesque, carnival figure of Hans Worst, later to be so memorably employed by Luther himself against Henry of Brunswick.[163]

Müntzer's positive images are, apart from the Biblical ones, rather less fresh and effective. Elijah is unforgettable, and the parallels with Christ and the Pharisees are cleverly drawn. As

---

[157] CW, 335/24f.; cf. also Luther's liturgical 'Nunc dimittis' to the martyrdom of others; CW, 342/5f.
[158] CW, 339/33f.
[159] CW, 341/16f.
[160] CW, 345/29–346/1.
[161] CW, 348/16ff., 346/19f.
[162] CW, 348/19ff.
[163] W 51, 461–572.

always in Müntzer it is remarkable to see how broad the sweep of his Biblical references is, and clearly they were not added here as a later 'armoury', as was sometimes the case, but belong to the integrity of his writing. Apart from John 8 and the apocalyptic books, there are quotations from the Pentateuch, the historical books, the prophets, the writings, the Gospels, and the Epistles. The image of Müntzer as the dove, wings silvered, and back gilded, is more than faintly ridiculous, and his continual identification of himself with Christ strains credulity, though he would have justified it by reference to the identical fate of master and pupil.[164] Other images, such as the dawn of truth, or the key to release sins, are hardly original.[165] An important image, as elsewhere in Müntzer's writing, is that of beginnings, of origins, of the source of faith. The way in which identical terms are used to describe the real source of faith, on the one hand, and the cause of the theft of God's creatures on the other is illuminating.[166] Here, as elsewhere in Müntzer's writings, we find the theme of the *coincidentia oppositorum*.

As a writing it is one and a half times as long as Luther's. Its language compares very favourably indeed with that of Luther's *Letter to the Princes*. It is much less conventional, not only in its dedication and conclusion, but throughout. Its three-fold orientation to Christ, Luther, and the elect makes it less one-dimensional than Luther's epistolary form. Its surrealist, carnival images of crow, fox and soft-living flesh sweep the reader along. In sheer creativity of language it far surpasses a writing of Luther's which is itself by no means uninspired! There are many more images, less heavy sarcasm, much less wearisome repetition, and a greater range of vocabulary. Its

[164]   CW, 328/22ff.
[165]   *Und nun die rechte warheyt wil auffgen*; MSB, 339/31; *den schlüssel der auflösung*; MSB, 328/28–329/1.
[166]   *den ursprung aller dieberey, die grundtsuppe des wuchers, Die ursach des auffrurß*; MSB, 329/15, 18, 27; on Müntzer's positive use of *ursprung, anfang, grundt*; cf. MSB, 326/4, 13; 327/1, 16.

weaknesses, which are considerable, lie in its continuity and in its argumentation.

Who is of the spirit, who of the devil? Which is Luther, which Müntzer? The terms 'devil' and 'spirit', used eighteen times and twenty-five times respectively in the *Vindication,* mirror the confusions and ambiguities of the Reformation era. Luther's main accusation was that Müntzer represented Satan in the guise of the spirit,[167] and his main linguistic device the repeated, derisory use of the term 'spirit': Müntzer is an arrogant, bold, defiant, lofty, giddy, lying, Pharisaic, rebellious, world-devouring spirit.[168] In the endeavour to win people's minds, to vindicate his position, and to refute Luther, to demonstrate that the 'spirit of God' was no devil,[169] Müntzer mints a new language, presenting the reader with a cavalcade of bizarre and drastic images. His words, indeed, often have the force of graffiti, ever the language of the outsider, sharp, striking and cruel. But his writing is also the testament of the humble folk, whose time is coming, and whose God is in ultimate control. Christ's grieving bride will soon embrace her gracious lord, her true protector and comforting saviour. Behind the graffiti lie the liturgies of Allstedt, the simple, triumphant language of prayer, the shared expectations of the elect. The real vindication will not be that of Müntzer, but of the poor people: of their rights to be heard, to judge, to go free; to bear not only the sword of justice, but the keys to the City of God.[170] The language of prayer, of the worshipping

---

[167] CW, 331/5ff.; WA 15, 211/11, 21.

[168] *welltfressergeyst;* CW, 214/16; this follows the references to the 'roast' and the 'brew' or soup, which Müntzer shuns, and no doubt triggered off Müntzer's cannibalistic fantasies at the end of his writing; CW, 348/16ff.

[169] CW, 329/24f.; 330/27; especially at the beginning of the *Vindication* there are frequent references to the Holy Spirit of Christ being despised and persecuted; CW, 327f.

[170] Note the marginal note on Beatus Rhenanus' *Admonitio ad lectorem de quibusdam Tertulliani dogmatis: Extra veram electorum ecclesiam nullum dimittitur peccatum;* CW, 411/8.

people of God, and of polemic against the blasphemous carnival of the enemies of the Spirit, is also a summons to an oppressed people to a 'justified uprising'. In articulating all three aspects, and not least in the genial combination of them, Müntzer's language breaks new ground.

Their language, then, played a quite vital part in the success of the Reformers. There is a sense in which we have always known this. Yet it is hard to overcome the tendency to discount their rhetoric as merely the relish on the meal, to identify their 'message' with the kernel of truth contained *within* the language. It is hard to remember that, far from being the external husk or frame of their thought, their language was the royal highway by which they walked into people's minds and souls, and simultaneously opened themselves to others. What they had to say was inseparable from how they said it. Luther's earthiness, Argula von Grumbach's directness, Müntzer's vivid images all attest to the way in which they accommodated themselves to people as they were, weaving what Künert calls the gritty, despised slang of the street into a 'new song'. Through their words the Word ran free. They spoke with authority, and not as the scribes, because the day of their language was not yet gone.

CHAPTER SIX

REFORMATION POLEMIC

Macht kaputt, was Euch kaputt macht!
Destroy what is destroying you!

Slogan of the 1968 Student Revolution

The Reformation had inherited a vigorous tradition of personal polemic, not least from the humanist tradition. Gerhard Ritter pointed out long ago that humanism took on the face of public opinion, and prepared the way for the Reformation.[1] Rummel has portrayed vividly the shift in humanist rhetoric from the playful epideictic stage, to the personal and professional jealousies which were aroused when humanists were seen to 'put their sickle into another man's crop', to trespass on the privileged realm of the scholastic theologians.[2] Stadtwald has amassed a fascinating documentation of humanist polemic against the Papacy, including Roman pasquinades, which both adumbrated and continued to complement the critique of Luther and the other Reformers. The Pope emerges as tyrant, as Antichrist, the patron of sexual deviations, the exploiter of German credulity. Gregor Heimburg's (1410–72) call on the princes not to bear the sword in vain, but to punish the popes, could be a direct quote from Luther's *Appeal to the German*

---

[1] Gerhard Ritter, 'Die geschichtliche Bedeutung des deutschen Humanismus', *Historische Zeitschrift* 127 (1923), pp. 428f.; very similar judgements in Gottfried Blochwitz, pp. 244–6.

[2] Rummel, 84–6.

157

Nobility. The ferocity of the polemic and its sharp polarities corrects any tendency to see the humanists as rather retiring intellectuals. What could be fiercer than the anonymous *Antithesis of Christ and the Pope*:

> Christ avoided kings, but the pope subdues cities.
> Christ wore a crown of thorns, the pope a triple crown.
> Christ washed feet, kings offer kisses to the pope's.
> Christ paid taxes, the popes exempt all the clergy.

Stadtwald argues that 'humanists created the Rome Luther loved to hate' and, more arguably, that the activist, political tradition of humanist polemic helped to convince Luther of the need to shed blood for the sake of the Kingdom.[3] The Reuchlin controversy produced the ripest of personal polemic in the shape of the *Letters of Obscure Men*, in which the Dominicans of Cologne were held up to merciless persiflage.[4] *Eccius Dedolatus,* a satire produced in 1520, is a very curious mixture of high cultured name-dropping, of 'in jokes' relating to current controversies, and of slapstick comedy, cacology and heavy sarcasm. It is as if *Playboy* and the *New Yorker* were within the one set of covers. While it claims to be offended by the crude polemics of the scholastics, it stops at nothing itself, not even sadistic fantasies, and the main aim is to destroy the credibility of Eck as a person by mockery and ridicule, not to focus on issues.[5] It reminds us that one of our difficulties in dealing with sixteenth-century polemics may be that the distinction between élite and popular culture, high and low, which we tend to presuppose was by no means cemented at this time.

[3] Kurt Werner Stadtwald, 'When O Rome Will You Cease to Hiss? The Image of the Pope in the Politics of German Humanism' (PhD, University of Minnesota, 1991), esp. pp. 57, 250f.

[4] *Epistolae Obscurorum Virorum* (London, 1909).

[5] T. W. Best (ed.), *Eccius Dedolatus. A Reformation Satire.* By Joannefranciscus Cotta Lembeergius (Kentucky University Press: Lexington, 1971); it is still generally attributed to Willibald Pirckheimer.

Important, however, as humanist influences were in form-
ing public attitudes, they were, of course, only part of the
'Manifestations of Discontent' preceding the Reformation,
what has been recently described as the 'disintegration' of the
power of the clergy.[6] Urban discontent has been well documented, but the rural or 'communal reformation' portrayed
by Peter Blickle, Rosi Fuhrmann and others, and to some extent
adumbrated by the older studies of A. G. Dickens, should not
be underestimated as a source for polemical criticism of the
ecclesiastical structures and as an explanation of their
extraordinary popularity.[7] Recently, for example, the closeness
of the concerns of the communal reformation and of the
antecedents to Hutterism has been demonstrated.[8]

Polemic, then, was far from being the prerogative of the
theologian, dialogue of the humanist. The picture is
infinitely more complicated. In the 1520s Luther was much
more aware than militant humanists such as von Hutten of
the need to bear with the weak and carry the case by the better
argument!

Our analysis, then, of why sixteenth-century sermons and
writings appealed so much to their contemporaries is still very
much in its infancy. What was it about their language and
style and structure that enabled them to wing themselves into

[6] R. W. Scribner, 'Anticlericalism and the Reformation in Germany',
in Scribner, *Popular Culture and Popular Movements in Reformation Germany*
(Hambledon Press: London, 1987), pp. 243–56.

[7] Peter Blickle, *Communal Reformation: The Quest for Salvation in
Sixteenth Century Germany*. Tr. Thomas Dunlap. *Studies in German Histories*
(Humanities Press: Atlantic Highlands, N.J., 1992); Rosi Fuhrmann,
'Dorfgemeinde und Pfründstiftung vor der Reformation. Kommunale
Selbstbestimmungschancen zwischen Religion und Recht', in Peter Blickle
and Johannes Kirnisch (eds.), *Kommunalisierung und Christianisierung.
Voraussetzungen und Folgen der Reformation 1400–1600* (Zeitschrift für
Historische Forschung, Beiheft 9; Berlin, 1989), pp. 77–112.

[8] Werner O. Packull, *Hutterite Beginnings. Communitarian Experiments
during the Reformation* (Johns Hopkins University Press: Baltimore and
London, 1995).

people's hearts? It was a century whose intellectuals idolised Cicero, drooled over Jerome, savoured Aesop's fables, read Quintilian avidly and enviously. Above all, one which was almost literally enchanted, spell-bound, by the lyricism of the Psalms, by the abrasiveness of the prophets, by the dialectic and rhetoric of Paul. In what way did such influences mould the form in which the new teachings were expressed? It has become a cliché that the Biblical message leapt fresh from vernacular pages, and was interwoven into everything from personal piety to domestic arrangements, to the reimagining of society. Equally importantly, however, contemporary issues were read back into Biblical space. Lay people, women, and the marginalised, as well as scholars and preachers made new connections between Old Testament and New, past, present and future, God and the human condition. They learned to 'read' their societies, as well as their Bibles, differently. We may be tempted sometimes to talk largely about the replacement of the *via dialectica* by the *via rhetorica*, of philosophy by the literary imagination, of scholasticism by humanism, and there is much truth to such observations. But the reality is far more complex. National sentiments, for example, shift not only cultural loyalties, but ultimate religious ones. An early pamphlet of Eberlin von Günzburg quite ingenuously assumed that Germany, not Italy or Palestine, was the heartland of Christianity.[9] Müntzer expected illumination to begin in Prague, and so on. We may have to examine much more closely what is meant by 'doing theology', ask where the resources were coming from, what the catalysts and restraints were, and begin to try to document the interplay of text and context.

To exemplify the dynamic thrust of polemic in galvanising public opinion and propagating reform programmes two

---

[9]   *Das hertz der christenhait; Ein klägliche Klag an den christlichen Römischen Kaiser Carolum . . . Der erst bundtsgnoß*, n.p., n.d. (Fiche 232/ 648) Ai.

writings have been chosen, Luther's famous 1520 writing on the sacraments, and that of his colleague Karlstadt on the adoration of images.

The Babylonian Captivity

In 1517 Luther's ninety-five theses had raised acute questions about the sacrament of penance, and about the authority of the Church. The *Appeal to the German Nobility* of 1520, as we have seen, went beyond such questions. It yoked a fairly traditional list of Gravamina, or complaints about abuses, with a new model for the Church, based on Pauline categories, especially those of the Body of Christ. The Church as institution, surrounded by its walls of privilege, was contrasted with a vision of the Church as the diverse, interactive community of the baptised, served by the priesthood of all believers. It ended with the promise that Luther would sing another song against Rome. This was to be the new *Prelude on the Babylonian Captivity of the Church*. The *Babylonian Captivity* harnesses these two concerns: to rethink penance and to recover the true vocation of the laity, but the context in which it sets them is a critique of the sacramental theory and practice of the late medieval Church. Its extraordinary radicality was illustrated by the fact that it was Luther's bitter opponent, Thomas Murner, who first translated it from Latin into German. He was convinced that as soon as people realised what Luther's views on the sacraments were they would reject them.

One theme dominated the whole writing. A theology of the Word replaced a theology of sacramental efficacy, or rather the power of the sacrament was that of the Word. This was to have far-reaching consequences for the role of the clergy, now envisaged primarily as preachers rather than priests, servants not lords. It also fundamentally altered the understanding of worship, and of the nature of the Church, the people of God. The truth question, for Luther, was also a power question, and he made this point with drastic, apocalyptic boldness. When the Church forgot that it only remained Church when it was under the Word, under its Lord, it became the synagogue of Satan.[10] Grace was not to be seen as being channelled through an institution for salvation, but the promises of God were grasped by the faith of the believer in the dominical signs of water, bread and wine. As Brady says, 'Luther's attack on this sacramental view of the church may well have constituted his most powerful contribution to the urban reformation; it was certainly his major contribution to overcoming late medieval anticlericalism.'[11]

In this writing Luther never lets the opponents determine the ground. They had been sniping at his views on administering the communion in both kinds. Early on in the writing, which is something of a *Forschungsbericht* on the current state of controversy, Luther toys with opponents such as Alfeld, running rings round them in terms of logic, showing how they contradict themselves, at one moment claiming that Christ said the laity should only have the bread, at another point that Christ's lack of injunctions on the issue meant he left it to the discretion of the Church.[12] For all the preliminary jousting, however, an underlying fury at what he sees as the arbitrary exegesis of John 6 and 1 Corinthians 11 keeps breaking through.

The humanist in Luther is very evident, as when he insists that the closer we return to the apostolic practice the better, and is contemptuous of the *nova grammatica* of his scholastic opponents, who seek to equate the dictates of the Church with those of Christ, calling them the *infallible foundation*. Luther drives a wedge where it was assumed no wedge could be driven: between the 'judgement of the Church, and the command of

[10]   *O principes, non catholicarum Ecclesiarum, sed Satanicarum synagogarum* . . . W 6, 565/28f.
[11]   Thomas Brady, 'You Hate Us Priests', in Peter A. Dykema and Heiko A. Obermann (eds.), *Anticlericalism in Late Medieval and Early Modern Europe*, Studies in Medieval and Reformation Thought, Vol. 51 (Brill: Leiden, 1993), p. 204.
[12]   W 6, 498f.

Christ'.[13] Again and again, he deploys the plumb-line of Scripture against the crumbling edifice of the hierarchy of the Church.

As so often, he emphasises his point by taking it to its logical or extreme conclusion: if we can play around with Scripture, and remove one institution of Christ, such as the celebration of the Lord's Supper in both kinds, we can remove all of them, whenever it suits us. The spare, punchy parallelism of the Latin, *si unam . . . iam universas . . .* sums up this argument in a few eminently memorisable words.[14] It is also engaging writing, interactive as always with Luther, anticipating the objections of the reader, bombarding opponents and supporters alike with questions; deeply personal, ringing the changes from logical or factual argument to emotional outbursts of despair or imprecation or prayer, appealing to Fathers such as Cyprian and Augustine, and to the history of the Church as a whole, wielding at times a sarcastic club at the 'unbelievable wisdom' of his opponents.

In some ways it is a re-run of the *Appeal to the German Nobility*. There is a brilliant central symbol, this time that of a Church in shackles, under tyranny, captive in far-off Babylon, having lost its freedom to know, to be, to serve God and humanity. This tyranny, which is repeatedly contrasted with the glory of Christian liberty,[15] is exercised by the Pope as the King of Babylon, or is it as Nimrod, the ruthless hunter from Babel?[16] In a daring use of the first person, Luther declares, as if he had just stridden down from Sinai: 'I say, therefore, that neither the Pope nor the Bishop nor any human, has the right to decide a single syllable for Christians without their consent.'[17]

---

[13] W 6, 499/18f.
[14] W 6, 503/13f.
[15] W 6, 535/27f.
[16] W 6, 498/5f.
[17] W 6, 536/6–8.

One notes the triple negative, which of course adds force to the declamation. One notes also the sharp contrast between tyranny and liberty, which is only one of the countless polarities which litter the writing: faith and works, articles of faith and mere human opinions, servants of and lords over the Word, clear Scriptural statements and figments, dreams, or fantasies, Christ's liberation and the reign of Babylon and the true Antichrist.[18] As in the wood-cuts and broadsheets of the day, the reader is confronted with an awesomely clear choice.

Corresponding to the three walls in the *Appeal to the Christian Nobility*, the central image of enslavement is spelt out in terms of the three successive captivities in the order of their seriousness: communion in one kind only, which separates off laity from clergy; the insistence, as a matter of faith, on the mere theory of transubstantiation, which binds faith to philosophy; and most ominous of all, making the Lord's Supper, Christ's gratuitous last will and testament, a work and a sacrifice, which only the priest can offer. These are demolished, one after another, by the application of the Scriptural principle.

Luther abruptly and starkly terminates his 'playing' of the small fish such as Alfeld by a staggering pronouncement which reduces the traditional seven sacraments of the Church to two, or at best three. A genially simple reconception of the sacraments justifies this. A sacrament is a divine promise, to which we have to respond in faith, bodied out in a sign which Christ has instituted. Together with the master image of captivity, and the apocalyptic contrasts already referred to, one of the greatest strengths of the writing is its countless aphorisms, brief, pithy definitions, or rather redefinitions, of faith, of Church and ministry and sacraments. The Church is the people of God, pastors are the servants of the Word, sacraments are dominical signs of God's grace received in faith. These definitions all mesh into one another. Often introduced by a

---

[18]   W 6, 537/24f.

poignant personal, subjective reference: 'As I have said', they claim Scriptural attestation, and are masterpieces of concision and clarity. The Mass, for example, is described as the gift of the divine promise, set forth (*exhibitum*) to all humanity through the hand of the priests.[19] These interlaced definitions effectively restructure the whole of ecclesial reality for the reader.

At a stroke they sweep away the sacraments of confirmation, marriage, ordination and extreme unction. These rites of passage, of incalculable importance for life's transitions, had evolved, of course, for excellent reasons. But because they were not Biblically based, Luther dismissed their claim to be sacraments. He was not unaware of the apparently Promethean elements in a programme which, as he clearly saw, recast the whole face of the Church. But in a good humanist phrase that may echo Reuchlin, he insists that truth is stronger than anything; *fortior omnium est veritas*.[20] Moreover, for pastoral reasons he could not stay silent, being accountable before God to warn the Church against error. He would be personally responsible before God for the souls of those to whom he did not communicate the light and truth he had so freely received. He sums up his confidence in the intimate personal testimony: *Christus meus vivit*, 'My Christ liveth'. The reader is drawn into Luther's own experience of grace, which is to be universalised.[21]

In this writing, then, Luther virtually reinvents Baptism and the Eucharist. Baptism refocused on death and resurrection, on drowning, *submersio*, and ascension, *emersio*.[22] It is portrayed in graphic terms not as one rite at the beginning of life, but as the constitutive reality of all Christian existence. Faith is seen as constantly looking back to God's initiative in Baptism. The adult constantly reflects on her or his infant helplessness. God's

[19] W 6, 523/3–5.
[20] W 6, 522/3.
[21] W 6, 512/20–5.
[22] W 6, 533/1f.

grace at the beginning is followed by our response to it in ever more conscious faith. We are, as he says succinctly, continually being baptised more and more.[23] Here is the basis for the priest-hood of all believers. Baptism, as it were, gobbles up ordination, renders penance redundant. A quite new paradigm for salvation opens up.

Post-baptismal sin no longer cancels out the grace of Baptism. Sin is not viewed quantitatively at all, as something committed in an episodic way. Sin is the condition of all human being. It is another way of describing our humanity. As long as we live, we will be dying and rising again, not only spiritually but physically, until when we finally shed life, we come to the Father and eternal life.[24] Baptism means God has adopted us unconditionally. All we need to do is to trust, to have *fiducia*, confidence, to hold, grasp on to the promise that is attested by our initial baptism. By it our whole life has resurrection quality.

The polemic in the writing is successful precisely because the positive, alternative vision of Christian life is so attractively presented. Christology drives the ecclesiology. Just as Baptism looks to the resurrection so the Eucharist is focused on the incarnation. Luther's immense seriousness about the earthiness of God, the fleshliness of Christ, the reality of the body and blood of the Lord, is dramatically conveyed. His deep reverence for the real presence of Christ in the sacrament of the Eucharist is something, of course, that he carries over from his monastic and priestly past. But it is a reverence that cannot be locked into philosophical speculations, that are forced upon a laity which cannot possibly understand them. This is a *nova impositio verborum*, a new coercive terminology. All we need to do is simply abide by the words of Christ, *verbis eius simpliciter inhaerens*.[25] True faith is simple. We have to accept the relentless mystery of the sacrament and not try to explain it away. It is

[23]   W 6, 535/15.
[24]   W 6, 534/38f.
[25]   W 6, 511/19f.

no heresy to believe bread and wine are still there, and that yet, by the power of the words of institution, Christ is truly present.[26] The Holy Spirit is greater than Aristotle, than all philosophy.[27]

So he turns, in intimate confidence, to *Christus meus*, to the simple words of institution, which are spelt out in dramatic terms as the testamentum, the last will or covenant Christ made just before his death. This, not Alfeld's reliance on the authority of the Church, is our infallible foundation. Christ left nothing behind but his will, his promise. Just as in the Old Testament God promises Israel the Land, so in the New Testament the forgiveness of sin is promised. This liberation is the good news exhibited by the Mass.[28]

The Mass certainly is a good work, but far from being of our doing, it is the good work of Christ. By this good work we become the new humanity, *novus homo*. Significantly, the lyrical passage in which our incorporation in Christ is so movingly described is almost immediately followed by one of his fiercest polemical utterances: there is no doubt that the false understanding of the sacrament as our work makes every priest an idolator![29] The polemic flows naturally out of the indignation at the obscuring and denial of the central wonder of our faith. It is the inversion of reality which outrages him, that we imagine, with unheard-of perversity, that the Mass is something we offer to God. So all the holding of Masses on behalf of others and the dead is revealed as a sad misunderstanding.[30] All we have to do is to listen, not act. To the practices of centuries we have to oppose the words and example of Christ. Rhetorically, in one sharp contrast after another, Luther sets out the polemical relation of the divine Word, *Adversarius noster*, to mere ecclesiastical realities.

[26] W 6, 508/27–31.
[27] *Maior est spiritussanctus quam Aristoteles*; W 6, 511/26.
[28] W 6, 513f.
[29] W 6, 515/33; 517/4–7.
[30] W 6, 520f.

The small print follows. There is no harm in ceremonies. Luther is no purist or primitivist. Nor does he urge rash, irredentist action. He is instructing the conscience of the believer. As he sums it up in one of his most striking aphorisms: 'Faith alone gives peace to the conscience.' His concern is to restore the simple heart of eucharistic faith, and in this writing he never tires of repeating the term 'simplicity' and its cognates.[31]

One clue to the success of this writing is that the intimacy of Luther's relation with 'his' Christ is conveyed to the reader. For all its wealth and precision of theological reflection Luther drives again and again to the core of the issue, and shares his simple, intimate faith with the reader. His own utter confidence and joy lends dynamic quality to the whole writing. Its intellectual credibility is undergirded by a personal credibility. No issues are fudged. No personal, or tactical, or prudential considerations are allowed to inhibit the radicality of the thought. No reader can be in doubt exactly what is meant. The readers would have been swept along by the affirmations, and found themselves nodding in agreement as they flowed imperceptibly into denunciation.

The shock with which contemporaries received this writing has already been referred to. The fearlessness of Luther's thought is staggering, but was such drastic polemic really necessary? One suspects that it may well have been. Much of our normal courtesies, after all, simply hides sloppiness of thought. Most of us have 'scissors in our head'. We censor our own thinking because we are apprehensive about how provocative and offensive it will sound. But the charm of Luther's polemic is that he writes without regard to what is acceptable, digestible, communicable, expedient or safe. Paradigm shifts in thought demand a certain relentlessness, and moralising or psychologising calls for more humility may miss the point. As the small print of his writing indicates, he meant to leave ample room for discussion about the modalities of reform.

[31]   W 6, 527/1.

If, like most of us, most of the time, Luther had permitted a sense of what was acceptable, 'communicable', to colour his thinking, if the presentation of his ideas had been permitted to influence their formation, he would not have achieved the same directness and clarity. How could the prophetic 'edge' of his insights have been brought to bear if it had been blunted by courtesy, respect and moderation? As it is, his formulations allow us to trace his innermost thought. By bracketing out all considerations of personality and practicality, blinkering himself to the hurt feelings of those loyal to the old ways, his theological critique is given free rein. Gradualism, in the end of the day, is not a tactic, it is a relationship to reality. We do not even allow ourselves to formulate thoughts if we are afraid how they may be received.

The uncompromising nature of this polemic reflects the distance Luther saw between Christ's last will and testament and the empirical development of the Church, between loyal exegesis of God's Word and current sacramental practice. The unforgiving quality of his polemic was necessitated by the seriousness and fatal consequences of the errors he confronted, part of what he perceived as a much larger cosmic struggle. Luther therefore thinks the unthinkable, and pursues the thread of his logic to the bitter end. His polemic, though never free from personal abuse, rises above considerations of persons and focuses on the matter in hand. Luther's God had a polemical relationship to all human realities, and how could the sword of the Spirit heal except by striking?

Karlstadt on Images

Another of the most dramatic examples of the power of the spoken and written word is afforded by the polemic against images. How on earth did some Reformers succeed in persuading people to abandon, as it were overnight, their beloved talismans and icons of holiness, the most hallowed of personal pieties? Who of us, today, scanning the scattered remnants of late-medieval art, carving, sculpture, stained-glass, weaving, can fail to be moved by them? How can we begin to explain how a new religious view was successful in convincing people to discard, even destroy them?

In 1522 Luther's colleague, Andreas Karlstadt, often seen as something of an academic clodhopper, wrote, in vernacular and lively German, his tract, *Von Abtuhung der Bilder*, *On the Abolition of Images*. We will use it as a vignette to exemplify the way in which the pamphlet represented a new form of polemic. It was, of course, a very topical mode of writing, reacting on the run, as it were, to some immediate provocation or incident. Guchmann emphasises its *Aktualität und Zeitgebundenheit*, its immediacy and time-conditioned character.[32]

Clearly its strengths lie partly in the intrinsic merits of its argumentation, which centred on the superiority of the Word, and the things of the Spirit, to the material and the fleshly. Here, however, our primary concern will be to examine the form, style and language of its polemic.

First of all, and very strikingly, the writing is a *conversation* poured into literary form. It is nothing if not dialogue. The second person singular dominates. From beginning to end the reader is addressed personally by a very persistent Karlstadt with a flood of exhortations and imperatives: 'Listen to this, now'; 'Learn this'; 'Now look'; 'See here'; 'Just take this in'; 'You have to admit'.[33] Sometimes it is opponents, dead or alive,

---

[32]   M. H. Guchmann, *Die Sprache der deutschen politischen Literatur in der Zeit der Reformation und des Bauernkrieges* (Akademischer Verlag: Berlin, 1974), p. 38.

[33]   Andreas Karlstadt, *Von Abtuhung der Bilder* (Kleine Texte für theologische und philologische Vorlesungen und Übungen 74; ed. H. Lietzmann; Bonn, 1911; hereafter VAB): *Nhu hore* – 5/17; *Das lerne* – 6/30; *Sih wie* – 7/24,5; 9/34; 14/11; *sih und mercke wol* – 13/8; *Nymb war* – 12/28; *Jetzo solstu endlich auch das eyn nhemen* – 10/10; *Du must mir auch tzugeben* – 14/6; *Endlich du must tzugeben* – 22/11; *sag mir* – 14/14; *ich frage dich* – 11/18f.

who are addressed: 'See here, you idolatrous un-Christian fellow
. . .'. 'Do tell us, dear Gregory . . .',[34] Karlstadt ironically
implores, drawing the reader onto his side over against Pope
Gregory. The issue is at once personalised. The reader is drawn
into this argument: Is one for Karlstadt or for Gregory?

Reader involvement is also ensured by volleys of *questions*,
sometimes as many as seven together, which are addressed to
the reader.[35] 'Why have we had [the images of the saints]
painted and coloured with velvet? With damask? With silver?
With golden clothes? Why do we hang them with golden
crowns? With precious stones? And accord them reverence and
love which we are reluctant to give to our children, wives,
parents, rulers, princes, and lords?' Sometimes the questions
are rhetorical,[36] but more often they are pointed, or ironic,
designed to draw out doubts, to raise eyebrows, to bore
surgically into accepted ways of thinking.[37]

Objections by the reader are anticipated – 'Maybe someone
will say: "But I don't worship the images"'[38] – only to be refuted
and the objection swept aside. Any tendency to side-step
the issue with fancy glosses or to minimise its importance is
rejected.[39] 'Try to help yourself, to cover yourself up, to crawl
away into a hidey-hole, to put the best gloss on your
action that you can, you'll still not escape from divine

[34] VAB, 12/12; 9/2; 'Note this, you saint-eaters!' 13/12.

[35] VAB, 5/1ff. et passim.

[36] Do you think [Jesus] would now give us a different teaching, one
contrary to that which he gave us in his life?' VAB, 13/29.

[37] How dare you be as bold as brass, bowing and scraping before an
image in my house?' VAB, 5/32–4; 'Isn't that a fine Papist teaching,
now?' 8/32; 'Don't you know that Paul says that those who do such
things will forfeit their salvation?' 10/3; 'Now I'm going to ask you a few
more questions . . .' 8/6.

[38] VAB, 7/29; 'No excuse or pretext will help you, though you say a
thousand times: "I don't revere these saints for their own sake . . ."' 18/31;
cf. also 21/15f., 32ff.

[39] *Glossiers wie du kanst*; VAB, 7/32.

judgement. . . .'[40] All the defenders of images use the same blocking technique: 'They just don't want to hear that we treat [images] as gods.'[41]

There is a relentless quality to the amassing of arguments and precedents; the words 'likewise' (*Item*) or 'moreover' (*ferner*) occur again and again. 'Now I'll go on to demonstrate . . .', says Karlstadt untiringly.[42] The arguments are taken from Scripture, especially the Old Testament Law,[43] whose clear and valid message is emphasised by Karlstadt,[44] and from the Fathers[45] and other 'unquestionably Christian writings'.[46] The points are stated clearly and simply, in non-technical language, and sometimes numbered: firstly, secondly, thirdly. . . .[47] It is asserted that it is not Karlstadt who is speaking, but Scripture,[48] and that the latter's message is quite clear, although the devious Papists frequently do violence to it *durch yre behendigkeit*, making white into black, good into bad.[49] In a period in which there was a crisis of belief the unchallenged authority of God's own revelation in Scripture was a trump card to be played for all it was worth. Frequently, however, Karlstadt does feel it necessary to explain exactly how Scripture applies to the contemporary situation.[50] Habakkuk's woes upon those who

---

[40]   VAB, 18/36ff.

[41]   VAB, 17/29.

[42]   *Nhu wil ich beweißen . . .* ; VAB, 7/37; cf. 12/24f.; 18/15.

[43]   Above all, of course, the second of the Ten Commandments; VAB, 4/21f.

[44]   The last two pages of the tract refute the idea that the Gospel supercedes the Law by a string of sarcastic questions: 'Why don't you go on to say: "We want to condone adultery, theft, murder and such-like . . . because they are forbidden by the old Law?"' VAB, 22/1ff.

[45]   VAB, 11/3ff.

[46]   *auß gottlicher und unbetryglicher schriffte genhummen*; VAB, 4/7.

[47]   VAB, 10/10ff., for example.

[48]   *sol keyner von mir/ sonder aus der schrifft lernen*; VAB, 6/26f.

[49]   VAB, 7/27f.

[50]   He quotes Ezekiel 6 and 16 and applies it to the veneration of images, for example; VAB, 17/28ff.; cf. 18/17ff.

tell a piece of wood to wake up refers to those in the present age who venerate images.[51] Interestingly, there is also a reference to the Jewish understanding of the Scriptures. How, Karlstadt asks, are the Jews' legitimate questions about the veneration of saints to be answered?[52]

Then at the end of a chain of arguments will come the clinching phrase: 'Therefore it follows that. . .'.[53] The reader has been hooked and caught, and is soon to be landed. One senses throughout the seriousness of the whole exercise. Salvation itself is at stake.

Yet why does the fish take the lure? Partly at least because the language is seductive. In Karlstadt's prose nouns, verbs, adjectives seldom occur alone, they almost always march in twos,[54] and sometimes in long, jingling columns, one after the other. Ritual processions are aped by the verbal ones; '. . . they bring to the images precious incense, bread, wine, beer, hens, geese, and horses. Yes, and their children too, and their sick friends . . .'.[55] 'You present waxen offerings in the shape of your sick leg, arm, eyes, head, feet, hands, cows, calves, oxen, sheep, house, yard, fields, meadows . . .'.[56] Chains of verbs, adjectives, adverbs are also frequent.[57] Alliteration is never far away: *kun und keck* (bold as brass); *betrügliche bilder* (deceiving images); *Witwen/Weßen* (widows and orphans).[58]

In other words, the imagination as well as the mind of the reader is addressed. Neologisms hint that matters are so urgent and shocking that language has reached its limit and new terms

---

[51] *Das ist bald gesagt wan du andacht tzu eynem holtz hast*; VAB, 10/28f.

[52] VAB, 5/29f.; an issue Thomas Müntzer also raised frequently.

[53] *Drumb ists . . .* ; iVAB, 4/25; *volget/das . . .* 5 /10; *Alßo . . .* 6/3.

[54] Countless examples include: *anbeter und breysser; pflicht und bewegnis; buleten und bubten; verderben . . . und verdammen* (note alliteration); VAB, 4/30; 17/23; 15/5.

[55] VAB, 18/10ff.

[56] VAB, 5/36ff.; cf. also 3/18f., 5/5, 6/17 and countless other examples.

[57] VAB, 4/25,27; 9/11ff.

[58] VAB, 5/32; 9/12; 12/31; 3/27.

have to be coined.[59] Dramatic, offensive, surprising collocations of terms such as 'created god' make the same drastic point.[60] The upside-down world of corrupt practice has to be reflected in the language.

It is indeed ironic that in a writing which is directed so massively against the misuse of material images, there is a curious naivety about the way in which verbal images, similes, and metaphors are used to create vivid visualisations which provoke pity, derision, disgust, outrage and anger.[61] Traditional piety, for example, because of its monetary aspects, is described as a flea-market, a *grempell marckt*.[62] Towards the climax of the writing the sexual theme becomes prominent; the image-worshipper is described as a whore, the Church as a brothel.[63] The technique of association is frequent: the Pope is associated with the devil, the priests' teachings with the plague.[64]

There is a tendency, also, to take everything to its logical limit, to drive matters to extremes, and then to encapsulate this in a vivid analogy or metaphor. Images of the saints, for example, are characterised as violent. They choke and violate us, or kill our spirit, while they insult and denigrate God. A Church with images is a den of murderers.[65] Likewise the image

[59]   E.g. *bildpreißer* (image-praiser); *olgotzischer preyßer* (idol praiser); *heylig fresser* (saint-eater); *Olgeck* (holy-oil fool); *Olfratzen* (holy-oil mask); *bildekusser* (image-kisser); VAB, 10/16; 15/2; 13/13; 13/21; 19/11; 21/15.

[60]   VAB, 6/24; similarly 'godless Pope' 17/34; 'heretical sermon' 21/17; on a different note cf. 'evangelical Prophets' for Isaiah and Jeremiah, 22/7.

[61]   Pity, for example, for the terminally ill, *wan sie yn tods stricke tzappeln*, who are given a crucifix instead of the word of salvation; or for the poor who waste their scarce money on trinkets; VAB, 10/29ff.; 11/36f.; disgust at the thought of someone lying or standing on the altar; 8/13; anger at the affront to God's House; 6/21f.

[62]   VAB, 9/22; this is a very common topos of pamphlet literature, both in North and South Germany.

[63]   VAB, 18/2ff., 33; the godless fondle the images, like whores their lovers; 17/19f.; they are the Devil's whores; 18/6; 18/15.

[64]   VAB, 8/32f.; 20/1.

[65]   VAB, 4/29; 5/12ff.

is vividly described as a 'painted devil'.[66] People are said to flock to idols as birds of prey are drawn to a corpse.[67] One has to linger over such images to appreciate their full force.

Pope Gregory VII's description of images as 'books for the laity' was a widespread topos in late-medieval literature and art. For Karlstadt this was to imply that lay people should be fobbed off with outward, external things, to remain in bondage to the devil, indeed to be excluded from discipleship altogether. For it is the truth alone which sets one free.[68] Interestingly, for Karlstadt, the book does not appear to be seen as an external thing. Clearly there is a close connection between Karlstadt the advocate of books and education for lay people and Karlstadt the opponent of images. This has sometimes been characterised as the shift from a visual culture to a verbal one. There is much truth in this, yet, as we have seen, such a statement is much too simplistic. Elizabeth Eisenstein has pointed out that the 'cultural metamorphosis produced by printing was really much more complicated than any single formula can possibly express'.[69] We are talking, rather, about a fundamental shift in imaginative paradigms.

As the writing proceeds, the emotional tone is continually raised, partly by the adjectives describing images as 'mad, foolish, harmful, dangerous, treacherous, deceptive, and devilish'. Now and then Karlstadt bursts out with an ejaculation: 'O how ill will it be for those . . . !' Or again, 'Dear brothers, God preserve you from this heretical

[66]   *eyn gemalter teuffel*; i.e. a creature of fantasy; VAB, 19/26; this again is a quite common topos; the German *gemalt* renders the Latin *fucatus*, used in humanist polemic to describe a purely cosmetic, or superficial, reality.

[67]   VAB, 6/13ff.

[68]   VAB, 9/27ff.

[69]   Elizabeth Eisenstein, *The Printing Press as an Agent of Change: Communications and Cultural Transformations in Early Modern Europe* (Cambridge University Press: Cambridge, 1979), Vol. 1, p. 67; cf. Bob Scribner, 'Popular Piety and Modes of Visual Perception in Late Medieval and Reformation Germany', *The Journal of Religious History*, 15.4 (1989), pp. 448–69.

utterance . . .'.[70] But perhaps the most striking feature of such polemic is its dualism. The world is divided between true worshippers and idolatrous non-Christians.[71] God and the devil confront one another. Everything is seen in terms of black and white, of extremes, of the sharpest of contrasts. Moses forbids the adoration of images; Gregory VII commends it.[72] God is faithful, while Israel constantly rebels.[73] The language continually rams home the message that the reader has to make a radical choice between the things of the Spirit and the things of the flesh,[74] between outward appearances and inner reality or power;[75] between pretence and authentic truth; between mere images, *Bilder*, which seduce, and books, *Bücher*, which instruct (note the alliteration in the German!);[76] between the authority of the Pope and that of God;[77] between Scripture and the devil, decked out in human customs and authority.[78]

The ultimate dualism is that of the transcendence of God and the materiality of images, which are but stick and stone, are deaf, dumb and blind; they can neither teach nor learn; are flesh, and nothing but flesh.[79] God alone, *gott allein*, is to be obeyed, heard, honoured, worshipped.[80] Images are alien gods,

[70]   VAB, 14/28; 21/17.

[71]   *du abgottyscher unchrist*; VAB, 12/12.

[72]   The parallelism is sharp: 'Moses declares: "You should teach your children God's Word from their youth up." But Gregory declares: "The laity should use pictures instead of books."' VAB, 9, 1ff.

[73]   VAB, 6/3ff.; cf. 15/25f.

[74]   The contrast of *fleisch* and *geist* is perhaps the most foundational in the whole writing; VAB, 9/5ff.

[75]   Those who support images cannot get beyond the *how* (*wie*) of the crucifixion: the body of Christ, his wounds, his beard even; but they completely fail to teach about the *why* (*warumb*) – his power; VAB, 10/16ff.

[76]   VAB, 17/11ff.

[77]   VAB, 8/30ff.; 11/17f.

[78]   VAB, 12/7f.; 19/38–20/3.

[79]   VAB, 9/11ff.; again much alliteration here!

[80]   VAB, 4/27; 5/25ff. – the word *allein* occurs three times.

and God, who is jealous, hates them.[81] We cannot worship both. We cannot set a creature side by side with God.[82] One's sole comfort is in the Word of God.[83] God's exclusive claim on us is thus closely related to the saving power of the Word, of speech, of the very mouth of God – *gotis mund*.[84]

The advocates of images are made to look absurd and stupid: for they take a lump of wood, chop off a bit to cook their meat, and then fashion the remainder into a god and fall down and worship it.[85] 'They seek help, advice and health from brainless fools.'[86] They end up by becoming what they revere – a hateful abomination in God's eyes.[87]

The apodictic note is unmistakeable. Karlstadt does use Scripture for proof texts, to quote Solomon or the prophets, or to give examples, like King Josiah, of true worship.[88] Generally, however, Scripture comes alive as the direct colloquy – or is it polemic? – of God with the reader. The Ten Commandments are cited as the very mouth of God speaking to us.[89] God addresses a string of questions to priest or lay person: 'How can you be so audacious as to let images and idols stand in my house?'[90] Karlstadt speaks, as it were, for God.[91] He has the 'infallible testimony' of the Holy Spirit.[92] His prose, drenched in Scripture, reads at times like a litany.

---

[81] VAB, 11/18.
[82] VAB, 13/9f.
[83] VAB, 10/36f.
[84] VAB, 15/25.
[85] VAB, 13/1ff.
[86] VAB, 6/20f.; 'bowing and scraping' before them; 7/39, 12/33f.
[87] VAB, 5/8ff.
[88] E.g. VAB, 19/2; 'Learn this by an example', that of the Exodus; 6/30ff.; the example of Peter, when mistaken for a god; 13/23ff.; King Josiah; 20/38ff.
[89] VAB, 4/21ff.
[90] VAB, 5/31ff.
[91] VAB, 5/8; 20/4 – *Und got beklagt sich senlich und schmertzlich.*
[92] *unbetruegliche beweyßung nemlich getzeugknis des Heyligen geistes*; VAB, 20/4.

'The ox knows its master, and the plodding donkey its lord's crib, but Israel . . . does not know me.'[93]

On the heels of the testimony follows the threat. The tract is dedicated to Count Wolf Schlick of Joachimstal, and is a defence of his reform programme, but the threat applies to individuals, too. Karlstadt can be quite specific in warning private individuals.[94] If we hear God so clearly in Scripture, but fail to obey, we will have to suffer the consequences, and we will perish like the sons of Aaron.[95] The decision for or against the Reformation is a life and death affair. The argument is never allowed to remain on the theoretical plane. Again and again Karlstadt refers to the daily life and experience of the reader. One example after another is used to ram home the message. These can be quite vivid and homely ones from daily life.[96]

As the little tract moves towards its end there is a shift from argument to emotional appeal; the surge of anger is based on God's own abhorrence of images, and with it comes an urgent call to action. For God is a God who speaks and expects to be obeyed.[97] The eyes of all the world are upon the Germans.[98] A reformation, a genuine Christian order, is urgently needed.[99] Repetitions hammer home the main points.[100] Final hesitations are dealt with, and then the reader is provided with simple arguments to refute the objections.[101] In a passage of con-

---

[93]   VAB, 6/9f.

[94]   VAB, 18/3ff.

[95]   VAB, 15/25ff., 36; 20/27.

[96]   The popular rhymes recited to the traveller's saint, Christophorus, for example: *Christoffore sancte virtutes sunt tibi tante/ qui te mane videt de nocte ridet oder vivet.* VAB, 13/36ff.

[97]   VAB, 20/12ff.

[98]   VAB, 4/3.

[99]   *eyn nottliche reformation; warhafftige und Christliche ordenung*; VAB, 3/14; 4/1.

[100]   From p. 14 (C1) onwards, about two-thirds of his way through the pamphlet, Karlstadt repeats his main points.

[101]   VAB, 16/9, 11.

siderable psychological empathy Karlstadt confesses his own
nervousness, indeed fear, when he contemplates abolishing
images. Reverence and fear of images, after all, he says, are one
and the same thing. Having been brought up from his youth
to fear them Karlstadt knows 'how deeply and firmly embedded
in my heart images are'.[102] The real images are in our hearts.[103]
The more we fear them, he says in language reminiscent of
Luther, the smaller is our God.[104] In this way he shows his
solidarity with the reader's own fears, and emphasises that only
God's grace can help us.

But action is now required. The language becomes cruder
and even violent, mirroring the need to destroy, knock down,
burn the images.[105] Karlstadt admits that he has become 'crude
and stupid', *grob und unnutz,* but defends his coarseness. It is
no cause for shame, or prudishness. It is the very language of
Scripture, which likens those who adore images to whores and
their lovers, shamelessly flirting and whoring.[106]

None of us, of course, can reconstruct how a sixteenth-
century reader would react to a writing like Karlstadt's. Perhaps
enough has been said to show that they would have been caught
up in a highly realistic dialogue or conversation with a particular
person, Karlstadt, faced with situations they knew, challenged
with the alarming authority of Scripture, nudged by argument
after argument, and finally, having been excited and alarmed
by appeals to their emotions, urged to come to a costly, but
apparently inescapable decision. This dialogue with the reader
was clarified and sharpened by the polemic against the 'Papists'.
Karlstadt cleverly draws the laity onto his side. They stand to
benefit by his anti-clericalism. Without the sharp demarcations
he has drawn for them between truth and error, the spiritual

---

[102]   VAB, 19/32f.
[103]   VAB, 19/3f.
[104]   *got bey mir ßo klein ist alß gros mein forcht ist gegen den Olfratzen;*
VAB, 19/10f.
[105]   VAB, 20/16.
[106]   VAB, 17/20ff.

and the material, God and the Pope, the choice before them would not have been so clear. In the past they had been exploited and misled by being fobbed off with mere images; now they, the laity, were being offered teaching, not Karlstadt's but that of Scripture, of God, of the Holy Spirit.[107]

The pamphlets of the Reformation function, then, not unlike the 'anxious bench' of the nineteenth-century American revivalists. They put their readers under enormous pressure to listen intensely to a chain of argument, to a succession of images, to work their way through, in a very short time, the whole gamut of emotions. All these experiences are presented by and focused in and through a particular person, who comes right into their minds and hearts and lives and asks them to review their most cherished beliefs and customs. Karlstadt becomes priest and confessor for his readers, as they engage on their own inner dialogue and prepare to make their difficult decisions. It is an intensely personal 'sharing' at an individual and group level, and the term 'propaganda' is not helpful to describe it.

The sermon, of course, was the normal locus for this process. 'The voice is the soul of the word', as Luther said.[108] The pamphlet or book lacked the personal presence and charisma of the preacher. All the more necessary, therefore, to perfect its array of weapons. It had, however, the advantage that it could be read and re-read – often within a group. One can imagine the spirited interruptions and discussion which would follow. Polemic promoting dialogue! Dialogue prompting further polemic or even collapsing into abuse.

It is worth thinking about other analogous situations in the sixteenth century, in which people reviewed their past lives, saw them in a new light, and were given the will and the resources to change them. The later *Spiritual Exercises* of Loyola, for example, given to people facing a turning point in their

---

[107]   *sol keyner von mir sonder auß der schrifft lernen*; VAB, 6/27.
[108]   *cum vox sit anima verbi*; W 5, 379/6f.

lives, were not too dissimilar, but had the incalculable advantage of a guide and mentor at hand. What evidence have we of books and pamphlets being used in this way, too? How specific were the expectations of reformers about the way in which their books would change people's lives, not just their opinions on this or that? Do we know how they imagined this would happen, and how intentional they were in structuring their books and tracts with this end in view?

CHAPTER SEVEN

THE DOWN-SIDE OF POLEMIC

They make their tongue sharp as a snake's,
and under their lips is the venom of vipers.

Psalm 140:3

There is a curious ambivalence about Biblical attitudes to polemic. They portray the evildoer's tongue as being sharp as a snake, and yet the same psalmist who condemns it lashes out at his enemies in terms equally trenchant. Psalmist, prophet and apostle regularly cut down their opponents. To prepare him for his prophetic calling Isaiah's mouth was honed like a sharp sword, a polished arrow.[1] The line between incisiveness and destructiveness would appear to be a fine one. This is especially the case when one sees one's own rage as a channel for God's righteous wrath. In an illuminating passage towards the end of the *Appeal to the German Nobility* Luther admits that his attacks have been too swingeing and that they will alienate many. He would prefer, however, to bear the world's anger than God's.[2] Many different elements come together here. There is the fear he has had to overcome to reach this point of fearlessness: all the world can do, he knows, is end his life. There is the disdain for contemptible opponents. While he 'sings', they howl and yell. Above all, however, there is his sense of a triangular relationship between God's wrath, his duty to

---

[1] Isaiah 49:2f.
[2] *Es ist mir lieber die welt zurne mit mir/den got*; W 6, 468/35.

183

articulate it, and the way in which the world will receive it. We only have in our hands the finished product of Luther's text. The *Anfechtungen*, the despairing struggles which underlie it, which can only be imagined, have to be borne in mind.

When we turn to look at the negative features of polemic, we have, of course, to attempt to see and hear it through sixteenth-century eyes and ears. The academic and ecclesiastical worlds, still often sheltered from much of life's importunities, may be particularly ill fitted to do it justice, since they tend to abhor the drastic and the emphatic, valuing conventions of courtesy and decency which 'serve to render life bearable and light in defiance of its dark horrors'.[3] The rougher, directer world of modern cinema or theatre or novel may be much closer to the popular literature of the sixteenth century.

Moreover, much that is offensive to us today did not offend against the conventions of sixteenth-century discourse. Popular and 'genteel' culture had not yet separated out. Scatology and bestial language provide the relish in the satirical literature throughout Europe at this time. The ferocity of the personal attacks of humanists, Reformers and apologists for the Old Church takes our breath away.

Satire has always used parody, sarcasm and burlesque to nail its victims.[4] When, however, as often happens in Reformation literature, apocalyptic categories bracket the discourse, satire tends to become one-dimensional, the tension between pretence and reality can be lost, humour may become plodding and flat-footed. The ludic dimension is forfeited. What had once been entertaining, serious enough but lively, becomes

---

[3] Hans Speier, 'The Communication of Hidden Meaning', p. 296.

[4] *Eccius Dedolatus*, the ferocious humanist attack on John Eck in 1520, probably by Willibald Pirckheimer, has already been mentioned; cf. p. 156; it commutes between high culture and crude, slapstick comedy, and does not stop short of sadistic fantasies about flaying and emasculating Eck. Heavy sarcasm is interlaced with crude puns and cacology; insult is added to injury by a dismissive rejection of the crude polemic of the theologians!

'*tierischer Ernst*', deadly serious. The papacy *becomes* the devil, distortion *is* description.

It is one thing to see oneself involved in a life and death battle with Satan. It is another to identify one's opponents with the devil, for once the 'other' has been demonised there is no room for reasonable argument or careful differentiation and scant need for precise attention to detail. One notes, for example, Müntzer's carelessness about facts, not least his global accusations about Luther's soft-living, or Luther's absurd claim that Müntzer wanted to abolish Scripture and the sacraments. Large generalisations such as these are developed from one or two particular instances. Divergent voices are tuned out. Statements are not read in context. Distinctions become blurred, as for example, when Luther fails to distinguish between the pacific Karlstadt and the militarily activist Müntzer.

Such polemic rests on a reality deficit, a penchant for wild generalisations. There is an incapacity to do justice to the complex untidiness of people and situations, or perhaps an impatience with the effort required. At all events the Other is viewed through distinctly grimy lenses. In the cut and thrust of polemics the battle went to the strong. It was, as the word suggests, a form of war. The humanists had laid particular blame on the obstinacy of the theologians, with their 'old women's quarrels', their curious and obscure speculations. A new method, they knew, would be hard to introduce, given such gladiatorial proclivities.[5] The humanists themselves, of course, frequently succumbed to similar temptations, not least due to their 'skill with the quill'. Verbal polemics were bad enough, but they vanished into thin air and could be withdrawn at day's end and some attempt at reconciliation made. Committing differences to writing hardened the conflict into permanent form, while launching it into a much wider public

---

[5] Cf. Jacob Spiegel's prologue to Peter Mosellanus' oration at the Leipzig Debate of 1519 in which he speaks of their *pertinaciam, rixarum conviciorumque parentem. De Ratione disputandi, Praesertim in re Theologica, Petri Mosellani Proregensis Oratio* . . . Fiche 1534/3991; Ai^v.

arena, through the medium of print, took it a step farther still. The contenders tended to become implacable foes.

One sad example of the 'down-side' of polemic is the relatively early clash between Luther and his one-time disciple, Thomas Müntzer. Gordon Rupp made the point long ago that Luther and Müntzer were in many ways kindred spirits, but failed to recognise this.[6] Luther's theology of the cross in fact may well offer many parallels to Müntzer's emphasis on the 'bitter Christ'. Yet they became quite unable to hear what the other said, and the vitriolic controversy between them leads with sad inevitability to the desperation, massacre and disillusionment of the Peasants' War. For a long time Müntzer had appealed for Luther's understanding and support. Then he broke with him. In the end, quite correctly, he saw Luther as determined to break and destroy him.

The differing views of the two on Scripture, the relationship between Law and Gospel, issues of social justice, have often been analysed. Here we will confine ourselves to observing the negative influence of their polemic on their perception of themselves and of one another, on their attitude to supporters and to neutrals, on their world-view generally.

Siegfried Bräuer, the doyen of Müntzer scholars, has compared Luther's and Müntzer's self-understandings and analysed their attitudes to one another.[7] He argues that it is unhelpful to lose sight of the fundamental theological differences between them, and to reduce their confrontation to one of personality or psychology. This is surely correct. Yet one notes in both Luther and Müntzer the greatest difficulty

---

[6] Their controversy is 'a flagrant example of historical misunderstanding, and proof that there was no real dialogue or confrontation between the two men'. Gordon Rupp, *Patterns of Reformation* (Epworth: London, 1969), p. 282.

[7] Siegfried Bräuer, 'Selbstverständnis und Feindbild bei Martin Luther und Thomas Müntzer', in Günter Vogler, *Wegscheiden der Reformation. Alternatives Denken vom 16. bis zum 18. Jahrhundert* (H. Böhlaus Nachfolger: Weimar, 1994), pp. 57–84.

in separating issues from personalities. Each identifies the opponent with a particular place, Allstedt or Wittenberg, as well as with particular views. Both regard the criticism of their views as attacks on their own personal integrity, on their 'place' and space, and on their 'reformation'. Both move from attacking the teachings of the other to attacking their personal credibility. It was, for Luther, the first major challenge to his 'gospel' from within the reformist camp, and shook at the very fundamentals of his understanding of Scripture. For this reason it was no doubt inevitable that issues had to be personalised. Opponents were viewed within the apocalyptic categories by which the *causa reformationis* itself was interpreted. The struggles on earth are but a dim reflection of the battles being waged in the heavenly sphere.

As a result polemic ceased to be a heuristic tool. It became a blunt weapon. Legitimate, discussable differences in opinion developed, in this case, as in so many others, into a confessional fracas between hostile forces. It became difficult to distinguish between *adiaphora*, marginal issues, and central ones, because stances were so closely identified with particular people, with their incarnation in particular prophets, who were seen to be endowed with a particular 'spirit'. Even the robust Luther claimed to feel like a defenceless wild flower in the face of Müntzer's rampaging actions,[8] while it is no accident that Luther was accused by his radical opponents of being a new Pope, even a new Messiah, a new Christ.[9]

Polemic, of course, is very satisfying for those who unleash it, but can be quite mortifying for its victim if it hits home, as we say. The accusations of stupidity, corruption, incoherence and incompetence would emerge in the night hours to haunt and distress their targets. The cruel nicknames with which one was lampooned stuck in the public memory, but also in one's

---

[8]   *Meyn blo(e)der und armer geist/hat mu(e)ssen frey stehen/als eyne fellt blume/* ... ; Hans-Ulrich Delius, Siegfried Bräuer, etc. *Martin Luther. Studienausgabe* (Evangelische Verlagsanstalt: Berlin, 1983), 3, 96/6f.

[9]   *er will ein newer Christus sein*; MSB, 335/29–32.

own gullet. Karlstadt's or Erasmus' writings make it clear how deeply such insults pained the more sensitive spirits, how pertinaciously the insinuations rankled. One had been made to look ridiculous before one's peers, before one's patrons or parishioners. One had been represented 'before the world', in this alarming new medium of print, as quite other than one was, or believed oneself to be. One could no longer be perceived on one's own terms.

Such accusations compromised one's status, livelihood, reputation, security, and could even endanger life itself. For the marginalised they could be fatal, indeed. Without implying any direct causal connection, one thinks of the peasant rebels who were lashed by Luther's writing, *Against the Murderous Hordes of Peasants* one day, and hung up to die the next. Though unapologetic, Luther himself recognised that his writing had unleashed a storm of criticism on all sides. All his achievements seemed to have been forgotten, he complained, while he himself had been threatened with death. He took a strange, defiant pleasure in provoking his critics to still more inarticulate rage by choosing this time of crisis to abandon his vow of celibacy and marry.[10] The interplay of word and symbolic action is interesting. The dynamics of hostility begin, it seems, to run their own course, and become an end in themselves.

Such reactive polemic may simply stir the pot of existing hostility. Luther, however, used this image of the 'stirring of the pot' to indicate that it is all the work of the devil, incarnated in the person of Müntzer, which has turned the peasants into beasts, into mad dogs.[11] Both sides thus become caught up in

[10]   *Welch ein Zetergeschrei, liebe Herren, hab ich angericht mit dem Büchlin wider die Bauern! Da ist alles vergessen, was Gott der Welt durch mich gethan hat. Nu sind Herren, Pfaffen, Bauern, alles wider mich, und dräuen mir den Tod.* Note the reference to his opponents becoming *toll und töricht*; W Br3, 531/4–8.

[11]   *Wohlan, wer den Münzer gesehen hat, der mag sagen, er habe den Teufel leibhaftig gesehen . . . Denn der Teufel fühlet vielleicht den jungsten Tag, darumb denkt er die Grundsuppe zu rühren . . .* ; W Br3, 536/35–9.

a whirlpool of accusation and counter-accusation, and the convenient alibi of the devil prevents any cool analysis of the situation.

Truth, we are told, lies in process as much as in content. Peter Brown has recently reminded us that the Christianisation of the Roman world owed less to spectacular edicts and acts of coercion and intolerance by the state, than to a winsome style, which accommodated itself to people where they were.[12] It should be remembered that one of Müntzer's fiercest objections was to the manner in which Luther contended with him. Instead of admonishing him in a brotherly way, Luther had resorted to hateful denunciation, combining this with the quite unfair tactic of calling upon the Saxon princes to suppress him.[13] Müntzer saw this as a 'tyrannous' abuse of power. Müntzer himself, of course, was not without a certain reputation for colourful denunciation, but he had a right to be aggrieved that he was never taken seriously theologically by his opponent. A debate had become a declaration of war.

Nearly all the participants in such disputes experienced an agonising dissonance between their own high sense of calling, and the dark imputations of infamy directed at them. Lies blackened their reputation, at a time when the function of 'naming' was taken much more seriously than today. Müntzer, who saw himself in the prophetic lineage of Elijah, Daniel, John the Baptist, indeed of Christ himself, found himself dismissed as a fanatic, a cannibalistic monster, as the Satan of Allstedt. This was an age which burnt offenders alive for blasphemy against God. Such polemic adumbrated this, and was experienced as a violation of the image of God in one's inmost soul.

The polemical language of the bestiary dehumanised the opponent into an ape, donkey, predatory wolf or repellent bird of prey. All the pigs of Bavaria, Luther once declared, had

[12] Peter Brown, *Authority and the Sacred. Aspects of the Christianisation of the Roman World* (Cambridge University Press: Cambridge, 1995).
[13] MSB, 430f.

moved to take up quarters in the theological faculty at Ingolstadt.[14] Luther could sometimes see himself as a hunter, on the chase after dangerous pests (*unzifer*); his opponents Cochlaeus, Mensing, Wimpina and others, constituted a howling, barking, grunting menagerie of wolves, dogs, foxes, pigs, grotesquely trying, under pressure from the huntsman, Luther, to apply themselves to Scripture.[15]

The writer often pinpointed precisely those weaknesses which one had preferred to keep hidden, even from one's own self, especially from one's own self. The aim was to embarrass, to wound, to discredit. There was no more effective polemicist than an erstwhile pupil or friend who knew precisely where to put the dagger in. Family violence, verbal and actual, is always the worst![16] Kindred spirits, such as Luther and Müntzer, may well have projected onto the other their own unresolved anxieties. Luther as the Wittenberg Pope; did this reflect Müntzer's deepest doubts about his own authority? One can but wonder.

One cannot read such polemical writings, and the apologias or vindications which countered them, without noting the hurt, self-pity, sense of betrayal and injustice with which they overflow. The language is frequently modelled on the courtroom, the *genus iudicale*.[17] The writer is both prosecuting or

[14]   *Wider das blind und toll Verdammniß der siebzehn Artikel von den elenden schändlichen Universität zu Ingolstadt ausgangen . . . 1524.* W 15, 125/16–19.

[15]   W 26, 531/21–35.

[16]   One thinks, for example, of Edward Albee's alarming play, *Who's Afraid of Virginia Woolf?* (New York, 1962); Erasmus' indignation at Geldenhouwer's doctored editions of his works was all the greater because the latter had once been on friendly terms, and precisely because of that could do him the greater harm; *Epistola contra Pseudevangelicos,* and *Epistola ad fratres inferioris Germaniae* in *Opera Omnia Erasmi Roterodami.* IX–1, 263–309; 311–426.

[17]   Many pamphlets are entitled *Schützrede,* speech for the defence, apologia; cf. Bubenheimer's analysis of the rhetoric of prosecution and defence in Luther's *Letter to the Princes of Saxony* and Müntzer's

defence counsel and judge, and often acts as witness as well. The readers constitute the jury. Those who found themselves 'in the dock' must have experienced this as unbelievably traumatic, almost unendurably humiliating and grievous. Memorable images branded one as a thief or murderer, a spreader of plague, poison, filth, sexual depravity, corruption and death.

There were no libel laws. This was no academic disputation in which conventions were clear, boundaries were recognised and 'Marquess of Queensberry rules' observed. Printing brought a new power to wound. The thousand duplicates of each printed tract meant that the 'game' was fought out time and time again, in the market, the parish, the home, the court. Old rivals and enemies would be sniggering at one; family and friends would be embarrassed. At stake was no winner's crown, but one's dignity and self-respect. Nor was there any outside instance to which to appeal for mediation. Pope, Council, Emperor were distant abstractions. The city magistrates might eventually come down hard on abusive ditties or tracts, but by then the damage would be done. There were no grounds for confidence that a proper 'debate' could be facilitated, that an impartial mediator existed, that one's response would be respected, that the questions and anxieties of one's parishioners, followers, dependents would be attended to. Frequently, therefore, it seemed that the only way to deal with personal or group hurt was to respond in kind, to channel one's indignation into rage, and fire off a reply. Thus the vicious circle continued. It is interesting to note that by 1524 Eberlin von Günzburg, once noted for his forthright criticism, was so alarmed at the indiscriminate rejection of ancient customs, and the lack of respect for opponents, that he warns against a premature polarisation of issues and a confusion of the cause of the Gospel with one's own glory.[18]

Vindication as noted in Bräuer, 'Selbverständnis und Feindbild', pp. 65–72; Bubenheimer may overstate a good case.

[18]   *Von Missbrauch christlicher Freiheit.* Fiche 442/1187; Grimma, 1522.

Luther himself frequently admitted that he had been carried away by outbursts of rage; sometimes during angry and sleepless nights he would dash down some all too human thoughts which after cooler reflection he would have withdrawn. Sometimes, however, it was already too late, for they had already been spirited away by someone and appeared in print.[19] At other times the rage and fury of his opponents spurred him on; he glowed inwardly with satisfaction at the thought that he had stirred the devil and his minions to such mad contortions.[20] At best, however, this sounds like a self-protective mechanism. It could not be sustained indefinitely.

Such dark polemic can perhaps be seen as the language of despair. In Luther's case there was never a total loss of hope. Even at the height of the Peasants' War he could remind himself that one should never despair about a fellow-human, and extend the olive-branch to an opponent such as Karlstadt.[21] There are frequent references, right to the end of his life, for example, to the wonderful way in which the pure teaching of the Gospel is being spread by a new generation of preachers and teachers.[22] Today's young boys and girls know more about the faith as a result of his Reformation than all the universities had known before.[23] But his prevailing attitude to the penultimate realities of this world is increasingly gloomy, for all his ultimate confidence. The devil was omnipresent. Reason seemed out of place once the opponent had been demonised. The Pope was Antichrist, Müntzer the Satan of Allstedt. These are to be understood as descriptive categories, not terms of abuse. They are an attempt to 'name' reality.

[19]   W 45, 422–3.
[20]   W 51, 469/17–26, 29f.
[21]   For all his fierce doctrinal disagreements with Karlstadt, *mein höchster feind . . . der ler halben,* Luther was willing in 1525 to trust his word on worldly matters, knowing that we may never despair of anyone: *Es ist auch an kainem menschen/weil er lebt/zuverzweiffeln.* W 18, 436/37f.
[22]   Cf. for example his letter to Wenzeslaus Link in June 1543: W Br 10, 335/13–17.
[23]   W 26, 530/26–8.

In one of his stories Franz Fühmann, little known in the English-speaking world, but one of the most perceptive literary analysts of National Socialism, describes how a common soldier, appalled at the lynching of two innocent girls during the Second World War, suddenly sees his 'comrades' taking on the heads of wolves, hyaenas and pigs, their faces becoming snouts, tiny red eyes appearing buried in layers of fat. He had 'recognised', 'named' them as animals.[24] We are not far here from Luther's perception that only exceptional language can describe the exceptionally evil. At times he drew the logical enough conclusion that his opponents were so devilish that there was no point in arguing with them at all, even polemically. It was not necessary to reply to the devil. He would leave it in the hands of God, who was the true judge. 'For who can stop the mouths of everyone, yes, of every devil.'[25]

Luther was following a long tradition of interpreting Church history which went back to Bernard and beyond when he regarded the Church as always having been plagued not only by outward persecution and violence, but by dissent, schism and heresy.[26] Like so many of his contemporaries Luther saw the Reformation period in these apocalyptic terms, with the final battle between right and wrong imminent, already upon them. Whenever God's word appears, so does the devil.[27] Müntzer, likewise, quite literally thought of everything in terms of black and white. Luther was the evil black crow, while he was an innocent silver dove.[28] Whenever Christ appears, Herod surfaces, too. Supreme goodness and ultimate evil always coincide temporally.[29]

---

[24]   Frans Fühmann, *Den Katzenartigen wollten wir verbrennen. Ein Lesebuch,* p. 43.

[25]   W 26, 145/3–10.

[26]   The Word of God is always plagued *non modo vi, sed et haeresibus novis* . . . WBr 3, 284/22f.

[27]   W 15, 210.

[28]   CW, 333; MSB, 327/18–25.

[29]   CW, 280; MSB, 283/3–10.

The frustration of such apocalyptic hopes naturally generated quite awesome grief or rage. A good example is Argula von Grumbach's extraordinary letter rebuking the Regensburg Council for its censorship of Reformation views.[30] The desperation of Müntzer, after losing his 'voice', his printing-press, and his home base at Allstedt, his 'ground to stand on', can also be easily imagined, indeed it is evident in every page of his last writing, the *Vindication*.[31] Such writings are penned in the wilderness, by the waters of Babylon. Like exiled or expatriate leaders of every age, their writers had lost their old home without having arrived at their new Jerusalem. Only the splendour of the apocalyptic vision kept them going.

Although geographically the older Luther kept his footing in Wittenberg he, too, had become an exile in a metaphoric sense, increasingly alienated from the pedestrian realities around him. One ominous sign of this is the readiness to summarily dismiss any opposition.

A recently discovered sermon of Luther's against young people making secret engagements to marry without consulting their parents, delivered at the very end of his life, shows him at his least attractive, insisting on his personal authority, on his right to determine what should happen in 'his' church, to identify the Gospel with 'his' gospel.[32] It illustrates not only his increasingly authoritarian attitudes, with all the prejudicial effects for his followers, but the way in which relatively trivial issues could be blown up into matters of life and death importance.

There seemed to be no room any more for a middle ground on any question. One result of this polarisation of views,

---

[30]   AvG, 150–9.

[31]   CW, 327–50; MSB, 3211–343.

[32]   *So sag ich: nicht Teufel, las mir meine Kirche rein* . . . ; Uwe Czubatynski, 'Der zörnige Luther auf der Kanzel. Eine neugefundene Nachschrift seiner Predigt vom 20. Januar 1544', in Matthias Köckert (ed.), *Der Wahrheit Gottes verpflichtet. Theologische Beiträge aus dem Sprachkonvikt Berlin* (Wichern Verlag: Berlin, 1993), p. 56.

stemming from grief as well as rage, is the escalation of the vocabulary of polemic. Since ordinary terms appeared to be incapable of doing justice to the gross and all-encompassing nature of the evil he saw all around, he minted neologisms, and lurched into the most lurid of sexual and anal abuse. Unfortunately this attempt to find a new language came close at times to a loss of all language.

Language ceases to be descriptive, and comes to cloak reality, or, even more ominously, to create a conspiratorial reality! The fatal effects of this in Luther's later anti-semitic writings has often been noticed. Few have analysed these more cogently than Oberman, though it is impossible to accept Oberman's contention that the negativity of his polemic is consistent throughout his life.[33] His apocalyptic 'blik' remains remarkably constant, but there is a self-indulgent loss of emotional control which clearly grows with age.[34]

No doubt part of the reason for the negativity and lack of creativity of Luther's later polemic was his physical ill-health. The growing catalogue of ailments he had to contend with, 'the stone', angina, headaches, acute indigestion and especially the dizzy spells and roaring in the ears associated with Ménière's disease was formidable.[35] But there was also a weariness of spirit. He had argued the case so often before on Biblical, logical, historical grounds; he had used all his formidable humour and charm and powers of exhortation to no effect. So all that

[33] Heiko A. Oberman, *The Impact of the Reformation* (T. & T. Clark: Edinburgh, 1994), pp. 81–172; of particular interest is his ingenious, if not wholly successful attempt to deny that the excesses of Luther's polemics relate to the disillusionment of old age: 'Teufelsdreck: Eschatology and Scatology in the "Old" Luther', pp. 51–68.

[34] The analysis of Luther's polemic by Joseph Lortz, *Die Reformation in Deutschland* (Herder: Freiburg, 4th ed. 1962), pp. 409–30 still repays study; Luther, he argues, was not master of his moods, they mastered him; less convincing is his moralistic critique of Luther's pride; pp. 428, 421.

[35] A good summary in Hans-Joachim Neumann, *Luthers Leiden. Die Krankheitsgeschichte des Reformators* (Wichern: Berlin, 1995); significantly, his illnesses, too, were interpreted as the work of the devil.

remained to him was to trump his opponents' polemic, and perhaps deter any potential supporters by trouncing them. He could, and did, resort to prayer, but succumbed too often to the temptation to do something, say something, when silence might well have borne better fruit.

The main reason for the degeneration of polemic, however, was that every issue came to be viewed in cosmic, or apocalyptic terms. 'Enthusiasts', Papists, Jews appear in the end to be interchangeable. There is no eschatological suspension of ultimate judgement any more. The choreographer, to adapt Leroux's categories, has become drunk or crazy. Insult is performative language. It has a cultic dimension, and once a certain point has passed it moves from being a piece of literary abuse to a religious curse.

Brecht has pointed to Luther's occasional use of a literary 'excommunication'.[36] Luther actually declared on one occasion that he had killed Müntzer off, and that he took responsibility for this. He had acted thus because Müntzer had sought to 'kill my Christ'.[37] Especially in the religious sphere polemic could be intended, perceived and experienced as a deadly weapon, pronounced in ritual form, a charismatic excommunication, calling down upon its object not only the derision of the onlooker but the wrath of God.

The battle-ground analogy becomes very vivid when this happens. R. H. Tawney has talked of the 'deadly space' of 'no man's land' in the First World War, territory of extreme danger, and yet of elation: 'Most men, I suppose, have a palaeolithic savage somewhere in them, a beast that occasionally shouts to be given a chance of showing his joyful cunning in destruction.'[38] The beast, one suspects, was released most

---

[36]   Martin Brecht, *Luther als Schriftsteller: Zeugnisse seines dichterischen Gestaltens* (Calwer Verlag: Stuttgart, 1990), pp. 68–73.

[37]   *Sic occidi Muncerum etiam, der todt ligt auff meinem hals. Feci autem ideo, quia ipse voluit occidere meum Christum*; WTr 1, 195/18–20.

[38]   R. H. Tawney, *The Attack and Other Papers* (Allen and Unwin: London, 1953), p. 15.

alarmingly in disciplined figures such as Luther and Müntzer (and Thomas More) when pent-up passion broke through the strongest flood-gates.

One may, therefore, have to modify somewhat the view of Miriam Chrisman, surely one of the best authorities on Reformation literature, that polemic at least in principle always assumed a rational base and a two-way argument, but that by the middle of the century this had given way to a much more manipulative, often anonymous propagandistic literature, whose aim was to secure social control for one's own party and to create a stereotype of 'The Other'. She suggests that propaganda of this type emerged when the Reformers saw the Peasants' War as indicating the failure of their more rational polemics. Chrisman believes that the Reformers felt they had been misunderstood. They realised also that they had failed to create a new society, and so they stopped writing in the previous way, and began to turn to broadsheets, news-sheets, songs and wood-cuts of a propagandistic nature, inciting fear, stirring sexual anxieties, and creating a monolithic image of their opponents.[39]

Clearly, there is much truth in this analysis, and the distinction between polemic and propaganda is a salutary one. Certainly, too, some explanation is required of the remarkable decline in pamphlet literature after 1524. Yet the subjective considerations mentioned by Chrisman may have been less important than the social, political and ecclesiastical changes as state-building proceeded, and confessionalism got under way. The shifts in literary techniques will have reflected these more fundamental structural factors. The interests of the mass of the laity, of what Blickle calls the communal cause, became

---

[39] Her first table shows that nearly three hundred polemic pamphlets, about forty-nine each year, were published in Strassburg from 1520 to 1525, but only nineteen, about five each year, from 1526 to 1529. Miriam Chrisman, 'From Polemic to Propaganda: The Development of Mass Persuasion in the Late Sixteenth Century', *Archive for Reformation History* 73 (1982), pp. 175–95.

subordinated to those of the professionals, the clergy, the lawyers, and state interests. One church system came to be set against another, each seeking to weaken and ultimately to destroy the other side.

An absolute distinction between polemic and propaganda may not be possible; the boundaries between the two were anything but precise; the evidence suggests there was a gradual shading of polemic into propaganda, with the Peasants' War a real watershed. The clichés of the propagandist embraced as gospel the apocalyptic images of the polemicist. As polemic lost its heuristic edge, as despair about the morality or rationality of the opponent took over, it degenerated into propaganda. More and more attention was given to strengthening the morale of one's supporters, and to attacking the credibility of opponents. Wiegmann reminds us that successful rhetoric requires at least a minimal consensus among participants as to the nature of reality and values. Where this collapses, all real dialogue, even polemical dialogue, becomes impossible.[40]

The aim in theory may still have been to put the record straight, to appeal to the middle ground, to protect the cause of the Gospel. But many of the features later found in confessional propaganda begin to be apparent in the polemical writings. They, too, polarised and caricatured, engaged in endless point-scoring, heroised or ridiculed, used sexual

---

[40]   Hermann Wiegmann, 'Allgemeinbegriff und Rhetorik. Zur theologischen, politischen und literarischen Argumentation im frühen 16. Jahrhundert', in Joachim Dyck, Walter Jens and Gert Veding (eds.), *Rhetorik,* Bd. 5 *Rhetorik und Theologie* (Max Niemeyer: Tübingen, 1986), pp. 87–96; his comments about the growing recourse to *exempla,* or generalising instances, in later sermons in comparison with Melanchthon's warnings to preachers to contextualise, and pay attention to the hearers' daily perception of reality, would be another illustration of a shift from dialogue to propaganda; *Nam ad bene dicendum in primis requiritur perfecta earum rerum cognitio, de quibus oratio instituitur, Elementorum rhetorices libri duo; Corpus Reformatorum* XIII, 418.

innuendo, and whipped up the emotions.[41] The truth question is increasingly being edged out by the power question. A good example of this is Luther's very late piece of polemic, *The Papacy at Rome founded by the Devil*, written in 1545. Interestingly, Eric Gritsch has described it as 'a key instrument of Protestant propaganda against papal diplomacy'.[42]

The Papacy at Rome founded by the Devil

The historian seeks to put text in context, to read even the unreadable in the light of its genesis, its surroundings and out-comes, and to move self and reader towards understanding, as far as this is possible. Texts such as this one, however, stretch and strain our categories to breaking-point.[43] It is offensive, in the end of the day, not only to our moral and literary sensi-tivities, but to the whole historical enterprise. Luther's own black despair, if such it be, is inaccessible to the ironic detachment in which we would find ourselves. We wonder, perhaps, if we have either the will or the wit do it justice. Dialogue with this ugly and what has been proved to be dangerous polemical material seems less possible than a polemic of our own against it. Yet as a testimony to Saturn, or rather to a Promethean attempt to cope with acaedia, melancholy and depression by polemical aggression it has its poignancy as well as, in the fullest sense of that word, its tragic dimensions.

It was occasioned by a stinging rebuke by Pope Paul III to the Emperor. Charles V, in need as usual of financial support for his war against France and the Turks, had, inter alia, agreed

---

[41]   R. Po-chia Hsia, 'Anticlericalism in German Reformation Pamphlets: a Response', suggests there may be similarities between anti-clericalism and anti-semitism, and points to the misogynist features of the former. Peter A. Dykema and Heiko A. Oberman (eds.), *Anticlericalism in Late Medieval and Early Modern Europe*, pp. 496f.

[42]   LW 41, 260.

[43]   English text in LW 41, 263–376; *Wider das Papsttum zu Rom vom Teufel gestiftet*; W 54, 195–299.

at the Diet of Speyer in 1544 to summon a free, Christian Council in Germany to settle the religious conflict. Paul III not only condemned this as a quite improper intrusion into religious matters but warned him in no uncertain terms to desist from such actions in future. When this missive, together with an even more incendiary earlier version, fell into Protestant hands, Luther's fury boiled over.

From an early point Catholics and Protestants alike had taken offence at Luther's polemical excesses. Ickelsamer, for example, points to what he calls its murderous and tyrannical quality.[44] Close friends and allies such as Melanchthon were frequently embarrassed at the language and tone Luther affected. This writing sets new standards even for Luther, however.

Mark Edwards points to the political context. Luther is indeed drifting alarmingly near to becoming the Saxon Elector's tame propagandist, as the Schmalkaldic League geared up for war.[45] Oberman highlights Luther's apocalyptic reading of events.[46] Both political and apocalyptic perspectives are certainly in evidence. We note that there are no references to the Jews in this tract, though many to the Turks. Why not? Can Luther's anger only focus on one target at a time? Are the frustration and rage at twenty years of persecution of the evangelical cause boiling over, as he writes of innocent Christians being borne off to 'fire, water, sword, dungeons, into exile from house and home, wife and family'?[47]

He is writing not to convince the Papists, but to strengthen the conscience of his 'brothers', to encourage, to empower the

---

[44]   Valentin Ickelsamer, *Clag ettlicher brieder* (Tübingen?, 1525), Bii^v quoted by Carlos Gilly, 'Das Sprichwort "Die Gelehrten die Verkehrten", oder der Verrat der Intellektuellen im Zeitalter der Glaubensspaltung', in *Forme e destinazione del messaggio religioso. Aspetti della propaganda religiosa nel cinquecento* (Olschki: Florence, 1991), p. 275.

[45]   Mark U. Edwards, *Luther's Last Battles. Politics and Polemics 1531–46* (Cornell University Press: Ithaca, 1986), pp. 163–202.

[46]   Oberman, *The Impact of the Reformation*, p. 66.

[47]   LW 41, 354; W 54, 281/3–13.

laity to sit in judgement on the Pope. The apostle Paul had, after all, given Christians authority to judge even an angel from heaven if his message were contrary to that of the Gospel.[48] The German laity must continue to insist on a free, Christian German Council, or at least to reject a papally steered one, despite the Emperor's opposition. For kings and emperors have been seduced to betray and murder by a Pope who is acting on behalf of the devil.[49] There is a certain programmatic echo here of the *Appeal to the German Nobility*, though the hopes of a Germany united under its emperor have disappeared. Luther even incites the secular powers to take up arms against the Papal States, to 'yank out the pope's tongue'.[50] Luther's life project had been to turn the traditional understanding of the Church upside down, in the light, as he believed, of that Gospel of the Cross which always upturns fleshly values. Pope and Emperor, however, had resisted this to the end. In the nightmarish perspective of this writing, therefore, Pope and Emperor, the traditional pillars of Christendom, have to be unmasked as 'possessed of all the devils'.[51] The Pope has become completely arbitrary, accountable to none, setting himself above the judgement not only of all fellow-Christians but of the very Word of God.

Luther's identification of the Gospel as 'my Gospel' now has an ominously exclusive ring. He saw his crusade for the true understanding of Scripture and against the Pope as part of a cosmic struggle. Before the day of the Lord comes, the lawless one must be revealed, the 'man of sin', Satan in disguise, the blasphemer against God, the source of all idolatry, the child of abomination, who has set himself up to be worshipped in place of God. The pun in the first sentence of the tract, which loses none of its effectiveness in English, sums it all up: the Holy

---

[48]   W 54, 294/17–21.
[49]   W 54, 265/20f.
[50]   W 54, 243/13.
[51]   LW 41, 285.

Father becomes the Hellish Father.[52] Yet there is an unmistakeable sense of personal grievance as well.

Our concern here is less to outline his arguments, which has often been done before, but to account for the black ecstasy of the language. Luther sees his task as that of a demolition worker on an ecclesiastical structure which has become life-endangering. He has to smash ancient taboos, using words alone. But what words are equal to what he so often describes as the inexpressible horror of the situation? How can Christians be liberated from their false understanding of Church and ministry, from the deeply engrained preconception that Church leadership is recognisable by prestige, wealth, hierarchical status? Nothing short of a comprehensive verbal demolition, a catalogue of accusations and questions of unprecedented ferocity will suffice. What, he asked, are the true marks of catholicity on the one hand, and of sectarianism on the other? Who is to lead the Church, be the 'head of all the churches and lord it over the Christian faith?'[53] Christ alone, not the Pope. The Pope imagines the Holy Spirit is bound to Rome, but can the Holy Spirit be bound to any institution?[54] Is not any baptised child authorised to judge the Pope and his God, the devil?

The questions recall his horror at Tetzel's Indulgences twenty years earlier, and there is the same genuine pastoral concern for people who have been duped, the 'credulous crowd' whose salvation is endangered by such idolatry, by this 'murderer of souls'.[55] The torridness of the polemic was necessary in Luther's view to challenge the myths of continuity and authority, and

[52]   W 54, 206/3, 216/29; cf. LW 41, 263, 275; the reference to the 'accursed dregs of the Devil', *verfluchte grundsuppe des Teufels zu Rom*, suggests that Psalm 75, with its vivid confrontation of the good and the evil, is a key passage; W 54, 220/18f.

[53]   *aller Kirchen Heubt und Meister des Christlichen Glaubens*; W 54, 257/9.

[54]   W 54, 258/17.

[55]   W 54, 239/19–27; 255, 8–19; 269/23.

to shake the nexus of Matthew 16, Peter, Rome, subsequent bishops of Rome, the primacy of honour, the magisterium, and above all to raise the question of power. For it is not just a question of truth. Power is at stake here from beginning to end. Even the power of the Turk is not so ominous, because it is confined to the external, political realm. But the Pope is arrogating to himself the very power of God.[56] Over against this Luther sets the power of his language. He cannot convince the Papalists, but he hopes to destroy their credibility. In a breathtaking comparison he implicitly likens his polemic to the breath of the mouth of the Lord Jesus, destroying, annihilating the lawless one of 2 Thessalonians 8.[57]

One is struck by the constant reversion by Luther in this writing to his initial steps as a reformer. At the end of his life, he is reflecting on his beginnings; he is still haunted by the authoritarian and uncomprehending reaction of the Papacy at that time, the inquisitoral intervention of Eck at Leipzig in 1519, the Indulgence controversy, with which the whole 'quarrel' (*hadder*) or 'game' (*spiel*) began;[58] by the failure to take up his challenge to use rational and Scriptural arguments. The unexpected interventions of those such as Karlstadt and Müntzer are also described. It is interesting, incidentally, that the Papacy is ranked with them as sectarian.[59] He unravels once again the endless postponements of the Council, the refusal to reform the Curial abuses of dispensations. The writing can be seen, then, as an act of stocktaking of his whole career as a reformer, in a sense an apologia for it. It may be so passionate because he is not only seeking to convince others, but himself as well, that his life has not been in vain. It is

---

[56] W 54, 274, 26; 269/15f.
[57] Cf. LW 41, 361: '. . . we with a good conscience teach and pray against him, dare to spit at him, avoid him and flee from him as from the devil himself, remove him from our hearts, and sink him into the depths of hell . . . '.
[58] W 54, 231/10–12; 293/4, 23.
[59] *Rotten*; W 54, 285/36.

vindication spilling over into vindictiveness. It is, of course, also the writing of an ageing and pain-wracked man, though this aspect should not be over-emphasised. Perhaps more relevant is the question: How does Luther keep his rhetoric fresh, given the fact that nearly all the issues had been dealt with by him so often before? How, at least, does he try to keep fresh?

Conscious that he is at the end of his life, he seeks to strengthen the hesitant, and remind everyone, perhaps for the last time, of the arguments against the papal claims. The Diet of Speyers in 1544 had granted concessions to the Protestants and foreshadowed another national Diet to plan a Christian reformation of Germany. The Papacy's rejection of this had been uncompromising. The idea of a separate German settlement of the religious issue had been denounced in the strongest terms. Once peace between France and the Emperor had been concluded in September, the Papacy had responded by summoning a General Council to Trent. In Luther's terms this meant that it would neither be German, nor free from Curial direction, nor Christian, using Scripture alone as a norm.

To counter the Roman ecclesiology Luther offers substantial amounts of Biblical, historical and rational argument. It begins lucidly and quite entertainingly, offering a not unreasonable analysis of the delays in calling a Council. His portrayal of the polity of the Early Church has much to commend it.[60] His anger about the forged Donation of Constantine, to which Hutten's edition of Valla's work had alerted him, is understandable.[61] The analysis of the growing power of the medieval Papacy is not without merit.[62] There are fine theological reflections on the nature of the keys, and of penance. He offers a summary of the main doctrinal issues, and seeks to spell out the choice between spiritual tyranny and spiritual freedom.

[60]   W 54, 228–30; 275–8; LW 41, 346–9.
[61]   W 54, 264.
[62]   W 54, 296–9; LW 41, 371–6.

Luther believes, however, that he has to go on to alert those reponsible, especially the rulers, to the gravity of the crisis. This cannot be done on a purely rational level, since the other side, in his view, is totally impermeable to argument. Stadtwald suggests that the writing expresses Luther's conviction at this time that it may be necessary to shed blood for the sake of the Kingdom.[63] Whatever the truth of this, the struggle transcends political and military considerations for Luther. It is directed against the powers of darkness themselves. He has to shock people into a new decisiveness. There can be no middle ground. All who defer to the Pope strengthen his abominations.[64]

His raging polemic against papal error is the flip side to his vision of a servant Church, and his advocacy of a theology of the cross. The Christ who speaks to the Church has sucked the Virgin's milk, and exercises dominion from a filthy stable and an accursed cross.[65] The lies of the Papacy are the more appalling because their theology of glory makes God, the source of all truth, into a liar. 'What can we theologians do, when we have to see and hear such great lies, all dressed up in God's words?'[66] His rage and his love are in counterpoint, arguably in necessary counterpoint, just as, on a much more banal level, his hatred of the Italian curia is paralleled by his love for Germany.

Perhaps it is the vocabulary of the tract which dismays us most. It must be conceded that there is positive language a-plenty about true pastoral care, about Christian freedom and salvation. It is also true that the language remains lively,

---

[63]   Kurt Werner Stadtwald, 'When O Rome Will You Cease to Hiss? The Image of the Pope in the Politics of German Humanism' (PhD, University of Minnesota, 1991), p. 251.

[64]   W 54, 294/6; the English tr. reads 'horror', but *greweln* is better rendered by 'abominations'; LW 41, 370.

[65]   W 54, 290/7–10; LW 41, 365.

[66]   W 54, 239/2, 242/30–32; *Denn da macht der Teufel Gott zumlügener* . . . .

innovative and inventive. New words are coined, such as 'soul-murderer', 'monastery-muncher', 'key-thief'. Language is still used with bite and precision, though at times, as Luther himself admits, he becomes prolix and repetitive. 'Old age is forgetful and garrulous.'[67]

The overwhelming impression given by the writing, however, is of a language straining at the very edge of meaningfulness. The drastic title itself, mirrored in the illustration on the title page, the 'devil count' on virtually every page, the prevalence of obscene or abusive language all indicate a loss of emotional control. One recurrent image is that of farting. The Pope's language in the decretals is for Luther one long, stinking, disgusting fart. The Pope is the 'farting donkey at Rome', he is the 'donkeypopefart'. There are countless references to dirt and to stink, to sealing documents with faeces, to licking the arse of the Pope.[68] The sense of smell is the primary one evoked, although the senses of sight, hearing and touch are also addressed. The reason for this cloacal obsession appears to be the immediacy of the sense of disgust which it conjures up. Another reason is the continual word play between the papal decretals and the term *dreck*, or filth.

The imagery used is extraordinarily vivid. The central image is meant to be that of the devil, who is the father and mother of the Pope, who has founded the Papacy, who wears the Pope's Christian mask, who mouths Christian words, but personifies evil. The Pope is *Satanissimus*, the bodily incarnation of Satan, *Satans leibhaftige wonung*.[69] Again, note the intimate counterpointing with the gentle, suffering incarnation of Christ. Closely associated with the reference to the devil is the image of Antichrist, although for Luther, of course, Antichrist is no more an image than the devil, but terrible reality, squatting on the Holy of Holies, having usurped the Temple of God.[70]

[67]   *Vergessen und wesschicht*; W 54, 283/27.
[68]   Probably the crudest is W 54, 273/16–25.
[69]   W 54, 288/36.
[70]   W 54, 269/5–24.

In reality, however, the central image becomes that of the Papal Donkey, trying to skate on thin ice, loud, dumb, coarse, unlearned, big-mouthed, and – of course – farting. This alone robs the treatise of some of its serious intent. There are many other subordinate images, frequent references to the Pope as *gaukler*, juggler, jester, clown. At his creative best Luther had once gloried in his own 'clowning', but no longer. Animal imagery is not so varied as in other writings, though the Pope does appear as a monstrous werewolf, who rages, rips, tears and devastates the flock; the good pastor, by contrast, feeds the sheep. Most puzzling and alienating are the frequent anal references: the Pope and his entourage are born from the devil's anus; the Papalists are encouraged to foul their pants, to hang the chain of turds around their necks and sniff them appreciatively.[71] Looking up the Papal arse expressses his abhorrence of Papal evil. It is out of this mouth that the decretals are issued.[72] The crudity of the language is obviously closely related to the strength of the disgust Luther feels. He keeps having to tighten his trousers to keep his farts in![73]

Like the language, the style of the writing could hardly be seen as elevated. It is worlds removed from that of Erasmus or Melanchthon! It does, however, have many strengths, largely related to its oral quality. The reader is drawn in by being addressed in the second person singular: 'You see!' 'Look at this! ' 'Work it out for yourself!' Such vocatives or imperatives make for interactive reading.

Sometimes Luther answers a possible objection by the reader, or develops a mini-dialogue either with the reader or with his opponents.[74] The Pope, for example, has direct speech put in his mouth, and is made to appear completely hypocritical, talking peace incessantly, but in fact fomenting war between

---

[71]   W 54, 288/31; 220/28–30.
[72]   W 54, 218/27; 221/19.
[73]   W 54, 239/35f.
[74]   W 54, 221/9ff.; 224/8–12; 282/18–283/5; 287/23ff.

France and the Empire.[75] The realism is sometimes enhanced by the use of Italian phrases or terms,[76] or the opponent is directly taunted or teased: 'Dear little virgin Pope', *Liebes Jungferlin Bepstlin.* This heavy-handed humour soon becomes wearisome. Rather more effective use, however, is made of brief quotations from Papal decrees, the Pope being made to condemn himself from his own mouth: even if the Pope leads many to hell he cannot be judged![77]

Like all Luther's writings, this one is peppered with questions, sometimes rhetorical ones, which keep the readers on their toes. Luther also draws from his own personal experience, for example, his visit to Rome, or his knowledge of how the Roman Church works. There is an anecdotal quality to the writing. He refers to the burning of paper effigies of the Pope.[78] Graphic examples are given of superstitious practices, such as processing around Rome with the alleged heads of the apostles Peter and Paul.[79] Discursive or descriptive writing is frequently interrupted by ejaculations or adjurations with a strong emotional tone.[80] This can develop into lamentations or curses: 'Woe, woe, woe!' Little arrow prayers to God also flow naturally from the prose, as Luther shifts his attention from his opponent, to his 'brother', or to God. There is little abstraction. Instead of criticising the Papacy's neglect of scholarship, for example, he doubts whether the Pope or his followers could recite the Ten Commandments, say the Lord's prayer, or remember the Creed. The language is concrete, specific, incident-related. There is lively use of popular proverbs and sayings; 'If you have eyes don't hide them in a purse'.[81] As so often in Luther's writings, long chains of adjectives or proper

[75]   W 54, 216/22–217/6.
[76]   W 54, 282/29.
[77]   W 54, 262f.
[78]   W 54, 219/13–26.
[79]   W 54, 255/8–12.
[80]   W 54, 243/3.
[81]   W 54, 247/9.

names or substantives reinforce a point by their cumulative effect.[82] The energy of spoken language still comes through. The word 'full' (of devils) is, for example, repeated four times.[83] Sometimes the impact is strengthened by the use of alliteration and/or rhyme, as in Sodomy, Simony, Scorn. It reminds one that such writings were often read out aloud.

On occasion an issue is dramatised by being taken to extreme lengths, *ad absurdum*; for example the Roman misinterpretation of Scripture is caricatured by fantastic interpretations of popular songs, or texts from the Latin Classics, which allegedly support Papal claims. A donkey, it is said, should be permitted to judge the Pope, for it at least recognises itself as a donkey, while the Pope does not.[84] Only determined adherents, one suspects, however, will have found any of this particularly funny.

As always in Luther, sharp contrasts or polarities shock the reader. Sometimes this is done by simple collocation of words: the Pope is an 'earthly God', though this characterisation is not original to Luther; more often by phrases contrasting Christ and the Pope, God and the devil, the Bible and the decretals, dominion and service.[85] Puns and plays with words, as we have seen, are frequent.

Figures of speech such as similes and metaphor are not so frequent as in other writings. The canon-lawyers, patching together a case, are like furriers working with little scraps of fur. The Popes make a charade of the faith, dressing themselves up in the name of Christ and St Peter, but resorting to violence and extortion.[86] Analogies can be rather forced, as in the comparison of the Curia with Eli's sons.[87] An unusual feature of this writing is the sadistic fantasies about the fate awaiting

[82] W 54, 217/20f.; 243/22f.;268/1f.; 269/32f.
[83] W 54, 218/19f.
[84] W 54, 286/25–32.
[85] W 54, 263/13; 279/5.
[86] W 54, 218/18–21.
[87] W 54, 225f.

the Pope and his followers: they will be chained up and marched into the ocean with all their Canon Law tomes, their tongues will be pulled out of the back of their heads; they will be skinned like foxes; *fuchs recht spilen*.[88]

Sarcasm is quite common, as, for example, about the Pope's alleged concern for his dear son, the Emperor. Such humour as there is is pretty heavy-handed, or should one say, heavy-arsed. It is a mortal sin not to worship the Papal farting, or to kiss his arse. An interesting feature is the solemn, liturgical damnation of the Pope and all his works.[89] Overall, however, Luther's writing seems to lack orchestration or dramatic unity.[90] It evinces little of what Leroux has called the choreographical skills of Luther's earlier polemics.[91] The material is poorly mustered, and apart from this deficit in organisational skills is the loss of emotional control which has already been identified. Luther himself is aware of the coarseness of the writing. He knows it is unseemly for a minister of the Gospel to curse, instead of blessing. 'But I have to talk of my great *Anfechtung* (the Papacy's very existence provokes one to doubt and despair) with unfitting words.'[92] He is a 'rough customer', and has jumped in like a peasant, with heavy boots. But when he has been stirring around in the papal stink for a while he just cannot take any more and has to stop and yell.[93] 'Look, look, how my blood is thumping in my body, how it longs to see the Papacy punished.'[94] He still feels he has fallen far short of finding

---

[88]   W 54, 283/ 6–25; 243/11–15; 292/17–20.

[89]   W 54, 290/16–23.

[90]   As the analysts of style would put it; cf. Kenneth Burke, *Counter-Statement* (2nd ed.; Berkeley, 1968).

[91]   'Luther does not merely act as lecturer . . . ; he functions like a choreographer.' Neil Richard Leroux, 'Style in Rhetorical Criticism: The case of Martin Luther's Vernacular Sermons' (PhD, University of Illinois, 1990), p. 267.

[92]   W 54, 277/23.

[93]   W 54, 263/13–15.

[94]   W 54, 292/20f.

language bad enough to express what he thinks about the monstrosity of the papal abominations.[95] The very length of the treatise is an attempt to do justice to the unspeakable and unending abuses of the Papacy.[96] The Pope's lies have to be shown up for what they are. As someone called to lead the Church he has done his best to reveal the truth. He sees it as part of his preaching ministry.[97] His fierce words should at least force people to come to a decision: whoever doesn't want to listen, can leave. 'Whoever wants to stink, let them stink . . . His blood be on his head.'[98] Such polemic separates out godly sheep from stinking goats. It is indeed a battle to the death: 'Let battle commence.' If we die we will live in Christ, if the Pope dies he will perish miserably with all the devils.[99] One is reminded of Luther's denunciations of the rebellious peasants in 1525. How could a 'heretic' like himself, Luther asks, have remained alive, and his ideas have survived if he had not fought for them? How could the Papacy have been made accountable?[100]

The effect of such polemic is to personalise. The unendingly complex crisis of faith and polity and authority is reduced to the devilish origin and nature of the Pope. This is easy for the reader to grasp, but leaves all the structural and most of the personal questions untouched. The leap from pure theology to foul polemic betrays the impatience with careful analysis.

---

[95]   W 54, 261/13–22.

[96]   W 54, 272/24f.; an interesting parallel is the Jewish author Jizchak Katzenelson's desperate attempts to find a language adequate to the apocalyptic horrors of the Warsaw Ghetto: 'Wie soll man Sachen beschreiben, die die Menschheit noch nie erlebt hat – man müsste sich ja eine spezielle Sprache dafür ausdenken!' Wolf Biermann (ed. and tr.), *Dos lied vunem ojsgehargetn jidischn volk: Grosser Gesang vom ausgerotteten jüdischen Volk* (Kiepenheuer & Witsch: Köln, 1994), p. 201.

[97]   W 54, 295/13f.

[98]   W 54, 284/6–9.

[99]   W 273/13–15.

[100]   W 54, 288f.

Secondly, it moralises in an abusive, tedious and unedifying way. Luther at his best had avoided cheap moralisation. Particularly sad are the sexual allusions. There seems to be an anti-feminine bias, in, for example, the repeated references to the legendary Pope Paula.[101] There are also barrow-loads of references to sodomy and bisexuality.[102] This is not the thought of a theologically alert and creative mind, but is reliant, in a derivative way, on some of the worst anti-curial abuse of the fifteenth- and sixteenth-century German humanists and indeed the pasquinades issuing from Rome itself.

Another outcome of such polemic is that it creates strong negative associations in the reader's mind between, say, Canon Law and filth, between the Pope and the devil, between the Curia and sodomy. It creates a negative image of the Papacy, and undermines its authority by derision. Unfortunately such images were to persist for centuries.

Fourthly, it polarises. The demonising of the Papacy rests on a notably weak argument: since the Papacy is based neither on spiritual or temporal authority, it must derive from the devil.[103] Exaggeration runs riot: the Pope would prefer a blood-bath in Germany to one soul being saved.[104] It is assumed that Paul III's motivations are entirely negative. He is deliberately leading Christianity astray. The Pope and his 'crew' are portrayed as complete unbelievers, hypocrites and pleasure-lovers, contemptuous of the Germans; they lead them around like a bear with a ring in its nose.[105] No acknowledgement is made of the reformist nature of Paul III's papacy. The attempts at Regensburg in 1541 to mediate between Catholic and Protestant are ignored.

This is polemic which is well on the road to propaganda, reflecting and encouraging the drift towards dividing

[101]   W 54, 223/22.
[102]   LW 41, 282–9; W 54, 222–7.
[103]   W 54, 238/1f.
[104]   W 54, 224/35–7.
[105]   W 54, 219/27–34; 283/1f.

Christianity into two ideological camps, two armed camps. The polemic will soon be replaced by actual warfare. The heuristic value of such polemic seems quite minimal. Its function, which had some considerable success, was to consolidate the Protestant camp. The Lutheran tradition has been too slow to recognise that in the process it also represents the acute politicisation of religion.

The language and thought of Luther's anti-Jewish tracts appals one. For not a few of this writer's students reading them has made it virtually impossible to engage in any way with the remainder of his theology. The over-blown imagery and the sprawling self-indulgence of the arguments against the Papacy, on the other hand, provoke that very derision which Luther hoped to direct at his Roman Antichrist. Such ungoverned rage becomes ridiculous, an unintended theatre of the absurd.

Polemic has become almost entirely counter-productive. It is no longer used 'playfully' to nudge or prod the reader into challenging conventional ideas or entertaining new ones. Nor is it any longer a hand-maid to the larger theological enterprise. Indeed, one of its most disquieting features is that, as in the anti-Jewish writings, it draws heavily on contemporary prejudice, mopping up anti-clerical and nationalistic themes and images in an uncritical way. Luther's writings become not only repetitive, but derivative. The representation of the Papacy is based on the poisoned pen of Ziegler and his like. As Stadtwald has argued, when he thought of the Pope and of Rome it was their images which flashed into his mind, images of unbridled sexual licence, of rapacity and unscrupulousness.[106] This particular debt of Luther to humanism has been too little regarded.

The interesting question, of course, is why he was so eager to believe the worst, why the formidable journalistic skills he had shown in his earlier writings deserted him, why critical acumen disappeared. His polemical stance, both in its political

---

[106]   Stadtwald, 'When O Rome Will You Cease to Hiss?', p. 240.

and apocalyptic aspects, had increasingly unhinged his grasp on the complex, untidy realities of ecclesiastical and political life. The activities of the devil became the sufficient explanation for everything.[107] As we would say today, he bought into conspiracy theories. This distorted his exegesis of Scripture, his reading of history and tradition, and ultimately his theological judgement. One might have considerable understanding if this happened to a lesser man, and if his early polemic had not driven such a splendid cleaver though the confusions and absurdities of his time. There is a German phrase, *tierischer Ernst*, which sums it up, 'bestial zeal'. Too much zeal for God simply leads us to forfeit our humanity. Luther's later polemics are no mere warts on a magnificent countenance, which a magnanimous eye should overlook. They are malignant growths which no surgeon can prune, an awesome warning against the abuse of polemic.

---

[107] Cf. Miriam Chrisman, *Lay Culture, Learned Culture, Books and Social Change in Strasbourg, 1480–1599* (Yale University Press: New Haven, 1982), p. 265, commenting on the bitter anti-papal propaganda of Johann Fischart in the later decades of the century in Strassburg: 'The pope became the scapegoat for all the evils suffered by mankind.'

CHAPTER EIGHT

MEDIATION AND RECONCILIATION: ESSAYS AT COLLOQUY

Der Vogel Wunschlos fliegt nicht weit.
No bird flies far without a goal.

Dorothee Sölle[1]

The alternative to polemic and confessional demarcation was dialogue, the path to peace. In the Classical tradition dialogue could either be Plato's quest for the truth or Cicero's pursuit of a probabilist best option. In rather similar fashion apocalyptic certainties jostled uneasily during the Reformation period with the reverent agnosticism of the mystic, while the more pragmatic concerns of the politician, the publicist and the populist for a consensus which provided stability could not be easily silenced.

An awareness of these varieties of Reformation discourse is imperative, though the *Zeitgeist* fostered confidence about access to ultimate truth and justice. Advocates of tolerance, moderation and dialogue tended to be cast in the role of trimmers and time-servers.

The various Reformation movements, Catholic, communal, Lutheran, radical and Reformed, often in close association with humanist enthusiasms, had spawned a wide spectrum of linguistic options. One of the fascinations of the early 1520s is this exciting and confusing clash of views, made possible by

---

[1]   Dorothee Sölle, *Berliner Dialoghefte* 6.2 (1990), pp. 54–6.

the temporary weakness of the authorities in Church and state and by the unparalleled access to, and unrivalled mana of Scripture. Biblical, patristic, apocalyptic, mystical and anti-clerical varieties of discourse vied for customers in the market-place. In any one individual or group, of course, several of these components were often combined. It took time for precisely demarcated orthodoxies to form, as laity and clergy, country-folk and town-dwellers, opinion-makers and individual readers or worshippers gradually sifted through the options on offer to discover which community of discourse best articulated their interests. There was often considerable reluctance to accept that Erasmian and Lutheran or radical emphases were in tension. Many declined in principle to line up behind any single teacher or authority, and held themselves accountable to Christ and Scripture alone.

We now know that it was to prove impossible for Christendom as a whole to recover anything like a common discourse. Yet this was altogether unclear at the time to the participants in the drama, to the apocalyptic Luther, or the spiritualist, Karlstadt, or the Catholic evangelical, Contarini. They all assumed universal reference for their own particular version of the truth. There was almost no cognizance of what we may recognise today as a new, emerging, denominational pluralism.

Options, therefore, were limited. One could mobilise all the resources of pulpit and school and printing-press to win over the middle ground and rally support for one's cause. One could rely on censorship, social pressures and varying degrees of coercion to suppress competing views. One could seek by prayer, exemplary life and winsomeness of argument to commend one's stance to others.

Or one could, as Erasmus and many like him did, argue for a moderate, mediating position, which tolerated differences on non-essential matters, and sought an amiable, rational consensus on the others. Theology then became a discipline for players rather than gentlemen, which could and should discuss the more controversial matters, and had to be given its own space to pursue this. This professional game had, however, to be sharply differentiated from the need for all Christians to adhere to the credal basis and confessional certainties of the Church, which could not be shaken. This irenic stance was taken further by a few choice spirits, such as Bucer and Gropper, who attempted, at least sporadically, to use the new theological tools and resources of humanism and reformism to fashion a new confessional discourse. Their dialogue is reminiscent of the young Augustine's dream of the patient, learned colloquy of the friends of truth.

Peter Mosellanus' opening speech at the far from patient gathering of disputants at Leipzig in 1519 sums up well the hopes of the Erasmian party. All obscure and subtle terms should be avoided and hospitality given to the clarity and simplicity of the philosophy of Christ. All bitterness and boasting and contumely should be shunned. Any errors should be pointed out gently. Otherwise one would be a *rixator*, a propagator of strife, a gladiator fighting for human glory. We have to remember, with Paul, that the mysteries of God are beyond us, that there are definite limits to our human understanding. There is no disgrace about confessing one's past errors. Self-knowledge means being aware of one's own fallibility, or as he puts it, fragility. Let the contest between Eck and Karlstadt be the beginning of true Christian peace and concord![2] Ironical, indeed, the chasm between such rhetoric and the emergent realities of the disputation.

But how was language used during the early years of the Reformation? Manfred Hoffmann has pointed out that for Erasmus all language had a mediatorial function. Since the cosmos was a harmonious one, good language should reflect this. Words mediated, analogically, between the hearer and

---

[2]   *De Ratione disputandi, praesertim in re Theologica, Petri Mosellani Proregensis Oratio* . . . Fiche 1534/3991 (Leipzig, 1519?), Aiiii[r], Bii, Biii[r], Cii, Ciii[r].

reality and reflected this reality accurately. But this linguistic realism, Hoffmann argues, cohabited in Erasmus with a philosophic dualism of letter and spirit. Only allegory provided the necessary bridge to talks of the deeper things. Through allegory spirit could accommodate itself to material realities.[3]

These concepts of accommodation, *sunkatabasis,* and mediation are fundamental to Erasmus' understanding of language. Just as God's very self is accommodated to our understanding in the person of Christ, the Word, so we have to accommodate our discourse to that of one another. Moderation is less a seemly mode of behaviour than a necessity for all communication. We should use conciliatory speech, one which springs from the milder affects, from *ethos,* not the passionate *pathos.* Colloquy implies respect, openness to the good sides of the other, awareness of one's own shortcomings, a sense of balance and equilibrium. Otherwise justified indignation at one set of abuses may well usher in still worse abuses, not least those of schism, disorder or heresy. One's personal opinions may be legitimate but they should not be absolutised. The firm beliefs of the Church universal are embodied in its creeds and councils, and are few in number. Only the latter command the allegiance of all.

A carefully controlled, structured discourse reflects a structured, hierarchical society, and a harmonious cosmos. The God of Erasmus was one of order, not Luther's God of apocalyptic renewal. The social vision of Erasmus, too, was relatively conservative. The vulgar, the common people, the mob, always flocked to false ideas, indeed to licence and violence, and needed to be protected from themselves. The good, whose union in a good cause constitutes what Erasmus

---

[3] Manfred Hoffmann, *Rhetoric and Reality: the Hermeneutic of Erasmus* (Erasmus Studies, 12; University of Toronto Press: Toronto, 1994); idem, 'Language and Reconciliation: Erasmus' Ecumenical Attitude', *Erasmus of Rotterdam Society Yearbook* 15 (1995), pp. 71–95; my debt to Hoffmann's appreciative yet critical assessment of Erasmus in what follows will be obvious.

means by harmony,[4] tend to be identified with the scholarly, and therefore with the middling to upper reaches of society.

For Erasmus language also had a definite moral dimension. Good language expressed a good heart. Good style offered clarity; but it also expressed purity of heart. Its outcome was useful and edifying, or, as we would say today, 'positive'. Impious people, on the other hand, revelled in conflict and accusation, produced invidious language and engaged in a point-scoring which was detrimental to others. Erasmus believed, not without ground, that his bad name on both sides of the confessional fence was attributable to his exhortation to both parties to be peaceable. He sought to be of use to both sides. *Ego sum moderatior*[5] was his watchword. He suggested as a pragmatic guide for settling the religious conflict that whatever assisted piety, morality and peace should be promoted. The finer doctrinal definitions could be left to the judgements of the professional theologians. In the meantime we should concentrate on the urgent need for moral and educational reform.[6]

Lurking behind this view was a degree of learned agnosticism. Storming life's mysteries, or rather, God's mysteries, could be counter-productive. The most appropriate language about God was not logic-chopping dialectic, with its relish for precise definitions, but metaphorical language, the many-roomed mansions of rhetorical amplitude and allegorical image.

---

[4] Cf. the section on concord or harmony in *De Ratione Concionandi*, Raymond Himelick (ed. and tr.), *Erasmus and the Seamless Coat of Jesus: De sarcienda Ecclesiae concordia* (Lafayette, Ind.: Purdue Research Foundation, 1971), pp. 215–19.

[5] Letters 1341A; quoted in Hoffmann, *Rhetoric*, p.143.

[6] Cf. his guidelines for colloquy: *Epistola ad fratres inferioris Germaniae*, *Opera Omnia*, IX–1, *Desideriii Erasmi Roterodami* (North Holland: Amsterdam, 1982), pp. 406/695–701; however it is better to be sinful within the true Church, than to live in schism, however righteous, outside it. Himelick, *Erasmus*, p. 82; *Opera Omnia*, IX–1, 301/503–5.

His intention was to be Christ-centred, to trust in the promises of God, as seen in the face of Christ, to foster the *harmonia Christi*. He was impatient of any confidence in mere externals,[7] and though the Reformation crisis constrained him in the end to give considerable credence to such 'externals' as the decisions of Councils and church leaders and the consensus of all times and all places, it was never his intention to support a triumphalist ecclesiology. Truth emerged by the careful comparison, or *collatio*, of what might at first appear to be differing, or even contradictory views.

Erasmus had a lively awareness, too, of the psychological reasons for people becoming entrenched in their positions, once they had adopted them. He was much less aware of how vain and touchy he himself could be. The sad truth is that he often used his writings to insinuate that the motivations of all who disagreed with him were less than honourable. In writings such as his *Letter to the brothers of Lower Germany* his argument frequently gets lost in cheap jibes, sarcastic comments, reactive defence and self-justification.[8] His *Profitable Admonition against Lying and Invective* is a still sadder piece of apologetics.[9] The real issues are lost sight of, as eminently forgettable details of actual and imaginary accusations and slights and insults are mulled over at interminable length. We tend, of course, to forget how alarming it was for a lonely individual such as Erasmus to be caught in the glaring searchlight of publicity as the flak of criticism flew at him from all sides. His moralising and at times devious refutations have to be read in the context of his struggle for credibility and independence in a rapidly polarising world.[10]

---

[7] Cf. Hoffmann, *Rhetoric*, p. 151.

[8] *Epistola ad fratres inferioris Germaniae. Opera Omni*, IX–1, 311–425.

[9] *Utilis admonitio adversus mendacium et obtrectationem.* LB 10, 1683D–1692B.

[10] As Augustijn points out in his introduction to the *Epistola ad fratres*, p. 326.

One notes a growing emphasis in Erasmus on the authority of the Church as he became older, and as the consequences of the Reformation became clearer. The Church had been entrusted with adapting the unchanging Gospel to changing times and circumstances. The discussion and resolution of disputed theological issues pertained to the experts, to the bishops and their theologians, not to lay people. A certain idealisation of the leaders in Church and state is a natural concomitant of this attitude.

Theologians and historians of doctrine tend to equate humanism with Erasmus, but we should remember that Erasmus was more conservative in his social and religious views than many other humanists. Some became eloquent advocates of the Protestant, or the Catholic, or the radical cause. The impact of humanism on the reform movements was extremely varied.[11] In some radical circles, for example, an interest in dialogue could take intriguing forms. Thomas Müntzer is one of several radicals who advocated dialogue with Jew and Turk. His concept of the *ordo rerum*, God's harmonious ordering of the universe, a grasp of which in some ways relativised Scripture, is an interesting variation on Erasmus' understanding of cosmic harmony.[12] Unlike the Church's rule of faith the 'order of things' offers a transcendent norm by which heretics and non-Christians can be convinced. The need to take the other seriously leads to a fundamental re-evaluation of theology's traditional criteria. Once the Bible comes to be seen as the Christian's Koran, one needs to look beyond it.

Humanism also won much popular support. If Mark Edwards' rewriting of Reformation history on the basis of the

[11]   Cf. Peter Matheson, 'Humanism and Reform Movements', in Anthony Goodman and Angus McKay (eds.), *The Impact of Humanism on Western Europe* (Longman: London, 1990), pp. 1–15.

[12]   Cf. Gordon Rupp, *Patterns of Reformation* (Epworth: London, 1969), pp. 292–5; CW 357 n. 6; Peter Matheson, 'Thomas Müntzer's Marginal Comments on Tertullian', *Journal of Theological Studies* 41 (1990), pp. 76–90.

mass support given to Scriptural reforms is anywhere near the truth,[13] Erasmus' priorities may have been much nearer to those of the majority of the Reformation's supporters than the crusading zeal of the theologians who debated the nature of the Eucharist in the 1520s and 1530s, or who made life and death issues out of what might appear to be rather recondite doctrinal points. Erasmus' irenic views on the value of confession, or how to deal with idolatrous practices, for example, would be shared by most people today.[14]

Much of Erasmus' thinking about dialogue was taken aboard by what Friedrich Heer has called the 'Third Force' in the Reformation period.[15] In countless individuals, at the local, civic and imperial levels, the idea of a religious 'accommodation' was welcomed. Catholics such as Pflug and Gropper, and Protestants such as Bucer and Melanchthon tried to find a new discourse which maintained the essentials of catholicity, provided a basis for joint reforming activity, and allowed for tolerance on matters which did not enter into the substance of the faith. Bucer's *Consilium*, written at the beginning of the 1540s, shows that an interim policy of flexibility and tolerance and dialogue could even be advocated for dynamic, missionary reasons.[16] Melanchthon tenaciously struggled to maintain the bridge of humanist friendship across the confessional divide, and had no patience with *logomachia*, mere battles of words. The impressive group of Catholic evangelicals, with Contarini and Pole at their head, sought to reform Catholicism from within, thus keeping open the door to dialogue with the Protestants.

[13]   Mark Edwards, *Printing, Propaganda, and Martin Luther* (University of California Press: Berkeley, 1994), pp. 163–73.

[14]   Himelick, *Erasmus*, pp. 88–90; *Opera Omnia,* IX–1, 305–7.

[15]   *Die Dritte Kraft: Der europäischer Humanismus zwischen den Fronten des konfessionellen Zeitalters* (Fischer: Frankfurt a. Main, 1959).

[16]   Pierre Fraenkel (ed.), *Consilium Theologicum privatim conscriptum* (Brill: Leiden, 1988); Peter Matheson, 'Martyrdom or Mission. A Protestant Debate', *Archiv für Reformationsgeschichte* 80 (1989), pp. 154–72.

Detailed descriptions of the religious colloquies of the Reformation period have been given elsewhere and need not be repeated here.[17] Some key points can, however, be highlighted. The indomitable pursuit of reconciliatory formulae on the Eucharist, for example, which resulted in the Wittenberg Concord between the Lutherans and south German Protestantism in 1536, was partly motivated by the necessity to set doctrinal differences in a wider perspective, which took account of social, political and cultural concerns. All of these concerns had their importance, in Bucer's mind, for the upbuilding of the Kingdom of God, and were not regarded at all as marginal, secular issues. This raises an important, but seldom considered problem: the degree to which theological controversies subverted other catholic and evangelical priorities, not only by diverting energies from them, but by creating an atmosphere in which the common weal became harder and harder to perceive.

Bucer's eschatological perspective sometimes led him to operate tactically, accepting, for example, a particular formulation such as that of the substantial or corporeal presence of Christ in the Eucharist which he personally regarded as unhelpful, but which was necessary to maintain the momentum of the overall project, and to prevent the 'Romanists' exploiting divisions within the Protestant camp.[18] He could accept practices for an interim period, or at least tolerate them being

[17] Recent studies include Cornelis Augustijn, 'Bucer und die Religionsgespräche von 1540/1', in Christian Krieger and Marc Lienhard (eds.), *Martin Bucer and Sixteenth Century Europe* (Studies in Medieval and Reformation Thought LIII; Brill: Leiden, 1993), pp. 671–80, which offers a useful review of current scholarship.

[18] . . . *putavimus memorata verba: substantialiter et corporalem praesentiam, quando ea, in quo sensu posita sunt . . . admittenda quo minus Pontificiis occasionis esset, eos qui idem quam Evangelii profitentur, cum totius orbis offendiculo, a se invicem divellendi*; J. V. Pollet (ed.), *Martin Butzer: Etudes sur la correspondance. . . .* (Presses universitaires de France: Paris, 1958), 1, 97.

embraced by others, provided that in the longer term the pure Word of God was going to prevail. He argued, for example, at the Regensburg Colloquy of 1541 that the reservation and adoration of the host, and even the term 'transubstantiation', could be tolerated in previously Catholic territories in the meantime.[19] The same is true of the intercession of the saints.[20] He accepted the need to move circumspectly in order not to affront the weak, and to provide time to educate people in new insights. Even on the issue of the so-called private Masses, that is, ones in which only the priest took communion, Bucer and Gropper could see their way to a toleration of varying practice.[21] As long as the common people were given positive teaching about the essentials of the faith, there could be agreement to disagree on finer points of doctrine. It is worth noting that there was a considerable consensus at Regensburg, including that of the Imperial chancellor, Granvelle, that it was unnecessary to perplex the ordinary person about such technical issues as transubstantiation.[22]

Still more important, perhaps, than his tactical flexibility was Bucer's awareness of the heuristic value of theological dialogue. The disagreements within the Protestant camp about the Eucharist, after all, went back to deeper christological issues, to what was meant by the human and the divine and their interaction, to what was meant by flesh and spirit, and to philosophical questions about the nature of space and time. Most of these issues are still with us. The unflagging energy which Bucer devoted to bringing together the Lutheran understanding on the real presence with the south German emphasis on the spiritual presence of Christ appears to owe much to his awareness that both parties were saying something of crucial importance and that by listening to both of them a

[19]   Codex Musculus 113v (in Fraenkel, 'Les protestants'), p. 101.
[20]   ARG 6, 54, 81.
[21]   ARG 6, 82.
[22]   Cf. Elizabeth C. Gleason, *Gasparo Contarini: Venice, Rome and Reform* (University of California Press: Berkeley, 1993).

new and more adequate discourse could be found. While, for example, Christ in his divine nature was at the right hand of God the Father in Heaven other Scriptural texts made it clear to Bucer that Christ was present wherever two or three were gathered together. Bucer realised that any language we use to describe this presence, which is also distance, can only be an approximation. His Erasmian bent is seen in the metaphorical language he brings to play: as the rays of the sun in Heaven, truly reach us here on earth, so is the heavenly Christ with us.[23] The task of mediators such as Bucer involves endless pertinacity and imagination in finding such a language.

This wrestling to find an accommodation between Luther and Oecolampadius, or between Wittenberg and Rome, does not necessarily lead to reductionism or indifferentism, to a watering down of the truth. In Bucer's view, it can lead us closer to God's accommodation to us in the incarnation. Unlike Erasmus, the primary concern of Bucer and Gropper was not for the advancement of piety or educational or pastoral reform or even for unity, but for unity in the truth, understood in a broad sense as the confession of the Christian Gospel. For them careful attention not only to the Scriptures and the Early Church but to the discourse of sincere fellow-Christians of a different persuasion was the way to the truth. Patience is required so that the others have the chance to explain exactly what they mean. The relationship of trust between Bucer and Gropper was itself a significant factor in the dialogue. For example, when one is prepared to give one's partner in discussion the benefit of the doubt, more flexibility in language and thought becomes possible.

Another significant point may lie in the personalities of Bucer and Gropper. Luther combated his despair through aggressive polemic, Erasmus through idealisation and petulant

[23]   Pollet, *Etudes*, 1, 225–7; I am grateful to my student, Mr Nicholas Thompson, for drawing this, and the next quotation, to my attention, in his thesis, 'The Eucharistic Articles of the Worms-Regensburg Book', University of Otago, 1996.

complaint, Melanchthon through agonising indecision. Bucer, in particular, appears to be of sterner mettle. When he found himself stymied he did not vent his indignation on others, but looked for another way through the impasse. He was less inclined to personalise issues, and to demonise opponents. This must have taken considerable courage, especially when peer pressure from colleagues was so strong. He was certainly aware of the possible pitfalls of mediatory work: '. . . my conscience assails me, lest in our concern to serve Christ through this colloquy we do not end up by serving the devil'.[24] The accusation that he was being devious and using ambiguous language was seldom slow in coming.[25]

He was cautious about identifying the cause of the Gospel with his own formulations. He could detach himself from the latter, and act as an intermediary between two sets of views, neither of which he may have fully shared, yet with which he could empathise. It is almost as if he and Gropper saw it as their vocation to act as theological mediators, as the 'voices' to their own companions of the opposing party.

Bucer's characteristic concern for the *gemein nutz*, the common weal, appears to have overridden the natural tendency to be over-defensive and reactive. This is not to suggest that he did not engage in polemic. The opposite is the case. He could be trenchant in his criticism of opponents. What was most unusual was his willingness to revisit issues repeatedly, to believe the best of the partner in dialogue, to revise formulations, and to explore new formulations which might lead to a common ground. In the crisis of authority which the Reformation precipitated his ability to combine firmness on the central issues

[24]   20 December 1540, Bucer to Phillip of Hesse; Lenz I, 101, 278.
[25]   Cf. Melanchthon's letter to the Emperor about the *flexiloqua*, the two-tongued formulations, in the Regensburg Book; CR 4, 321; Calvin included Melanchthon with Bucer in his condemnation of the dangerous *flexiloquentiam* of the Book; CR 39, 217; on the Catholic side not only Eck, but the irenic Contarini condemned Bucer's position as an incoherent mish-mash, *garbuglio*; HJB 1, 376.

with flexibility was no mean feat. One is reminded of his great Biblical mentor, Paul, who managed to remain on the whole in dialogue with those with whom he passionately disagreed, and who, of course, did succeed in developing a whole new discourse of his own.

Bucer and Gropper left, as has often been observed, no form of church life or polity behind them, but they did make significant progress in laying the basis for a new, mediatorial ecumenical discourse. Their emphasis on Scriptural and patristic language and concepts, and above all their championing of the Regensburg Book, a formulation of the faith which could not be identified with either of the parties at Regensburg, pointed the way forward. The agreement on justification by faith showed a flexibility about vocabulary as well as concepts. As far as the Eucharist was concerned Gropper apparently was ready to concede that the term 'transubstantiation' was not indispensable, and may have suggested the term 'transmutation'.[26] For his part Bucer met this concession by coining the improbable term, 'transconditionation', to characterise the changed spiritual condition of the bread after consecration.

Bucer was aware that on many issues Scriptural language varied, or was less than precise, and that we should not attempt to go beyond it in our precisionism. Patristic precedents could on occasion persuade Melanchthon, too, to be open-minded about legitimate interpretations of the sacrificial nature of the Lord's Supper, if this helped to stem controversy and bring peace to the churches.[27]

For a while the promotion of religious colloquy even became Imperial policy. At the Diet of Regensburg in particular Imperial, Papal and Protestant humanists co-operated with Imperial counsellors to promote the cause of dialogue. At this Diet some of the conditions for genuine dialogue to take place

[26]   CR 4, 261f.
[27]   CR 4, 314f., 318.

had been created. The Papal Legate, Contarini, represented a reforming, evangelical Catholicism; Imperial policy favoured dialogue; an atmosphere of trust developed between Bucer and Gropper, both of whom were committed to a humanist approach to Scripture and the Fathers. The Regensburg Book, on which discussions were based, was a genuine attempt to find a middle ground between the two parties. The lay chairing of the colloquy by the Imperial chancellor, Granvelle, was another indication of the desire to transcend previous divisions, and offers an interesting analogy to the civic disputations in which magistrates acted as arbiters. Political concerns for a joint programme of national reform and unity and the need to secure subventions against the Turkish threat lent urgency to the resolution of the theological issues.

The agreement on justification achieved at Regensburg was the most remarkable fruit of this drive towards a viable compromise. Its importance has seldom been sufficiently recognised. The colloquy, however, always had something of a spectral air. Its polite words and fair intentions did not reflect the vested interests and intransigent attitudes of either Rome or Wittenberg. Truth issues and power issues were hopelessly entangled. The failure to agree on the authority of the Church and the nature of the sacraments may have been predictable, given the lack of will for accommodation in these centres. The pressures of time combined with unease at the political pressures being exerted on the collocutors. The limited resources of time and energy available, when compared with those poured into polemic confrontation for two decades, militated against the development of the new theological discourse which would have been required. The colloquy was unable to proceed beyond incipient moves towards an evangelical Catholicism, a Catholic evangelicalism.

There may, however, have been more fundamental reasons for the failure. Erasmus himself, it could be argued, had done little to prepare the way for a genuine reconciliation. His main interests lay in the realm of practical piety and educational and pastoral reform, not in theology as such. His undoubted Scriptural scholarship had the flair of Jerome, rather than the penetration of Augustine. His followers tended to have an idealised picture of the Early Church. His criteria for good dialogue – caution and moderation, flexibility and tolerance – gave little specific guidance to mediating theologians. At best Erasmian initiatives could have patched together a compromise, based on a fairly traditional understanding of the Church and society, and a rather moralistic reading of Scripture. Alternatively, they could have facilitated a toleration of a considerable variety of views, if the spirit of the age had not been such a confessional one. A genuine theological reconciliation, however, was beyond their purview, and it was this which was needed.

Likewise the *spirituali* or Catholic evangelicals in Italy, France and elsewhere often had a relatively narrow individualistic focus to their piety. One thinks of Lefèvre in France or Juan Valdes in Naples. There is a strong mystical as well as a Biblical dimension to both of them, which tended to relegate structural or ecclesiological questions to the periphery of their concerns. Others were in the Augustinian tradition which combined a high doctrine of grace with a strong sense of the authority of the Church. For such Rome remained a central focus of loyalty and a symbol of the unity of the Church. Few allowed their understanding of justification to modify their understanding of Church and sacraments.

Hence reforming figures such as Contarini or Pole were distressed and appalled when they discovered what the views of Protestants on the Church and the sacraments actually were. The preparatory ground for a new community of theological discourse had not been laid. The presuppositions of the parties remained poles apart.[28]

---

[28]   It would be an interesting exercise to compare the sixteenth-century colloquies with ecumenical discussions in the twentieth century.

The cases of Martin Bucer, and of Johann Gropper, in many ways such tragic ones, become all the more interesting by comparison. Like Erasmus they were aware of the need for moderation in language to prevent people talking past one another, but unlike Erasmus their primary interest was in theology. They were practically engaged in attempts at what we might call theological mediation. In Bucer's case this involved a long-term commitment to mediate between the breaches in the Protestant camp as well as between Protestants and Catholics. Both Bucer and Gropper owe much to Erasmus, and yet one detects a significant shift to specifically theological concerns.

The world from which the exegete speaks determines in large part how the text is understood. When two people, such as Bucer and Gropper, genuinely met their worlds also met. Their shared insights could then reflect the different worlds from which they came. Such a meeting of minds, however, takes grace as well as time, and is as rare as it is precious. It presupposes the willingness of those engaged to let a dialogue develop between their lives as well as between their minds. It can be argued, therefore, that the tentative ecumenical dialogues of the Reformation period did not fail. They were scarcely allowed to begin.[29] Words were exchanged, but worlds were not allowed to meet. Personal factors, the clash of what were rapidly becoming the rival institutions of Catholicism and Lutheranism, and a plethora of political issues militated against success as much as purely theological concerns. Their fascination, however, remains. To illustrate the mediatorial approach we turn to the famous writing of Erasmus on irenics, of 1533, *De sarcienda ecclesiae concordia*.[30]

---

[29]   Gleason, *Contarini*, p. 239; Basil Hall, *Humanists and Protestants 1500–1900* (T. & T. Clark: Edinburgh, 1989); Peter Matheson, *Cardinal Contarini at Regensburg* (Clarendon: Oxford, 1972).

[30]   *Opera Omnia*, V–3, 245–314.

On Restoring the Concord of the Church

Erasmus, it appears, had been importuned for a long time by his humanist friends, the Protestant Philip Melanchthon and the Catholic Julius Pflug, the later bishop of Naumburg, to write something which would 'calm the tempest' raging within the Church, following the failure of the Diet of Augsburg to settle the religious issue.[31] Following a common enough practice, he wrote his recipe for peace in the form of a Biblical commentary, on Psalm 84. This had the advantage of permitting an indirect and non-confrontational approach to the issue.

The key images of the Psalm pervade the writing: Zion is our dwelling-place, it is a nest, a place of safety, the peaceful haven where the sparrow finds its home. One senses the *Geborgenheit* which the catholicity and apostolicity of the Church offered Erasmus: being enfolded, hidden, rescued from life's vagaries and storms. The sub-title of the writing: *De amabili Ecclesiae Concordia*, echoes the first words of the Psalm: 'How lovely is your dwelling place.' In this Platonic vision beauty, harmony and truth all walk together.

The controlling image of the Church is that of one's 'home'. This is amplified by the analogies of friendship and marriage. Both demand give and take, a mutual toleration of faults. There is no worse sin than leaving home, forsaking the company of the faithful. The importance of good relations among family members is supreme. Although Erasmus has no truck with dour traditionalists, who reject something just because it is new, the tabernacle image is not understood in a dynamic way. The Church is not the pilgrim people of God, the Church on the move. It is an idealised construct. As the mystical body of Christ it is invisible, and known only to God. The true way to unity is to make Christ the focus of all our hopes.[32]

---

[31] As Robert Stupperich notes in his introduction, Erasmus' interest in finding a way to settle the religious crisis goes back to the early 1520s. *Opera Omnia*, V–3, 247–55.

[32] Himelick, *Erasmus*, p. 82; *Opera Omnia*, V–3, 300/504f.

Yet in another sense the Church is clearly a visible, historical one,[33] with deep roots back to the apostolic past, and a catholic network extending horizontally throughout the world which guarantees stability and continuity. Any rash departure from a tradition which has been tried and tested for centuries should be shunned.[34] To conserve such consensus patience and humility are required. The larger good is to be preferred to private agendas and group interests, and we should prefer to be modest doorkeepers in the house of the Lord, rather than insist on holding centre stage ourselves. This is no legalistic or institutional view of the Church. The gift of the prophet, the work of the teacher, the operation of the Spirit of Christ, are more important than formal office,[35] and Erasmus has no patience with clerical rivalries or pretensions. True honour depends not on some ecclesiastical pecking order, but springs from one's innermost motivations, and is demonstrated in the love of neighbour and enemy.[36]

Erasmus can talk movingly of the majesty and felicity and invulnerability of the Church.[37] This doxological dimension is pivotal. The Church is the community of those who praise God. True piety, spiritual worship, the sacrifice of praise are central. The language of music, of choral harmony and symphony, is often used. The eternal temple to which the Psalmist refers is the Catholic Church, which mirrors that heavenly Jerusalem where no cacophony of selfish voices will mar the melody.[38] Our human individualism, however,

---

[33]   Himelick, *Erasmus,* p. 43; *Opera Omnia,* V–3, 270/403–15.

[34]   Himelick, *Erasmus,* p. 86; *Opera Omnia,* V–3, 304/620–3.

[35]   Himelick, *Erasmus,* p. 43; *Opera Omnia,* V–3, 270/405–10.

[36]   Himelick, *Erasmus,* p. 6; *Opera Omnia,* V–3, 290/122.

[37]   *Tanta autem est Ecclesiae maiestas et felicitas, ut quod in ea contemptissimum est, longe praestet omnibus mundi splendoribus*; Himelick, *Erasmus,* p. 77, 49; *Omnia Opera,* V–3, 297/360–2; 274/583–275/585.

[38]   *Piorum enim concordia coelestis illius Ecclesiae imaginem nobis repraesentat, in qua nulla est opiniorum dissensio*; *Opera Omnia,* V–3, 269/ 382f., Himelick, *Erasmus,* p. 42.

threatens this harmony: Erasmus uses an impressive array of pejorative terms to characterise it: ambition, obstinacy, insolence, licence, blind partisanship, zealotry, thorny disputatiousness, gladiatorial combat about mere words, abusiveness, intemperance, animosity, coerciveness, personal hatred, intransigence, idolatry, lunatic contention, brawling, barbarism; discord, tempest, violence, tumult; the last four all stem from the uneducated, the masses, the untutored crowd.

The corresponding positive terms he uses are: peace, concord, faith, love, hope, tolerance, generosity of judgement, piety, simplicity, innocence, sobriety, learning, respectful submission, faithful obedience, peace-making truth; *sunkatabasis* or accommodation, condescension; flexibility, temperance, ingenuousness, emulation of the saints, forbearance, reasonableness, reform, renewal, wholesome counsel, healing relief, moderation, respect for tradition.

These two catalogues of opposing terms illustrate the definite limits to the tolerance of Erasmus. He is intolerant of much more than intolerance. His notorious anti-semitism does not figure prominently in this writing,[39] but he summarily dismisses as monsters and blasphemers such groups from the Early Church as Gnostics, Montanists, Marcionites, Arians, Sabellians, Eunomians. He did not even seem to be aware what a mixed bag of people he was condemning! There is no interest in their truth claims. In a manner reminiscent of I Clement's Letter to the Corinthians at the close of the first century a moralising criterion is applied: heretics are ambitious power-seekers, frustrated leaders who twist Scripture to suit their own thinking, *ad sensum humanum*. He feels genuine nausea when he reads the writings of people such as the Manichaeans.[40]

Erasmus, of course, cannot be expected to manifest post-Enlightenment attitudes. His brusque assertions suggest,

[39]   Cf. H. O. Oberman, *The Impact of the Reformation* (T. & T. Clark: Edinburgh, 1994), esp. pp. 102–6.

[40]   Himelick, *Erasmus*, pp. 39f.; *Opera Omnia*, V–3, 267/305f.

however, that he is not greatly interested in opening up theological debate as such, or even in suggesting ways to engage imaginatively with the views of others. His concern for peace and concord is the primary one, and rests on some unexamined presuppositions about the relationship between orthodoxy and ecclesial structures.

The Church, however, should restrict to a minimum what is confessionally binding on everyone. Erasmus' experience is that much theological debate, such as that on free will, tends to be a 'thorny' business, which bears little fruit.[41] Similarly, the endless debates about the mode of Christ's real presence in the Eucharist produce little but nausea (that word again!). The Eucharist, rather, should be providing the pious with its unique solace in their devotional lives.[42] On justification he attempts to steer between the parties by maintaining the necessity of good works and the legitimacy of merit, but seeing meritorious works as merely supplementary and ornamental to the justification which comes by faith.[43] This form of double justification is a good example of his concern that both parties, that is, the Reformers and the champions of the Old Church, should accommodate their views to one another.[44] For the sake of peace, concepts are often left deliberately vague. One wonders in which sense Erasmus believed, for example, that meritorious works benefited the dead.[45]

He appears to beat a tactical retreat from inter-disciplinary debate between theology and the liberal sciences, when this threatened the supreme value of concord. The dominant public discourse in Church and state was not radically questioned.

---

[41]   *Spinosa est verius quam frugifera disputatio*; *Opera Omnia*, V–3, 304/ 625; Himelick, *Erasmus*, p. 86.

[42]   Himelick, *Erasmus*, p. 94; *Opera Omnia*, V–3, 310/848–50.

[43]   Himelick, *Erasmus*, p. 87; *Opera Omnia*, V–3, 304, 633–7

[44]   *accedat illa sygkatabasis, ut utraque pars alteri se nonnihil accommodet, sine qua nulla constat concordia*; *Opera Omnia*, V–3, 304/617f.; Himelick, *Erasmus*, p. 86.

[45]   Himelick, *Erasmus*, p. 87; *Opera Omnia*, V–3, 305/654–67.

Sin continues to be seen as referring to particular acts, rather than one's whole relationship to God.[46] Traditional understandings of grace are not challenged. The nature of heresy and schism tends to be taken as given. If his solutions seem somewhat bland at times, the reason may be, as his exegesis of the Psalm suggests, that the ecclesiological tail wagged the christological dog.

What criteria does Erasmus suggest for good dialogue? Scripture is the key guide. Patristic precedents offer another criterion. The term 'sacrifice', for example, had already been used in the Early Church, and so there could be no objection to its use in the Mass to mean praise and thanksgiving.[47] Listening skills are important. Time and time again, he pleads for flexibility, a readiness for concessions and compromise. He argues against those who love to cry 'heretic' at every opportunity. One should err on the side of a generous interpretation of what the other person says or does.[48]

When confronted by two extreme positions, he often suggests that the final decision be left to an ecumenical council, that is, to the consensus of the bishops.[49] This 'expectant' position avoids premature polarisation, but could be regarded as too easy an option at times, given the widely different views of what constituted a proper ecumenical council. In the interim he pleaded for the reform of abuses in the adoration of the Mass, for example,[50] and for more scholarly debate. Finally, individuals should allow one another more latitude. The weak

---

[46]   Himelick, *Erasmus*, p. 90; *Opera Omnia*, V–3, 307/730–46.

[47]   Himelick, *Erasmus*, p. 92; *Opera Omnia*, V–3, 309/796f.

[48]   *in peiorem partem interpretantes quae dicta sunt ambique, per calumniam depravantes ea quae pie dicta sunt*; *Opera Omnia*, V–3, 302/575–8; Himelick, *Erasmus*, p. 84.

[49]   The question of celibacy and of vows, for example; Himelick, *Erasmus*, p. 90.

[50]   Himelick, *Erasmus*, p. 93; *Opera Omnia*, V–3, 309/816–310/829.

who still adhere to semi-superstitious practices should not be condemned. God loves the simple-minded, after all.[51]

Heroic remedies, in Erasmus' view, not only worsen the situation but encourage the masses to total cynicism and licence.[52] Attacking the bishops, who have been given to us as successors to the apostles, will simply lead to anarchy. He felt a particular repulsion for those who sought to force their novel views upon others.[53] The Emperor Charles and his brother, Ferdinand, mean well. If only moderation were embraced, it could pave the way for the General Council to settle the issues once and for all.[54]

The very manner in which Erasmus so often drifts from a discussion of doctrinal matters to ceremonial practice or moral reforms illustrates the point that his primary concern was less to encourage dialogue on doctrinal issues than to avoid or circumscribe it. There is, of course, much to be said for this point of view.

What, then, of the 'dream of an understanding'? At the Imperial religious colloquies, and on many other more modest occasions, the interesting attempt was made to instrumentalise dialogue to secure the peace that religion, society and empire required by the rational and amiable discussion of good people. In retrospect the chances must always have been slim, given the confusion of religion and politics, of truth issues and power issues, the clash of potent personalities, the uncertainty about final criteria and loci of authority. Understanding may, in any case, require a rather more costly reconciliation than was possible at this time, including a deep healing of memories, a quite daunting readiness for self-knowledge and self-criticism, and an awareness of the value of ongoing differences. Yet

---

[51]   Himelick, *Erasmus*, pp. 87f.; *Opera Omnia*, V–3, 305/671. This view is in line with his distinction between the learned and the masses in the Church.

[52]   Himelick, *Erasmus*, p. 84; *Opera Omnia*, V–3, 302/567–72.

[53]   Himelick, *Erasmus*, p. 95; *Opera Omnia*, V–3, 311/876–81.

[54]   Himelick, *Erasmus*, p. 97; *Opera Omnia*, V–3, 312/924–7.

irenic dialogue, in the longer perspective, does not have to succeed. That it took place at all is encouragement enough. Success, after all, as the Jewish wisdom reminds us, is not one of the names of God.

CHAPTER NINE

REFORMATION RHETORIC

hommage à rabelais
d'schöni
vo de wüeschte wörter
isch e brunne
i dr wüeschti
vo de schöne wörter.

The beauty
of wild words
is an oasis
in the wilderness
of beautiful words.

Kurt Marti, *Rosa Loui,* 1967

In the Library Hall of the Old College, Edinburgh, is the bust of an eighteenth-century professor, evidently known to his students as a 'dungeon of knowledge'. He had got his learning in, but could not get it out! The early 1520s were the exciting opposite of this. University walls cracked open, theological scholars turned outwards, and for the first time in European history something like a public opinion emerged, fed by a jostling variety of genial word-smiths, and of what we might call mini-media. The connection between theological faculties and religious leaders and this new animal, public opinion, is the event we call the Reformation.

In this book we have been trying to trace some aspects of the social history of ideas in this period, to approach the

239

Reformation as an intricate, fascinating and serious game, and to recognise the centrality of rhetoric in its choreography. This has led us to describe the spread of reforming views, to look at what is meant by literacy, and specially Biblical literacy, to discuss the appropriateness of the term 'propaganda', the legitimacy and limits of polemic, and the brave failures of the apostles of dialogue.

Netherlands historians in particular, following Huizinga, have encouraged us to think of the whole of Church history in terms of play, with its teams of competitors, its rules and umpires. It is not unhelpful to think of the councils of the Church in this light, for example. The Reformation 'game' succeeded because it lured onlookers into becoming participants, to join the dance. As we have seen, the word *spiel*, game, was often used by the Reformers to describe the events in which they were involved. The difficulty of course, was that the traditional referees – the bishops, councils, and Popes – had been sidelined, 'sin-binned'.

It was a game, therefore, in which the rules were being reinvented as it proceeded. The daring, passionate preachers, the initiators of communal liturgies, the authors of the smudgy, cheap pamphlets and broadsheets which landed on German laps in their tens of thousands in the 1520s were, of course, serious enough, ready to risk career and even life for their convictions. But on another level they were hucksters standing behind their several booths, enticing people to 'have a go', to sing along with the Wittenberg nightingale. 'If, then, you long for truth then come and join us in the dance', writes Thomas Müntzer to the people of Erfurt at the height of the Peasants' War.[1] As the old feasts and festivals of traditional piety, the razzmatazz of the Indulgence-sellers and the gladiatorial rituals of the scholastic disputation went out of fashion, in surged a flood of peasant dialogues, fables, songs, covenants, civic disputations, vernacular liturgies. The Reformation pamphlets

[1]   CW, 159/10.

caught the popular imagination precisely because they presented the age-old Christian game with poetic, mythic, dramatic originality, with verve and panache.

The Reformation, we have suggested, was primarily a paradigm shift in the religious imagination, not a structural reform, not even a doctrinal reform. Each pamphlet is witness to a collapsed consensus, and simultaneously signposts the dream of a new religious landscape and inscape. The broadsheets and wood-cuts of the period confirm this. They present the birth-pangs of a new age in visual terms: a drastic, simplistic confrontation of dawn and dusk, light and dark, discipleship and corruption, freedom and tyranny. Their striking images are littered with rhymes, slogans, catch-phrases which decoded them, above all with what we can call God's graffiti, quotations from Scripture.

We think of the Bible in terms of a text to be exegeted. The sixteenth-century Reformers saw it as the exegetical tool which illumined the whole of reality. Their cultural landscape, accordingly, was studded with these graffiti, the Biblical quotations from prophets, evangelists and apostles, the divine wisdom which seemed to settle every argument. In fact, however, Scripture's triumphal march was not a knock-down, logical one, but intuitive and imaginative. Scripture was certainly verbal enough, but it was also delivered orally from the pulpit and sung about in the new hymns. Karlstadt may seek to replace images by Scripture, but Scriptural language is itself image-laden, one might almost say, image-ridden. When Müntzer sums up his work as preaching, singing and printing, he reminds us that the Reformation unleashed a flood of images and of music, as well as of words. At the heart of Scripture for the ordinary believer were the Psalms, both song and word and an endless source for the imagination.

For Müntzer, revelation occurs when the exterior image of Scripture meets the interior image in the abyss of our soul. His writings are one long testimony to the collocation, or confrontation of the Word of God in Scripture with the work of God within us. The historical witness to prophetic and apostolic figures such as John the Baptist is 'tuned in' to resonate with the wilderness in our hearts. When 'one has not yet heard the clear words of God in the soul one has to have visions'. Authentic dreams and visions and Scripture are both catalysts, which complement one another and nudge the believer to be open to the work of God in the abyss of the soul.[2] While Müntzer, of course, has his own specific emphases here, the whole Reformation can be conceived as a comprehensive re-imaging of law, prophets, wisdom, Gospel, Church, sacraments and discipleship.

The first impression given by the Reformation may be that of iconoclasm, God's servants whirling a rod of iron among the old clay pots. Even an iconoclast such as Karlstadt, however, speaks in a succession of dramatic images. He attacks images of wood or stone, but mediates to lay people a vibrant Biblical mysticism. One image after another is offered to the passionate embrace of their memory. We may have to rethink our understanding of the Reformation. It may have been less concerned to reform a corrupt Church, or to restore pure doctrine than to encourage Christians to dream in a differing mode, to celebrate Baptism and the Eucharist eschatologically, to weave the daily business of living into the religious life. Erasmus' evocation of the Jerusalem Temple as a model of the Church, where even the sparrow finds its rest, shares this dream-like quality. The doxological dimension is as pivotal as the utopian one. The Catholic Church should mirror that heavenly Jerusalem where no cacophony of discordant voices can mar the melody.

And what of Luther himself? His language is a kaleidoscope of images. His Word of God is a tiny, helpless child, an agonised Messiah on a cross. In his theology of the cross God plays an elaborate game of hide and seek with us, concealing power under weakness, glory under the grime of earthy reality, joy

---

[2]   Cf. his *Sermon to the Princes*, CW, 241, 243.

under suffering. The language of paradox, the exaggerations of hyperbole, make their escape from the chains of logic. The sinner, by God's grace, is also the saint. *Simul justus et peccator.* Luther's teaching about the Real Presence or about infant Baptism is quite inaccessible to any logic. God is above mathematics. Grace cannot be calculated. Logic is a whore, anyway.

To understand the Reformation, therefore, we have to enter the world of its dreams, its utopias, its homely recasting of spiritual reality. The *Appeal to the German Nobility* is a vivid, dazzling dream of what the Church can be, the priesthood of all believers replacing the *olgotzen,* the oily idols of the consecrated clergy, the Jericho-like walls of Canon Law around clerical privilege collapsing before Joshua's trumpet. This is not a programme for reform. It is an invitation to an apocalyptic dance, to enter with Christ into his Kingdom.

As we begin, then, to recognise the genial choreography of Reformation thought, to use Leroux's term, the images of the wood-cuts begin to make sense. The Reformation is the new song proclaimed by the Psalmist, which celebrates freedom from enslavement to fear, the gracious exchange of Christ's righteousness for our turpitude, of Pauline ecstasy for Babylonian captivity. As Junghans has emphasised, the theology of the Reformation is structured by its rhetoric.

For the concrete, spoken word, in Luther's view, is the medium, the bridge, the waggon, which draws us into God's work as witnessed in Scripture, and draws it into us. Without the Word the grave remains empty! The historical events of Israel and the life and work of Christ are brought together with our present life by the Word. The stories of Scripture are to be told in such a way that the hearers identify with them, become part of them.

Accordingly, Bieritz describes Luther's sermons as a battleground of words, a *Wortkampf,* in which Christ, the devil, angels, disciples and the women all find a voice through the preacher. He does not affect the sermonic 'we', but is in continual dialogue with God and the devil, the Papists or the

'Enthusiasts', as well as with his audience. It is not the popular touch of Luther which is surprising, Bieritz argues, but the ambitious use of learned rhetoric to appeal to the emotions and transform the conduct of the 'ordinary' listener. The Holy Spirit deploys rhetoric to make exhortation more effective.[3]

Rhetoric, then, is far more than the ornamentation of thought. It is as we struggle for the 'right' words to reach out to others, to teach, delight and move them, that we discover what we ourselves really think. In the end of the day, as every speaker and preacher knows, it is not logic but rhetoric which really shifts thought, including our own. As Perelman and others have argued, figurative discourse is itself argumentative, bringing about a change in perspective, focusing the imagination, creating depth and presence, bringing to birth communion between writer and reader. Or as Deborah Brandt puts it, through the temporal flow of imaginative discourse a progressive interaction of the audience with the author takes place.

The polemic, the cut and thrust, spark and flash, of Reformation debate has to be revisited from this perspective. It is not reducible to a clash of ideas, of pure doctrine, of principles or values. It was, rather, a battle of credibilities and personalities, human and superhuman, of principalities and powers, of the German Hercules and the Papist bull, of Karsthans, the bluff, Scripture-toting peasant wielding his flail against injustice, and the pussy-footing theologian, Murner, *Murrnarr*. It was seen as an apocalyptic battle between Christ and Satan, God and the Devil. The competing visions of reality reflected a struggle for power, quite irreconcilable understandings of the role of clergy, laity, women.

This polemic was the weapon of the under-dog, of those who were hurting and those who were thinking. Such polemic

---

[3]   *Rhetoricatur igitur Spiritus sanctus iam, ut exhortatio fiat illustrior*: Karl Heinrich Bieritz, 'Verbum Facit Fidem – Homiletische Anmerkungen zu einer Lutherpredigt', *Theologische Literaturzeitung* 109 (July 1984), pp. 482–94; cf. W 29, 269–81.

rakes up the muck, lifts the lid to reveal the obscenities within, opens up a hole in the wall, so we can see what the 'big wigs' are on about, as so many pamphlets put it. It is a liberating tool; it topples the false consciousness of oppressor and oppressed; it empowers the marginalised; it lays bare the power-broking behind religious rationalisations.

At a time when the laity were supposed to obey, peasants to sweat, be fruitful and multiply, and accept their lot, when sixteenth-century women were forced to affect a rhetoric of humility to be heard at all, popular polemic subverted the whole social universe. When Luther said that Christ did not have two bodies, a clerical one and a lay one, he was stating the blindingly obvious. But the blindingly obvious had been obscured by the ghetto wisdom of the professionally learned; as the popular saw had it, the learned are perverted: *die gelehrten die verkehrten.*

Where reality has become offensive, language has to become angular. Another very popular topos in the Reformation pamphlet, 'Christ did not say: I am tradition, but I am the truth', has a similarly wicked edge. The time for soft-speaking had gone because, in Karlstadt's words, the Church had become a flea-market. The truth, therefore, had to be elicited at the cost of peace. Polemic developed a heuristic drive. In the simple slogans of the Reformers, ecclesiology and revelation are reinterpreted in simple, christocentric terms. The one body of Christ, uniting under its head, who is the truth, both lay and cleric becomes the compelling vision, epitomised by catch-phrases, like those mentioned above. The term 'catch-phrase' itself is worth reflecting on. It is always the mark of the genius to reduce the complex to the simple.

The courage to be simple, however, is a mark not only of the polemicist, but of the peacemakers as well, the apostles of concord. Erasmus, sophisticated through and through, was drawn in the end of the day to a quest for innocence, for the simple Gospel. The irenic dreamers of the Reformation, such as Erasmus and Bucer, Gropper and Contarini, cherished simple utopian hopes of harmony and continuity and concord and peace. These have conservative, even nostalgic dimensions to them. Yet they were also fired by an agonised awareness of the cost of division and distrust, and sometimes prompted determined and costly efforts to fashion a new universe of discourse.[4] From today's perspective they appeared to have the future on their side.

The marginalised also had their simple dreams. Argula von Grumbach could imagine a world in which a woman's baptismal vows would ensure that her views were treated with as much respect as those of a theology professor! Likewise, the struggles of the peasants and radicals were not primarily about social engineering or political change, but about personal dignity and community solidarity. 'Worship should be open and above board, not some private mumbo-jumbo, so that it can edify and set on its feet the whole congregation.' Müntzer's view that the entire congregation consecrates the sacrament symbolises the new communal reading of reality.[5]

The discourse of the Reformation, then, is that of prayer and protest and poetry and passion. It is not thought dressed up in rhetoric. It is rhetoric. When Luther turned from writing in Latin to German he focused, as the pastor he was, on the life and death questions about salvation which perplexed ordinary people. As a result the rhetorical, subversive, dangerous language of the Psalms and the prophets, the Gospels and the Epistles was released from its academic captivity and legal fetters and churchy continuities. By focusing on the themes of Luther which caught fire in the popular imagination, Mark Edwards

[4]   Hubert Jedin characterises them dismissively as 'dreamers' in his chapter, 'The Dream of an Understanding and the Reality of the Differences', *A History of the Council of Trent*, vol. 1 (Nelson: London, 1957), pp. 355–409; Augustijn rejects the term 'dream', because of this pejorative connotation: 'Bucer und die Religionsgespräche', in C. Krieger and M. Lienhard (eds.), *Martin Bucer and Sixteenth Century Europe* (Brill: Leiden, 1993), Vol. 2, p. 675.

[5]   CW, 174.

has assisted us to grasp this, and to challenge the traditional historiography of the Reformation, based on the gradually shifting perceptions of a Latinate minority about such issues as justification and the sacraments.

All this has raised sharp questions about how we are to understand sixteenth-century literacy. We frequently and quite correctly think of the Reformation as a Scriptural movement. This does not mean, however, that it was a textual one. It biblicised culture; but it also enculturated the Bible. Werner Packull, for example, has demonstrated that a situational reading of Scripture predisposed the emerging Anabaptist communities towards specific Biblical texts and interpretations.[6] Although Reformation pamphlets sometimes appear to be little more than loosely joined Biblical texts, we have to remember that sixteenth-century people did not read Scripture like us. They relied primarily on memory and association. They clustered texts together not unlike a revivalist preacher. Pull out one and a chain of others followed, prophetic and Pauline, Deuteronomic and Johannine texts all yoked together.[7] Argula von Grumbach read Lamentations, Isaiah, Joel, Matthew with the eyes of a mother, a woman, a lay person. She had her personal canon in her head, before she fired off her cannonades at her opponents. She, too, like Müntzer, married Biblical images to her own personal images.

Deborah Brandt argues, as we have seen, that literacy grows out of conversation, story-telling, song and dance, that semantic and social relationships are inseparable. Bob Scribner's image of the musical score supports this. Pamphlets and books, texts, all the gear of literacy – including, I would add, Biblical texts – only constitute one line in the musical score of the Reformation. Rumour, letter-writing and sermons, liturgies and

---

[6]   Werner O. Packull, *Hutterite Beginnings. Communitarian Experiments during the Reformation* (Johns Hopkins University Press: Baltimore and London, 1995), p. 16.

[7]   Peter Matheson, 'Whose Scripture? A Foray into Reformation Hermeneutics', *Mennonite Quarterly Review* 70 (1996), pp. 191–202.

symbolic 'happenings' are among the others. All this may have found its most complete expression in worship, a most significant social event in sixteenth-century life, but also a cultural event, and certainly the drama where literacy was most tellingly 'involvement'. In the iconography of the period the crucified Christ often hovers between the pulpit and people. It is a haunting image, which may tell us more about popular literacy at this time than many books.

I have argued, then, that it is a category mistake to see the literature of this period as propaganda. Perhaps the peasant dialogues, with their stock characters and predictable conversions, come closest to propaganda. Generally, however, the pamphlets are intimately personal and confessional, at the other end of the spectrum from the manipulation of the propagandist. They are also derived from real-life, interactive situations, from sermons, conversations, confessions, pastoral visits. The thousands of texts have to be seen in terms of their genesis in this landscape and 'inscape' and timescape. They bear the imprint of their oral culture origins.

Anyone who has lived in a society and a culture drenched in propaganda knows how people develop a cynical resistance to it. The unmistakeable enthusiasm for 'books in German', on the other hand, which pamphlet after pamphlet expresses, indicates that their readers found in them dignity, knowledge and empowerment. They have to be understood, of course, in terms of their very diverse reception. The Reformers' literature of aspiration was sifted through the gravel-beds of their readers' actual needs and capacities and hopes. However, its liberating power remained. Luther, as Ebeling has famously said, was himself a *Sprachereignis*, a language-event. Not a coiner of memorable language, but someone who forged a new universe of discourse in which people could discover anew who they were.

In turn all this poses a challenge to our hermeneutical skills. 'The time has come to speak out', said Luther at the beginning of the *Appeal to the German Nobility*. Yet the way in which that 'speaking' took place may elude us if we try too hard to keep our phenomenological distance, to sift its message through our reductionist categories, to 'cash out' its abrasive, apocalyptic, desperate, and lyrical language in terms which are acceptable to us, whether sociological or feminist, political or propagandistic. Sixteenth-century people tend to appear in some contemporary historical writing as denizens of an exotic zoo at whom we can gape from a safe distance. Where this happens the Reformation's rhetoric remains inaccessible to us.

And yet an ironic reserve has also to be maintained, not least because the Reformation game gradually slipped from being serious to deadly, from being creative to being drearily predictable. When its images became reified and its celebration of divine folly objectified, propaganda began to replace polemic and dialogue. Opponents were bestialised, Jews transmuted into well-poisoners, the Papacy depicted as the gaping arse of Hell. Apocalyptic imagery was read as divine documentation of everyday reality. Polemic no longer functioned as a heuristic, ludic and liberating tool but was the ammunition for confessional trench warfare.

This gradual declension of Reformation rhetoric into propaganda raises difficult interpretive issues and fascinating questions about the processes of social change. Given the mendacity of all human institutions how is the liberating potential of polemic best unleashed? How can its heuristic value be nurtured ? And what of the patient skills of dialogue? What extraordinary qualities of imaginative accommodation are required to shift boundaries and heal divisions? What models are available for wedding the scalpel of polemic to the soothing hand of dialogue? Are Luther the asserter, the confessionalist, the broker of salvation, and Erasmus, the educationist, the reverer of mystery, the ironic harmoniser, forever doomed to talk past one another?

BIBLIOGRAPHY

Cornelis Augustijn, 'Bucer und die Religionsgespräche', in Christian Krieger and Marc Lienhard (eds.), *Martin Bucer and Sixteenth Century Europe* (Brill: Leiden, 1993), Vol. 2, pp. 671–80.
———, 'L'Esprit d'Erasme au Colloque de Worms', in Jean-Claude Margolin (ed.), *Colloquia Erasmiana Turonensa* (University of Toronto Press: Toronto, 1969), 1, pp. 381–95.

David V. N. Bagchi, *Luther's Earliest Opponents: Catholic Controversialists, 1518–1525.* Fortress Press: Minneapolis, 1991.
Bernd Balzer, *Bürgerliche Reformationspropaganda. Die Flugschriften des Hans Sachs in den Jahren 1523–1525.* (Germanistische Abhandlungen, 42) Stuttgart, 1973.
Hermann Barge, *Andreas Bodenstein von Karlstadt.* 2 Vols. Leipzig, 1905.
Italo Michele Battafarano (ed.), *Begrifflichkeit und Bildlichkeit der Reformation.* (Ricerche di cultura europea, 5) Peter Lang: Bern, 1992.
Phillip N. Bebb and Sherrin Marshall (eds.), *The Process of Change in Early Modern Europe. Essays in Honor of Miriam Usher Chrisman.* University of Ohio Press: Athens, 1988.
T. W. Best (ed.), *Eccius Dedolatus: A Reformation Satire.* Kentucky University Press: Lexington, 1971.
Peter Biller, 'Heresy and literacy: the earlier history of the theme', in Peter Biller and Anne Hudson (eds.), *Heresy and Literacy 1000–1530.* (Cambridge Studies in Medieval Literature, 23; Cambridge University Press, 1994), pp. 1–18.
Peter Blickle, *The Revolution of 1525: The German Peasants War from a New Perspective.* Tr. Thomas A. Brady and H. C. Erik Midelfort. Johns Hopkins University Press: Baltimore, 1981.

Peter Blickle, *Gemeindereformation. Die Menschen des 16. Jahrhunderts auf dem Weg zum Heil.* R. Oldenbourg Verlag: Munich, 1985.

Gottfried Blochwitz, 'Die antirömischen deutschen Flugschriften der frühen Reformationszeit (bis 1522) in ihrer religiös-sittlichen Eigenart', *Archiv für Reformationsgeschichte* 27 (1931), pp. 145–246.

Heinrich Bornkamm, 'Luther als Schriftsteller', *Sitzungsberichte der Heidelberger Akademie der Wissenschaften.* (Philosophisch-historische Klasse 1965, 1; Heidelberg, 1965), pp. 7–36.

William Bouwsma, 'The Renaissance and the Broadening of Communication', in Lasswell et al. (eds.), *Propaganda and Communication.* Vol. 2, *The Emergence of Public Opinion in the West,* pp. 3–40.

Marjorie O'Rourke Boyle, *Erasmus on Language and Method in Theology.* University of Toronto Press: Toronto, 1977.

Thomas A. Brady, Heiko A. Oberman and James D. Tracy (eds.), *Handbook of European History 1400–1600. Late Middle Ages, Renaissance and Reformation.* 2 Vols. Brill: Leiden, 1994–5.

Deborah Brandt, *Literacy as Involvement: The Acts of Writers Readers and Texts.* Southern Illinois University Press: Carbondale and Edwardsville, 1990.

Siegfried Bräuer, 'Selbstverständnis und Feindbild bei Martin Luther und Thomas Müntzer: Ihre Flugschriftenkontroverse von 1524', in Günter Vogler (ed.), *Wegscheiden der Reformation. Alternatives Denken vom 16. bis zum 18. Jahrhundert.* Verlag Hermann Böhlaus Nachfolger: Weimar, 1994, pp. 57–84.

———, 'Die Reformation in Grafschaft Mansfeld', *Protokoll Band zum Kolloquium anlässlich der ersten urkundlichen Erwähnung Eislebens am 23 November 1994.* Vol. 1, Veröffentlichungen der Lutherstätten Eisleben, Stekovics: Halle, 1995.

Martin Brecht, *Martin Luther,* 3 Vols. Tr. James L. Schaaf. Fortress: Philadelphia and Minneapolis, 1985–92.

———, *Luther als Schriftsteller: Zeugnisse seines dichterischen Gestaltens.* Calwer Verlag: Stuttgart, 1990.

———, *Doctor Luther's Bulla and Reformation: A Look at Luther the Writer.* Valparaiso, Indiana, 1991.

Martin Bucer and Sixteenth Century Europe. Actes du colloque de Strasbourg, 28–31 août 1991. 2 Vols. Ed. by Christian Krieger and Marc Lienhard. Brill: Leiden, 1993.

Lawrence Buck and Jonathan Zophy, *The Social History of the Reformation*. Ohio State University Press: Columbus, 1972.

Otto Burger, 'Luther als Ereignis der Literaturgeschichte', *Luther Jahrbuch* 24 (1957), pp. 86–101.

Roger Chartier (ed.), *The Culture of Print: Power and the Uses of Print in Early Modern Europe*. Tr. Lydia G. Cochrane. Polity Press in association with Basil Blackwell: Cambridge/Oxford, 1989.

Miriam Chrisman, *Lay Culture, Learned Culture, Books and Social Change in Strasbourg, 1480–1599*. Yale University Press: New Haven, 1982.

———, 'From Polemic to Propaganda: The Development of Mass Persuasion in the Late Sixteenth Century', *Archive for Reformation History* 73 (1982), pp. 175–95.

Otto Clemen, *Flugschriften aus den ersten Jahren der Reformation*, 4 Vols., Halle, 1906–11.

Richard G. Cole, 'Reformation Printers: Unsung Heroes', *Sixteenth Century Journal* 15.3 (1984), pp. 327–39.

———, 'Pamphlet Woodcuts in the Communications Process of Reformation Germany', in K. C. Sessions (ed.), *Pietas et Societas: New Trends in Reformation Social History*. Kirksville, Mo., 1985.

Franziska Conrad, *Reformation in der bäuerlichen Gesellschaft: zur Rezeption reformatorischer Theologie im Elsass*. (Veröffentlichungen des Instituts für europäische Geschichte Mainz, Vol. 116); Steiner: Stuttgart, 1984.

Corpus Reformatorum. Melanchthons Opera. Ed. C. G. Bretschneider. Halle, 1834ff.

Uwe Czubatynski, 'Der zornige Luther auf der Kanzel. Eine neugefundene Nachschrift seiner Predigt vom 20. Januar 1544', *Der Wahrheit Gottes verpflichtet. Theologische Beiträge aus dem Sprachkonvikt Berlin*, Matthias Köckert (ed.) (Wichern: Berlin, 1993), pp. 47–64.

W. Phillips Davison, 'The Media Kaleidoscope: General Trends in the Channels', in Lasswell et al., *Propaganda and Communication*, Vol. 3, pp. 191–248.

Hans-Ulrich Delius, 'Und merken dass man deutsch redet. Germanistische Anmerkungen eines Theologen', *Luther* 61.2 (1990), pp. 91–105.

A. G. Dickens, *Luther and the German Nation.* Edward Arnold: London, 1974.

Hans-Joachim Diekmannshenke, *Die Schlagwörter der Radikalen der Reformationszeit (1520–1536): Spuren utopischen Bewußtseins.* Peter Lang: Frankfurt a. Main, 1994.

Gerhard Dünnhaupt (ed.), *The Martin Luther Quinquennial.* Wayne State University Press: Detroit, 1985.

———, 'Luther the Satirist: Stragegies and Function of his Satire', in idem, *The Martin Luther Quinquennial,* pp. 32–43.

Peter A. Dykema and Heiko A. Oberman (eds.), *Anticlericalism in Late Medieval and Early Modern Europe.* (Studies in Medieval and Reformation Thought, Vol. 51) Brill: Leiden, 1993.

Mark U. Edwards, *Luther and the False Brethren.* Stanford University Press: Stanford, 1975.

———, *Luther's Last Battles. Politics and Polemics 1531–46.* Cornell University Press: Ithaca, 1983.

———, *Printing, Propaganda, and Martin Luther.* University of California Press: Berkeley, 1994.

Elizabeth Eisenstein, *The Printing Press as an Agent of Change: Communications and Cultural Transformations in Early Modern Europe.* Cambridge University Press: Cambridge, 1979.

Desiderii Erasmi Roterodami Opera Omnia. 10 Vols. Leiden, 1703.

Desiderii Erasmi Roterodami Opera Omnia. North Holland: Amsterdam.

Flugschriften des frühen 16. Jahrhunderts. Eds. H. J. Köhler, H. Hebenstreit and C. Weismann. Zug. 1978–87.

Flugschriften der frühen Reformationsbewegung (1518–1524). A. Laube, A. Schneider and S. Loos (eds.). 2 Vols. Berlin, 1983.

Pierre Fraenkel, 'Les protestants et le problème de la transsubstantiation au Colloque de Ratisbonne', in F. W. Kantzenbach (ed.), *Hermann Dietzfelbinger zum 60 Geburtstag* (Augsburg: Minneapolis, 1968), 70–116.

——— (ed.), *Consilium Theologicum privatim conscriptum.* Brill: Leiden, 1988.

Alistair Fox, *Thomas More: History and Providence*. Basil Blackwell, Oxford, 1982.

Rosi Fuhrmann, 'Dorfgemeinde und Pfründstiftung vor der Reformation. Kommunale Selbstbestimmungschancen zwischen Religion und Recht', in Peter Blickle and Johannes Kunisch (eds.), *Kommunalisierung und Christianisierung. Voraussetzungen und Folgen der Reformation 1400–1600* (Zeitschrift für Historische Forschung, Beiheft 9; Berlin, 1989), pp. 77–112.

E. J. Furcha, tr. and ed., *The Essential Carlstadt*. Herald Press: Waterloo, Ontario, 1995.

Gottfried Geiger, 'Die reformatorischen Initia Johann Eberlins von Günzburg nach seinen Flugschriften', in H. Rabe, *Festgabe für Ernst Zeeden*, pp. 178–201.

Carlos Gilly, 'Das Sprichwort "Die Gelehrten die Verkehrten", oder der Verrat der Intellektuellen im Zeitalter der Glaubensspaltung', in *Forme e destinazione del messaggio religioso. Aspetti della propaganda religiosa nel cinquecento*. Olschki: Florence, 1991, pp. 229–375.

J.-F. Gilmont, 'Pour une typologie du "Flugschrift" des débuts de la Réforme. A propos d'une recherche entreprise à Tübingen', *Revue d'Histoire Ecclésiastique* 78.2 (1983), pp. 788–809.

Elizabeth C. Gleason, *Gasparo Contarini: Venice, Rome and Reform*. University of California Press: Berkeley, 1993.

Hans-Jürgen Goertz, *Pfaffenhass und gross Geschrei: die reformatorischen Bewegungen in Deutschland 1517–1529*. Beck: München, 1987.

———, 'Träume, Offenbarungen und Visionen in der Reformation', in Rainer Postel and Franklin Kopitzsch (eds.), *Reformation und Revolution. Beiträge zum politischen Wandel unter den sozialen Kräften am Beginn der Neuzeit*. Festschrift für Rainer Wohlfeil zum 60. Geburtstag. Stuttgart, 1989.

Ludger Grenzmann and Karl Stackmann (eds.), *Literatur und Laienbildung im Spätmittelalter und in der Reformationszeit*. (Germanistische Symposien, V); Metzler: Stuttgart, 1984.

E. W. Gritsch, *Martin – God's Court Jester: Luther in Retrospect*. Fortress: Philadelphia, 1983.

M. H. Guchmann, *Die Sprache der deutschen politischen Literatur in der Zeit der Reformation und des Bauernkrieges*. Akademischer Verlag: Berlin, 1974.

Jürgen Habermas, *Strukturwandel der Öffentlichkeit. Untersuchungen zu einer Kategorie der bürgerlichen Gesellschaft.* Luchterhand: Darmstadt-Neuwied, 1962.

Monika Hagenmaier and Sabine Holtz (eds.), *Krisenbewusstsein und Krisenbewältigung in der frühen Neuzeit . . . Festschrift für Hans-Christoph Rublack.* Peter Lang: Frankfurt, 1992.

Silke Halbach, *Argula von Grumbach als Verfasserin reformatorischer Flugschriften.* Peter Lang: Frankfurt a. Main, 1992.

Basil Hall, *Humanists and Protestants 1500–1900.* T. & T. Clark: Edinburgh, 1989.

Berndt Hamm, 'Das Gewicht von Religion, Glaube, Frömmigkeit und Theologie innerhalb der Verdichtungsvorgänge des ausgehenden Mittelalters und der frühen Neuzeit', in Monika Hagenmaier and Sabine Holtz (eds.), *Krisenbewusstsein und Krisenbewältigung in der frühen Neuzeit . . . Festschrift für Hans-Christoph Rublack.* Peter Lang: Frankfurt a. Main, 1992, pp. 163–96.

Eric Havelock, 'The oral-literate equation', in D. Olson and N. Torrance (eds.), *Literacy and Orality,* pp. 1–27.

Friedrich Heer, *Die Dritte Kraft: Der europäischer Humanismus zwischen den Fronten des konfessionellen Zeitalters.* Fischer: Frankfurt a. Main, 1959.

Raymond Himelick (ed. and tr.), *Erasmus and the Seamless Coat of Jesus: De sarcienda Ecclesiae concordia.* Purdue Research Foundation: Lafayette, Ind., 1971.

Manfred Hoffmann, *Rhetoric and Theology: The Hermeneutic of Erasmus.* University of Toronto Press: Toronto, 1994.

Louise W. Holborn, 'Printing and the Growth of a Protestant Movement in Germany from 1517–1524,' *Church History* 11 (1942), pp. 123–37.

Hubert Jedin, *A History of the Council of Trent,* tr. by Ernest Graf, Vol. 1. Nelson: London, 1957.

Ninna Jørgensen, *Bauer, Narr und Pfaffe. Prototypische Figuren und ihre Funktion in der Reformationsliteratur.* (Acta Theologica Danica vol. XXII); Brill: Leiden, 1988.

Andreas Karlstadt, *Von Abtuhung der Bilder* (Kleine Texte für theologische und philologische Vorlesungen und Übungen, 74); ed. H. Lietzmann, Bonn, 1911.

Hans-Joachim Köhler (ed.), *Flugschriften als Massenmedium der Reformationszeit* (Spätmittelalter und frühe Neuzeit, Tübinger Beiträge zur Geschichtsforschung, 13). Klett-Cotta: Stuttgart, 1981.

————, 'Erste Schritte zu einem Meinungsprofil der frühen Reformationszeit', in Volker Press and Dieter Stievermann (eds.), *Martin Luther: Probleme seiner Zeit* (Spätmittelalter und Frühe Neuzeit: Tübinger Beiträge zur Geschichtsforschung, Vol. 16). Stuttgart, 1986, pp. 244–65.

————, ' "Der Bauer wird witzig": Der Bauer in den Flugschriften der Reformationszeit', in *Zugänge zur bäuerlichen Reformation. Bauer und Reformation* Vol 1 (Zürich: Chronos, 1987), pp. 187–218.

Barbara Könneker, 'Vom "Poeta Laureatus" zum Propagandisten: Die Entwicklung Huttens als Schriftsteller in seinen Dialogen von 1528 bis 1521', in *Colloque international d'études humanistes: L'humanisme allemand 1440–1540*: XVIIIe colloque international de Tours. Fink: Munich, 1979.

Andrea Körsgen-Wiedeburg, 'Das Bild Martin Luthers in den Flugschriften der frühen Reformationszeit', in Horst Rabe et al. (eds.), *Festgabe für Ernst Zeeden.* Aschendorff: Münster, 1976, pp. 154–6.

H. Lasswell, D. Lerner and H. Speier (eds.), *Propaganda and Communication in World History.* 3 Vols. University Press of Hawaii: Honolulu, 1980.

Werner Lenk, 'Martin Luthers Kampf um die Öffentlichkeit', in Günter Vogler (ed.), with S. Hoyer and A. Laube, *Martin Luther. Leben – Werk – Wirkung.* Akademie Verlag: Berlin, 1986.

Friedrich Lepp, *Schlagwörter des Reformationszeitalters.* Leipzig, 1908.

Neil Richard Leroux, 'Style in Rhetorical Criticism: The Case of Martin Luther's Vernacular Sermons', PhD, University of Illinois, 1990.

Marc Lienhard, 'Mentalité populaire . . . à Strasbourg en 1522–1523', in M. Kroon and M. Lienhard (eds.), *Horizons Européens de la Réforme en Alsace.* Librairie Istra: Strasbourg, 1980.

Carter Lindberg, *The European Reformations.* Blackwell: Oxford and Cambridge, Mass., 1996.

Joseph Lortz, *Die Reformation in Deutschland.* 2 Vols. 4th ed. Herder: Freiburg, 1962.

Martin Luther: Probleme seiner Zeit, eds. Volker Press and Dieter Stievermann (Spätmittelalter und frühe Neuzeit, Tübinger Beiträge zur Geschichtsforschung, 16). Stuttgart, 1986.
Martin Luther. Studienausgabe, ed. Hans-Ulrich Delius. 4 Vols. Evangelische Verlagsanstalt: Berlin, 1979–.
D. Martin Luthers Werke, Kritische Gesamtausgabe. Weimar, 1883ff.
Luther's Works (the 'American Luther'), eds. J. Pelikan and H. Lehman. 55 Vols. Concordia: Philadelphia and St Louis, 1955ff.

Peter Matheson, *Cardinal Contarini at Regensburg.* Clarendon Press: Oxford, 1972.
———, tr. and ed., *The Collected Works of Thomas Müntzer.* T. & T. Clark: Edinburgh, 1988.
———, 'Thomas Müntzer's *Vindication and Refutation:* A Language for the Common People?', *Sixteenth Century Journal* XX. 4 (1989), pp. 603–15.
———, 'Martyrdom or Mission. A Protestant Debate', *Archiv für Reformationsgeschichte* 80 (1989), pp. 154–72.
———, 'Humanism and Reform Movements', in Anthony Goodman and Angus McKay (eds.), *The Impact of Humanism on Western Europe.* Longman: London, 1990, pp. 1–15.
———, 'Thomas Müntzer's Marginal Comments on Tertullian', *Journal of Theological Studies* 41 (1990), pp. 76–90.
——— tr. and ed., *Argula von Grumbach. A Woman's Voice in the Reformation.* T. & T. Clark: Edinburgh, 1995.
———, 'Whose Scripture? A Foray into Reformation Hermeneutics', *Mennonite Quarterly Review* 70 (1996), pp. 191–202.
———, 'Breaking the Silence: Women, Censorship and the Reformation', *Sixteenth Century Journal* XXVII/I (1996), pp. 97–109.
Hermann Meuche (ed.), *Flugblätter der Reformation und des Bauernkrieges:* 50 Blätter aus der Sammlung des Schloßmuseums Gotha, with catalogue by Ingeborg Neumeister. Insel: Leipzig, 1975.
E. C. Erik Midelfort, 'Toward a Social History of Ideas in the German Reformation', in Kyle C. Sessions and Phillip N. Bebb (eds.), *Pietas et Societas. New Trends in Reformation Social History (Essays in Memory of Harold J. Grimm).* Sixteenth Century Journal Publishers: Kirksville, Miss., 1985.

Bernd Moeller, 'Stadt und Buch: Bemerkungen zur Struktur der reformatorischen Bewegung in Deutschland', in W. J. Mommsen (ed.), *Stadtbürgertum und Adel in der Reformation: Studien zur Sozialgeschichte der Reformation in England und Deutschland* (Stuttgart, 1979), pp. 25–39.

R. I. Moore, 'Literacy and the Making of Heresy, c. 1000–1150', in Peter Biller and Anne Hudson (eds.), *Heresy and Literacy 1000–1530*. (Cambridge Studies in Medieval Literature, 23) Cambridge University Press: Cambridge, 1994.

Keith Moxey, *Peasants, Warriors, and Wives: Popular Imagery in the Reformation*. University of Chicago Press: Chicago and London, 1989.

Thomas Müntzer: Schriften und Briefe. In collaboration with Paul Kirn edited by Günther Franz. (Quellen und Forschungen zur Reformationsgeschichte, Vol. XXXIII) Gerd Mohn: Gütersloh, 1968.

Hans-Joachim Neumann, *Luthers Leiden. Die Krankheitsgeschichte des Reformators*. Wichern: Berlin, 1995.

Heiko O. Oberman, *Wurzeln des Antisemitismus. Christenangst und Judenplage im Zeitalter von Humanismus und Reformation*. Severin und Siedler: Berlin, 1981.

———, *Luther – Man between God and the Devil*. Tr. Eileen Walliser-Schwarbart. Image Books: New York, 1992.

———, *The Impact of the Reformation*. T. & T. Clark: Edinburgh, 1994.

David Olson and Nancy Torrance (eds.), *Literacy and Orality*. Cambridge University Press: Cambridge, 1991.

John W. O'Malley, 'Luther the Preacher', in Dünnhaupt, *The Martin Luther Quinquennial*, pp. 3–16.

Walter Ong, *Orality and Literacy: The Technologizing of the Word*. Methuen: London, 1982.

Steven Ozment, *Protestants: The Birth of a Revolution*. Doubleday: New York, 1992.

Werner O. Packull, *Hutterite Beginnings. Communitarian Experiments during the Reformation*. Johns Hopkins University Press: Baltimore and London, 1995.

Calvin A. Pater, *Karlstadt as the Father of the Baptist Movements: The Emergence of Lay Protestantism.* University of Toronto Press: Toronto, 1984.

Chaim Perelman and Lucy Olbrechts-Tyteca, *The New Rhetoric: A Treatise on Argumentation,* tr. John Wilkinson and Purcell Weaver. University of Notre Dame Press: Notre Dame, Ind., 1969.

Andrew Pettegree (ed.), *The Early Reformation in Europe.* Cambridge University Press: Cambridge, 1992.

Rainer Postel and Franklin Kopitzsch (eds.), *Reformation und Revolution. Beiträge zum politischen Wandel von den sozialen Kräften am Beginn der Neuzeit.* Festschrift für Rainer Wohlfeil zum 60. Geburtstag. Stuttgart, 1989.

James S. Preus, *Carlstadt's Ordinaciones and Luther's Liberty: A Study of the Wittenberg Movement 1521–2.* (Harvard Theological Studies XXVI) Cambridge, Mass., 1974.

Hans-Christoph Rublack, *Gescheiterte Reformation: Frühreformatorische und Protestantische Bewegungen in süd- und westdeutschen geistlichen Residenzen.* Stuttgart, 1978.

————, 'Anticlericalism in German Reformation Pamphlets', in Dykema and Oberman (eds)., *Anticlericalism,* pp. 461–90.

Erika Rummel, *The Humanist-Scholastic Debate in the Renaissance and Reformation.* Harvard University Press: Cambridge, Mass./ London, 1995.

Gordon Rupp, *Patterns of Reformation.* Epworth: London, 1969.

Oscar Schade, *Satiren und Pasquille aus der Reformationszeit,* 3 Vols.; 2nd ed., Hannover, 1856–8.

Heinz Scheible, 'Reform, Reformation, Revolution. Grundsätze zur Beurteilung der Flugschriften', *Archiv für Reformationsgeschichte* 65 (1974), pp. 108–34.

Joachim Schildt, 'Die Sprache Luthers – ihre Bedeutung für die Entwicklung der deutschen Schriftsprache', in Vogler, *Martin Luther,* pp. 307–24.

Klaus Schreiner, 'Grenzen literarischer Kommunikation. Bemerkungen zur religiösen und sozialen Dialektik der Laienbildung im Spätmittelalter und in der Reformation', in Grenzmann and Stackmann, *Literatur und Laienbildung,* pp. 1–20.

Johannes Schwitalla, 'Martin Luthers argumentative Polemik; mündlich und schriftlich', in Albrecht Schöne (ed.), *Akten des VII Internationalen Germanisten-Kongresses* (Göttingen, 1985), pp. 541–4.

Tom Scott, *Thomas Müntzer. Theology and Revolution in the German Reformation.* Macmillan: London, 1989.

Bob Scribner, *For the Sake of Simple Folk: Popular Propaganda for the German Reformation* (Cambridge Studies in Oral and Literary Culture, 2), Cambridge/London, 1981.

———, 'Flugblatt und Analphabetentum. Wie kam der gemeine Mann zu reformatorischen Ideen?', in Köhler, *Flugschriften als Massenmedium*, pp. 65–76.

———, 'Heterodoxy, literacy and print in the early German Reformation', in Biller and Hudson, *Heresy and Orthodoxy*, pp. 255–78.

———, 'Anticlericalism and the Reformation in Germany', in idem, *Popular Culture and Popular Movements in Reformation Germany* (Hambledon Press: London, 1987), pp. 243–56.

———, 'Popular Piety and Modes of Visual Perception in Late Medieval and Reformation Germany.' *The Journal of Religious History* 15.4 (1989), pp. 448–69.

Jerrold E. Seigel, *Rhetoric and Philosophy in Renaissance Humanism.* Princeton University Press: Princeton, 1968.

Dieter Seitz, 'Flugschriftenliteratur der Reformation und des Bauernkriegs', in Horst Glaser (ed.), *Deutsche Literatur: Eine Sozialgeschichte.* Reinbek bei Hamburg, 1991.

Kyle C. Sessions and Philip N. Bebb (eds.), *Pietas et Societas. New Trends in Reformation Social History.* Essays in Memory of Harold J. Grimm. Sixteenth Century Journal Publishers: Kirksville, Miss., 1985.

Ronald J. Sider, *Andreas Bodenstein von Karlstadt. Documents in a Liberal-Radical Debate.* (Studies in Medieval and Reformation Thought, XI); Brill: Leiden, 1974.

——— (ed.), *Karlstadt's Battle with Luther.* Fortress: Philadelphia, 1978.

Kurt Werner Stadtwald, 'When O Rome Will You Cease to Hiss? The Image of the Pope in the Politics of German Humanism', PhD, University of Minnesota, 1991.

Georg Steer, 'Zum Begriff "Laie" in deutscher Dichtung und Prosa des Mittelalters', in Grenzmann and Stackmann, *Literatur und Laienbildung*, pp. 764–8.

Birgit Stolt, 'Lieblichkeit und Zier, Ungestüm und Donner; Martin Luther im Spiegel seiner Sprache', *Zeitschrift für Theologie und Kirche* 86.3 (1989), pp. 282–305.

R. N. Swanson, 'Literacy, Heresy, History and Orthodoxy; Perspectives and Permutations for the Later Middle Ages', in Biller and Hudson, *Heresy and Literacy 1000–1530*, pp. 279–93.

Hella Trompert, 'Die Flugschriften als Medium religiöser Publizistik: Aspekte der gegenwärtigen Forschung', in *Kontinuität und Umbruch: Theologie und Frömmigkeit in Flugschriften und Kleinliteratur an der Wende vom 15. zum 16. Jahrhundert* (Klett-Cotta: Stuttgart, 1978), pp. 211–21.

Günter Vogler (ed.), with S. Hoyer and A. Laube, *Martin Luther. Leben – Werk – Wirkung*. Akademie Verlag: Berlin, 1986.

Lee Palmer Wandel, 'Strubelhans and the Singing Monks', in Hagenmeier and Holtz, *Krisenbewusstsein . . .* , pp. 307–15.

Hermann Wiegmann, 'Allgemeinbegriff und Rhetorik. Zur theologischen, politischen und literarischen Argumentation im frühen 16. Jahrhundert', in Joachim Dyck, Walter Jens, Gert Veding (eds.), *Rhetorik*, Bd. 5 *Rhetorik und Theologie* (Max Niemeyer: Tübingen, 1986), pp. 87–96.

Hannelore Winkler, *Der Wortbestand von Flugschriften aus den Jahren der Reformation und des Bauernkrieges*. Akademie Verlag: Berlin, 1975.

Rainer Wohlfeil, *Einführung in die Geschichte der deutschen Reformation*. Beck: Munich, 1982.

———, 'Reformatorische Öffentlichkeit', in Grenzmann and Stackmann, *Literatur und Laienbildung*, pp. 40–54.

Alejandro Zorzin, *Karlstadt als Flugschriftenautor*. Vandenhoeck & Ruprecht: Göttingen, 1990.

INDEX OF NAMES AND PLACES

INDEX OF THEMES